THE DEVON
FOOD BOOK

THE DEVON FOOD BOOK

Carol Trewin

PHOTOGRAPHY
Adam Woolfitt

EDITORS
James Crowden
Ann Wilson

FLAGON PRESS

First Published in 2010 by
Flagon Press
Forge House, Fore Street
Winsham, Chard
Somerset TA20 4DY
www.james-crowden.co.uk

Visit the Devon Food Book website
www.thedevonfoodbook.co.uk

ISBN 978-0-9557073-9-1

British Library and Cataloguing-in-Production Data.
A catalogue record for this book is available from
The British Library.

Design Andrew Crane
http://andrewcrane.posterous.com/
Typeset in Formata and Bodoni

Printed and bound by Butler Tanner & Dennis, Frome, Somerset
www.butlertanneranddennis.com/

▶
*Rainbow over the red
sandstone cliffs of
Salcombe Hill, Sidmouth*

Contents

Nutcombe on the edge of the Exmoor National Park above Combe Martin

Acknowledgements

Getting the Devon Food Book researched, written, photographed, designed and printed on time has been a major undertaking, not least because of the size of Devon, two coasts and two moors, as well as the depth and breadth of its history. Before she died, Carol Trewin had envisaged a book along the lines of *Gourmet Cornwall* but it soon became apparent that the Devon book would have to be far larger and more comprehensive.

The Devon Food Book has been published with sponsorship from a wide range of food producers and organizations. It is very much a community publication and has the backing of many Devon food and drink producers. In particular the publishers would like to thank all those that have contributed either financially or in kind: Michael Caines, Gidleigh Park and ABode, Devon County Council, Tamar Valley AONB, Brend Hotels, Mole Valley Farmers, Jilly Greed, One Voice Media & PR, Little Comfort Farm, North Devon Plus, Devon Farms, Food and Drink Devon, Occombe Farm, Riverford Organic Vegetables, Darts Farm Shop, Paul Parnell, Jack in the Green, Peter and Henrietta Greig, Pipers Farm, Andrew Maunder, Lloyd Maunder, Patrick McCaig, Otter Brewery, Luppitt, Richard Haddock, Churston Traditional Farm Shop, Plymouth Gin and Guy Crowden. The publishers would also like to thank all the other food and drink producers featured as well as the farmers and chefs, the market traders and shop keepers who gave up their time to be interviewed and photographed as well as members of Slow Food Devon who have all been incredibly supportive. In some ways the book has now evolved into a social history of Devon as well as a food document.

On the design side I am very grateful indeed to Andrew Crane for his patience and artistic flair in producing such a stunning book, to Adam Woolfitt for his breathtaking colour photography, style and precise eye. To Ann Wilson of George Nympton not only for copious research and editing but for her long hours of administrative work behind the scenes. To Jennie Rayment for trying out all twenty five recipes. To Chris Chapman for the Headland Warren and Three Rabbits photographs. To Sue Andrew for the stag roof boss photograph. To Tom Greeves for information on Dartmoor, warrens, rabbits, hares and tin mining. To Sally Vincent and Denise O'Leary for help with interviews, to Nell Barrington and Guy Crowden for proof reading and to Jenny de Gex for sourcing two pictures at short notice.

To Flaydemouse of Yeovil for scanning and to Butler, Tanner and Dennis of Frome for printing. To the eminent chefs and food writers who paid tribute to Carol Trewin and to Carol herself for persevering with the book when others might well have thrown in the sponge. To the staff and doctors of Derriford Hospital, Plymouth who tried their very best to accommodate having a writer on their ward and to all Carol's friends from the Western Morning News who kept her spirits up right to the very end.

The book is fine tribute to Devon's food and drink producers but also to Carol Trewin herself and the fine tradition of food journalism that she pioneered in the South West.

James Crowden

Chittlehampton Church near Umberleigh. North Devon

Tributes to Carol Trewin 1953-2009

"The story of food in Devon is a complex and intertwined one. As a journalist, Carol Trewin understood these complexities, drawing vital connections between farmers and fisherman, artisan food producers, chefs and ordinary food consumers. She had an innate understanding of the importance of such issues as regionality, traceability, and seasonality, long before they became popular buzzwords. Carol helped to define and redefine the food culture of our region. I have long maintained that Devon has the best larder in Europe. The Devon Food Book is magnificent proof of this and a lasting legacy to Carol's life and work."

MICHAEL CAINES MBE Executive Chef at Gidleigh Park,
The Bath Priory, and Michael Caines Restaurants

We were very lucky to have a journalist of Carol's calibre covering food and drink in Devon and Cornwall. She had a real love of everything local but because she was such a good writer whatever she chose to write about from local fishing and seafood through to her overriding passion for the Devon and Cornwall food industry was of great value. She was such a lovely person and will be sadly missed.

RICK STEIN Padstow

Carol was an amazing woman, her support and passion for the West Country food and farming industry was second to none. She was kind and generous and will be truly missed.

MARK HIX Hix Oyster and Fish House, Lyme Regis

Carol not only had the greatest in-depth knowledge of farming, food and drink in Devon, she was also such a talented writer who observed always with the utmost clarity and honesty. In The Devon Food Book, she explains and records myriad complex subjects objectively and totally without sentiment, placing food traditions and production within an historical, cultural and human perspective. Her keen, enquiring mind delves far beyond the surface of our beautiful Devon landscape to unearth and chart not just the glories of the Devon table, but also stories of the hardships, mistaken food policies, and politics that have inevitably had an impact on the foods that we eat and enjoy today.

MARC MILLON food, wine and travel author,
member of Slow Food Devon, Topsham

*Thatcher's tools
Newton Poppleford*

INTRODUCTION

OVERLEAF
*From Cadbury Cross looking
towards Chapeltown between
Bickleigh and Crediton*

HARTLAND POINT is majestic and stubborn. This rocky headland with its small lighthouse, set in the far north-western edge of the Devon coast, juts out into the sea at the exact spot where the North Atlantic meets the Bristol Channel. In the distance lies Lundy, an island famed for its puffins and pirates. It is hard to imagine, standing on the windswept cliffs that anywhere could be less hospitable on a grey winter's day. Giant waves pummel the cliffs three hundred and fifty feet below and relentless gales lash the rugged coastline. This, the most remote of Devon's parishes, is surrounded on two sides by the sea. Yet only a mile or two inland, in the Hartland Village Hall the monthly farmers' market gives a strong clue to the burgeoning food renaissance in this part of the county, not previously famed for either its fish markets or the lushness of its pastures. This was once one of the least fertile agricultural

Clovelly fishermen c. 1899

areas of Devon and proved a very tough coastline for fishermen endeavouring to make a living, because it was and still is, a very long way from any centres of population. This remoteness, local distinctiveness and need for survival has over the centuries changed the profile of not just the landscape but of the food that is found there. In Moortown Diary, Ted Hughes says that he thought Yorkshire was remote, until he saw the 'isolated self-sufficiency' of the old North Devon farmers, which was 'like nothing else he had ever encountered.'

At almost the diametrically opposite end of the county lies Beer, one of the last beach fisheries in England. Here a handful of boats catch their share of the rich South West stocks of fish and shellfish. Once the catch is landed, the boats are then winched or towed up the pebble beach by

*The Iron Coast: Shipload Bay
looking towards Hartland Point*

tractors and come to rest, their gaily painted hulls jauntily wedged in a ragged line. The dramatic chalk cliffs rearing up out of the sea are part of the historic Jurassic coast, but move slightly inland and the rich, fertile farmland of East Devon produces an abundance of livestock, crops and vegetables.

Beer- fishing boats and beach huts

This is the point about Devon. Although it is little more than 70 miles from coast to coast at its broadest point, it is a county of many contrasting landscapes. From north to south, east to west, the agriculture is finely tuned and in the centre, overshadowing most of the county, the great brooding granite mass of Dartmoor. It is this very diversity of the landscape that has created a rich larder of food and drink - ingredients that make Devon one of the most sought after destinations for gourmets, chefs and food connoisseurs.

It is a county of two moors - Dartmoor and Exmoor - two coasts, north and south and literally dozens of rivers, some running north-south through drowned river valleys, known as rias, and others finding their way lazily to the sea, meandering through traditional water meadows and lush pastures.

Take your pick from the Exe (the longest) and the Dart, to the Taw, Torridge, Teign, Tavy (the fastest), and the Tamar. Also not to be overlooked are the Otter, the Yarty, the Axe and a whole host of short, fast rivers

Widecombe-in-the-Moor

Drying the salmon fishing nets, on the Dart c 1899

running pell-mell down steep ravines from Dartmoor's peat laden and spongy bogs like the Plym, the Meavy, the Yealm, Avon and the Erme. It is these rivers connecting the moorland to the sea which make Devon's farming so varied. And this gave rise to a unique form of transhumance where most of the county had rights to drive their cattle and sheep up onto the high moorland pastures where they were looked after by the quarter men for most of the summer and then driven down to the markets in autumn. Tightly controlled common grazing often with hereditary rights. A form of extensive summer ranching, semi-nomadic in nature.

Over the centuries the development of farming crops and livestock has given rise to a well balanced agriculture, producing everything from beef to milk and clotted cream, to a wonderful range of cheeses. Sadly the traditional cycle between dairy and pig farming, using up surplus whey, has been largely lost, but pigs also came into their own as part of the orchard tradition, either eating unwanted windfalls or the lucky recipients of

South Devons tucking into pomace from Heron Valley Cider Farm, Crannacombe, Loddiswell

pomace and pulp at the end of cider making. Vegetables too have been a far greater part of Devon's agriculture than many realise - cabbages, broccoli and cauliflower are widely grown on the south coast, early potatoes as well as main crop potatoes, and for more than a century the market gardens of the Tamar valley were a centre for the earliest soft fruits and a great source of apples and plums. Even Seakale was first domesticated in South Devon.

Oliver Cromwell, who visited Devon on campaign during the Civil War in the autumn of 1645 and the spring of 1646, reckoned that 'the husbandry of Devon was the best he had seen in the whole country', and he should know, having to feed his troops at every town, village and farmstead. No doubt this was because of their early history of enclosures. Cromwell visited Ottery St Mary, Bovey Tracey, Ashburton and Torrington. It goes without saying that the Devon cattle, which eventually became the Red Rubies of the North and South Devons of the South Hams, would have been highly prized.

In the 21st century enterprising growers have extended not only the seasonal range of the crops but the varieties available - think Braunton asparagus, hemp (for seeds and oils). With one eye on future climate change, experiments have been conducted with olive growing in the Tamar

Treatise on Cider by John Worlidge 1678

A Devon Bull belonging to Mr W Porter of Hembury Fort, Buckwell near Honiton for which a prize of £30 was awarded at the RSA Meeting at Cambridge 1840

Valley and there are more than a dozen productive vineyards in the county.

Historically Devon was a county that for hundreds of years had also shown enormous ingenuity with development and a keen spirit of exploration. From the early fishermen taking enormous risks to sail to Newfoundland as part of the salt cod trade, to the men of war and pirates, such as Drake and Raleigh, Hawkins and Frobisher, who set sail for King or Queen and country or on behalf of merchant adventurers. One such ship in 1622 going out to Newfoundland from Exmouth to the cod fisheries took with it '2 firkins butter, 200cwt cheese, 2 hogsheads very good English beef - £10 and 2 hogsheads Irish beef - £5.'

On dry land many other industries had been very important since medieval times; a thriving trade in wool and cloth, with tin, copper, lead and silver mining in West Devon, the quarrying of china clay and granite, boat building and even paper milling, all made Devon a very prosperous county. In 1768, William Cookworthy, born in Kingsbridge and son of a Quaker weaver, patented his discovery of how to make fine porcelain from Cornish kaolin, as well as conducting other experiments including distilling sea water to provide fresh water on long voyages. In Plymouth the naval dockyard used to victual ships for long voyages and they had their own market within the dockyard, for farm produce. Cattle and sheep would be driven down from Dartmoor and

A day boat heads back up the Dart past Kingswear

even from North Devon. In the King William Yard in Devonport they employed over 100 coopers to make barrels for salt beef and storage of dry goods. They even had their own brewery capable of producing 30,000 gallons of beer a day and a state of the art 1840s steam driven flour mill with 27 millstones and a bakery with twelve conveyor ovens. Supplying the navy with food and victuals was big business and underpinned much of the local food economy in West and North Devon.

The arrival of the railways in the 19th century also gave access to valuable urban markets up country as well as bringing tourists down to the seaside, a thriving industry that has kept the Devon economy afloat for over 150 years and provided a ready market for ice cream.

For modern day chefs Devon has a rich larder which provides them with acres of produce, tons of cheese, hogsheads of butter, firkins of clotted cream, copious supplies of fresh local beef, mutton, lamb, venison, pork, crabs and even salmon. Agriculture and cookery are therefore locked into a single cycle and a growing number of these chefs, who have embraced their locality, are keen to source food locally and sing about it on their menus. A trend kick-started by Joyce Molyneux and Tom Jaine at the Carved Angel in Dartmouth in the 1980s. Sometimes the dishes will contain influences that are derived a long way from Devon, but if they are using locally grown or reared ingredients this is adding to the richness of the county's culinary heritage.

One of the key attractions to tourists is the county's unique landscape, but what they may not at first realise, is that the beauty they are looking at,

▶
Organic vegetables at the Riverford Farm Shop

the rolling hills and hedges, has been shaped and fashioned over thousands of years by hunter-gatherers and farmers intent upon survival. The terrain of Dartmoor is in effect an open history book of enclosures, reeves, farm boundaries and settlements going back to the Bronze Age. Food production therefore underpins the entire county's being and its economic purpose and has done for thousands of years.

But the future of that productive landscape is now at stake as leisure and tourism has, in many places, taken over from hard agricultural work. Even Dartmoor and Exmoor are now regarded by many as nothing more than a vast adventure playground. Farming inevitably continues to contract and there are far fewer animals on the moor than there were twenty years ago. Even the quarries, the rough landscape of gullies and the waste tips left over from centuries of tin mining are now often the only indicators of

The Warren House Inn, Dartmoor.... where generations of thirsty tin miners slaked their thirst.

heavy industry. Moorland is in severe danger of becoming overgrown and derelict, as there are no longer enough grazing mouths to counteract the spread of bracken, gorse and brambles which crowd out the young shoots of new grass.

The Devon Food Book looks at a wide variety of foods and farming techniques, coastal fishing, farm shops and farmers' markets; not just from Hartland to Beer but from The Horn of Plenty in the Tamar valley to the Blackdown Hills, from Heron Valley to Saunton Sands, from Salcombe to Clovelly. A rich diet of wild food, Devon's larder beckons. Not for nothing did the barefoot sailors returning from long arduous voyages around the world or the privations of blockading France during the Napoleonic War, call Plymouth and the cherry gardens along the Hamoaze, 'Guzz'. Devon kept them alive.

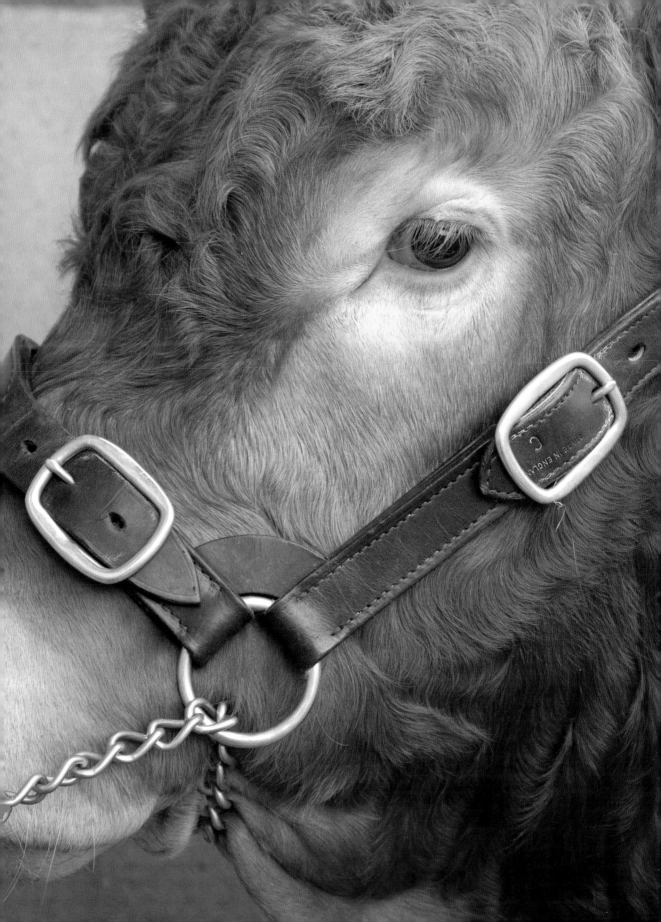

1/

FROM RABBIT TO RED RUBY

NEXT TIME YOU DRIVE THROUGH narrow Devon lanes and admire the countryside through a gateway on a summer's evening when the warm light is gently slanting across the green grass, spare a thought for the farmer. Without the rearing of cattle and sheep there would be no Devon landscape as we know it today. No fields, no hedges, no fine pastures and rolling hills. It has taken well over a thousand years to take the land in hand, to blend the semi-nomadic herding practices into a cohesive rural economy. The word Devon is derived, as that famous commentator W G Hoskins pointed out, from the earlier Celtic tribal name Defnas and Dumnonii, which means roughly 'people of the land or deep valleys.'

When you buy a good looking piece of dark beef in a butcher's shop that has been hung for at least three weeks, it is well worth thinking about which farm that beast may have come from and what grazing patterns led to its final texture and flavour. Understanding these things, these subtle nuances, is what makes a food culture vibrant. It is what top quality chefs are looking for and Devon, more often than not, gives them exactly what they want. Without meat our ancestors would not have survived in adverse conditions, it is an essential part of our hunter-gatherer history.

Traditionally meat comes from a very wide variety of sources. Some is truly wild and hunted, some is just feral, some is semi-domesticated, some is half wild and ranched on open moorland, some is almost tame and yet spends half its time in sheds. All of it has its own distinctive taste and flavour reflecting how it has been reared.

The first three chapters of this book take a close look at various forms of farming livestock which have shaped the countryside that we so admire

▸
Red Rubies at Pipers Farm near
Cullompton

◂
Richard Vines' Welsh Black
cattle being driven up onto
the open moor

and have given us the food that we need to survive. Meat is very definitely your maker and the history of meat production very much at the heart of Devon's agriculture. The finely tuned Devon landscape, the farmer's real inheritance, is a precious a gift that we can all enjoy.

Warrens and Rabbit Stew

But livestock does not just mean sheep and cattle. At one time Devon was also covered in rabbit warrens and deer parks, Dartmoor and Exmoor were well known as hunting forests. Slowly but surely distinct breeds of Devon sheep and cattle evolved in different ways to suit the climate and terrain. Some medieval methods of farming, like the great rabbit warrens on Dartmoor, only died out in the 1950s. Here land was temporarily enclosed and long artificial burys (burrows) were dug called coney pillows.

It was the Normans who introduced large scale rabbit warrening to Devon. This was the art of building special warrens in which rabbits lived, fed and bred - a mix of managed and wild rabbits. Henry 1 allowed the Abbot of Tavistock to keep warrens on his land. A warren on Drake's Island in Plymouth Sound was given to the Plympton Priory in 1135, and another was recorded on Lundy almost 30 years later. Lundy being an ideal location as the rabbits had nowhere to go.

The animals were bred for their meat and their fur, and during the Middle Ages were seen as a rare and expensive luxury, with one rabbit worth more than a craftsman's wages for a day's work. It was only in the 19th century that it was regarded as a poor man's food. Many thousands were sent on the train every day to the cities of Plymouth, Exeter and Bristol, even as far afield as London, Birmingham and Liverpool.

Lloyd Maunder used to send wicker hampers full of these creatures to London by train each week, supplying its major customer J Sainsbury.

At one time there were hundreds of warrens in Devon and many on

Mrs Ware in the kitchen at Ditsworthy Warren c 1930
▼

Dartmoor, suggesting that this was probably the centre of English rabbit farming. Rabbits remained an important commercial commodity right through the 19th and early 20th century. It was a highly efficient system: a man, two boys and several long legged dogs could control a warren with many thousand of breeding rabbits. They only had to watch out for weasels, stoats and foxes. On Dartmoor some of the famous warrens were at Ditsworthy, Huntingdon, Headland and Hen Tor. Many were medieval: Trowlesworthy Warren was reputedly set up as early as 1272.

James Hannaford and his family
at Headland Warren, North Bovey
c 1890. © Chris Chapman

Three rabbits roof boss from
Tavistock Church. © Chris Chapman

Rabbit therefore is a much underrated meat and for centuries was the staple meat for many Devon men and their families, particularly when out on the remote mining settlements. It was hard life being a warrener but not without its rewards. Indeed the three rabbits or three hares symbol with conjoined ears can still be seen in roof bosses of at least seventeen Devon churches such as Tavistock, South Tawton, Throwleigh, Spreyton, Chagford, North Bovey, Widecombe in the Moor and Cheriton Bishop to name but a few. One theory is that the rabbits were seen as a symbol of wealth and fertility, to counterbalance the wild excesses of the Green Man. For others they have a more religious and esoteric significance.

Whatever the true meaning of the medieval symbolism, rabbits meant money and they often used to say that the rent of the warren could be paid for in rabbit skins alone. But warrening had its financial risks. In the blizzards of 1891 Ditsworthy Warren lost nearly all of its rabbits and the snow drifts were so high that the dog was found pawing at the bedroom window to be let in.

Rabbit farming only came to an end in 1954 with the introduction of myxomatosis and Rabbit Clearance legislation. Half a century later wild rabbit is still popular as a cheap form of meat and can be found in high street butchers as well as on the menu in up-market restaurants. Sadly, the days of seeing scores of rabbits hung up by their hocks outside game dealers alongside the odd brace of pheasant are long gone. Rabbit stew is a fine dish. In Peter Brear's recent book on Cooking and Dining in Medieval England there is an excellent recipe for stewed rabbit 'Cony in clear broth' – stewed rabbit with ginger, saffron, red wine, parsley and thyme.

A brace of rabbit await skinning and jointing for the kitchen

Wild Venison and Deer Farming

For centuries game was the protected privilege of rich landowners who also had herds of park or fallow deer, whilst Red Deer were strictly Royal property. In our modern and more democratic era, commercial shoots and venison farms have made it readily available to all, and certainly pheasant and venison can even be found on some supermarkets' pre-pack shelves.

Up in North Devon, Paul Messenger of Beckland Game, Hartland, chairman of the South West Branch of the British Deer Society, is also a BDS trainer and assessor of stalkers - so guarantees that his venison has

Stag roof boss c 1500 Coldridge Church, near Crediton

Stag with hinds at Wallace's, Hemyock

been killed humanely by qualified stalkers. He sells at Hartland farmers' market, The Big Sheep December markets and from the farm gate. Also as a shoot manager, in addition he offers a variety of game – pheasant, wild duck, partridge, woodcock and snipe.

Many high street butchers also supply wild game and venison. The main thing is to check where the venison has come from, that it has been shot cleanly by a marksman and that it is not been poached. Poaching by gangs with dogs can be very destructive and the animals are often very stressed before they are killed.

Some farms, rearing conventional livestock, also specialise in supplying wild venison whether it be Red Deer, Roe deer or Fallow when it is season. Mark Bury, for instance, of Eversfield Organics near Bratton Clovelly, sells non-organic wild venison shot on his estate from small, local wild herds who roam free.

Venison pie

Over the past few decades deer farming has become increasingly popular with farmers who want to diversify. High in the beautiful Blackdown Hills lies Hill Farm, home for 25 years to the Wallace family, Graham, wife Ruth and Graham's mum Diana, and their red deer farming enterprise. Why Farmed Venison? Because, in Graham Wallace's view, "you always know the provenance of the product you buy and, because it is much younger, it is better eating quality."

The calves from their 70 strong breeding herd are reared on grass and a supplementary feed that is free from modern additives. When ready, at about 2 years, they are shot on farm, avoiding the stress of travelling to an abattoir. All the venison, along with their beef, lamb and pork, is processed in their on-farm butchery and sold through their own farm shop and café, at Taunton Farmers Market and to village shops in Devon, Somerset and Dorset. Amongst several other deer farms across the county is Deer Force 10, near Totnes, who rear organically and supply farm shops such as Riverford and Occombe Farm. Venison is a major part of Devon's game sales and is readily available throughout the county. These days you don't have to be Royalty to eat the finest venison. You just have to know the right people.

Beefing it up – Red Ruby or South Devon?

A brace

However, when you need a real feast to entertain your village and you need something slightly larger than rabbit, and you don't want to get caught poaching a deer, a good solid Devon beef animal fits the bill admirably, whether it be a Red Ruby from the North or a South Devon from the South Hams. The improvement of such pedigree livestock has played a vital part in the local economy in Devon. As one farmer said, rubbing his hand along the back of a particularly fine South Devon specimen at the Devon Show, "they do make I purr." Hubert Snowdon was brought up at Thurlestone on the south coast and remembers the great red tides of animals being driven up onto the moor for the summer grazing. They would then be under the control of the quarter men who looked after them and they were paid at the end of the summer when the cattle had fattened and were driven down again. These commoners' rights to graze on the moor were an integral part of the farming year and enabled the farmers to concentrate on their arable farming in the summer months. The South Devon was very much a dual purpose animal giving good beef and good milk. As early as 1625 a consignment of 500 Devon cattle were driven into Plymouth and sold to the Navy. No doubt some for salt beef but more likely as breeding animals to keep the fledgling colonies in

America up to the mark. Indeed some of the cattle societies in North America trace their roots back to these early years and the importation of Devon Cattle. No doubt the Pilgrim Fathers were not averse to a bit of Devon topside. Earlier still, in 1366 at Tavistock Abbey one red bull was noted as being accepted in payment for heriot or death duties on behalf of the manor of Werrington just over the border near Launceston. Some say the red cattle came across with the Saxons.

Apart from being draught animals, the South Devons, established as a separate breed in 1800, were also expected to produce ample milk to make cream, butter and cheese. The South Devon Herd Book Society was founded in 1891 and the breed went from strength to strength. For many years at Dartington Hall, near Totnes, there was a very successful South Devon cattle breeding centre and AI unit. Between 1944 and 1970 the

Some of Peter and Henrietta Greig's Red Ruby cattle at Pipers Farm near Cullompton

*Waddeton Poll Sunshine 4th a South
Devon bull entered in The Devon
County Show 2009*

breed flourished and by the late 1960s it had the distinction of being the only breed to qualify for milk subsidy and calf subsidy.

Sadly, however beautiful they were, they slowly went out of fashion as increased traffic, rules about animal movements and risk of disease, turned what had been a very natural pastoral tradition into something quite different, much of it designed to produce large volumes of cheap food quickly. The invasion of fast finishing continental beef breeds such as Charolais and Simmental and dairy breeds like Friesian and Channel Island Jersey and Guernsey breeds have also taken their toll on the breed. The South Devon is now predominately a beef animal again and its marbled meat is much sought after. South Devons have been exported to South Africa, Canada and America and can cope very well with extremes of temperature.

In the North of Devon, on the other hand, the indigenous breed is the Red Ruby also known as North Devon or Ruby Reds. These great beasts are linked to other red cattle of England such as Lincoln Red, Red Poll and Sussex.

These Red Rubies – one of the great Devon icons, were also used as draught animals for hundreds of years, but their milk and meat made them favourites in the colonies too. It is thought that the Saxons probably brought with them cattle that cross bred with native breeds to become ancestors of the Devon Cattle. In 1627 a bull and two heifers were exported to the New World and many of the earliest Devon bloodlines are still there. In the nineteenth century, the first corned beef was produced in Massachusetts from Devon cattle. They had an unusual ability to thrive in climatic extremes, in countries as far apart as South Africa, South America and Australia.

By 1794, writing in a 'General view of the County of Devon' Robert Fraser noted that "The breed of cattle in North Devon is remarkably fine

HRH Prince Edward meets Red Ruby cattle and breeders in the Judging Ring at The Devon County Show 2009

MEAT ON THE MOOR: DARTMOOR FARMERS' ASSOCIATION

Think of our cattle and sheep as environmental managers says Philip Coaker, fifth generation to farm at Runnage Farm near Postbridge. "Without them and other traditional moorland management techniques such as swaling (planned, selective burning of specific areas, to thin out old vegetation and allow new grass shoots to grow) the moors would be over-run by invasive vegetation such as bracken and scrub. By cropping the moorland vegetation, the animals are helping to maintain the moor landscape as we all know and love it."

Christine Malseed who farms at Frenchbeer Farm near Chagford puts it a different way. "We maintain the landscape and countryside through our farming activities and produce meat with exceptional flavour, almost as a by-product. Cattle and sheep are a management tool to keep moorland for public access, landscape value and wildlife diversity."

"Most farmers don't know just how good their meat is, we don't know what rubbish is out there, as we always eat our own animals. I've had some meat at restaurants which tasted like a washing up sponge! They add so many spices and flavourings to cover up the tastelessness of the meat. I firmly believe you should be able to taste the flavour of the meat without too much fussing."

and is perhaps the best in the Kingdom, many people preferring them to the famous Longhorn breed of Mr Bakewell"

In 1796, another keen eyed observer, William Marshall, who had travelled the whole country observing agriculture at first hand, declared that 'The Breed of Cattle in Devonshire is in many respects, the most perfect breed of Cattle in this Island.' At South Molton he noticed that out of six cows belonging to Mr Trigg at Barton on Great Hill, one cow was 'superior to the rest; remarkable in carcase, well loined, wide at the hips, and square in the quarters, with a fine head and bone. The horns also fine, and shorter than ordinary. The color a lightish blood-red, the rest darker and with smokey faces.' Red Rubies without a doubt.

Also in 1796 Francis Quartly, built the fame and national reputation of the breed by walking his best cattle from Molland to Bath which was then the home of major agricultural improvement. Today we still have the Royal Bath and West Show which was started in 1777. Not a few of its members came from Devon and were keen to showcase their breeds of cattle.

By the middle of the 19th century the Devon was well established and numerically surpassed only by Shorthorns. It was the post-war boom in supermarkets that almost did for the Devon and the South Devon. What they were looking for was leaner meat from bigger animals. To achieve this quickly meant that these cattle put on layers of fat which a skilled butcher would recognise as adding flavour, but did not suit the multiple retailers' buyers, whose customers wanted to buy ready-packed, bright red, lean meat. Continental bulls were introduced to achieve this and create larger carcases, marginalising the breed that could produce, and still does, the highest eating quality beef on grass alone, without the need for concentrated animal feeds. Given the forecast global food shortages perhaps the Devon's day has come?

Known as a '2rent paying' breed, for its ability to thrive where others could not and still produce quality beef, Red Rubies also lend themselves to parkland such as Forde Abbey which has a very good herd. Forde Abbey used to be in Devon until the 18th century but is now in West Dorset. Such are the vagaries of county boundaries.

Red Ruby has also become recognised by many conservation organisations as ideal for grazing conservation land, causing minimum damage to grassland.

Traditionally born on Exmoor, single suckled and brought down onto lower pastures to finish – a docile temperament, natural resistance to disease and the eating quality of their beef has led to a real resurgence in their popularity over the last 25 years. Grazing herds are a common sight in North Devon and can now be found throughout the county.

Chris Pouncey, of Brightly Barton, Umberleigh took over his father-in-

Prime ribs of their own Red Ruby beef at Pipers Farm butchery near Cullompton

Pipers Farm butcher preparing three week hung Red Ruby beef

law's herd 25 years ago. For him "the satisfaction of rearing – including the careful science of choosing the right bloodlines, their temperament, the sight of them with the afternoon sunlight on their mahogany coloured coats, the most superb end product – all makes them the most wonderful breed to work with."

Shapland & Searle, South Molton butchers, buy direct from local farmers and every week their blackboard says "This week's beef is Red Ruby from Mr Pouncey, Umberleigh". Michael Shapland is very clear why. "The texture and colour of lean and fat go together very well – a dark, rich colour. The balance of fat to lean is just the right, basting the lean meat during cooking for succulence and excellent flavour.

Our customers like to know where it comes from. They live locally and the Red Ruby is a local breed from a local farm. They always say 'I will have some of Mr Pouncey's beef'."

Moor Beef

For some beef farmers, black not red is the favourite colour. High on Dartmoor Richard Vines' Welsh Black cattle enjoy the best of the summer grazing. Welsh Blacks benefit from the extensive grazing on these unimproved grasslands. For Richard the breed is less important than the natural rearing methods and the range of grasses and herbs available in this unimproved grassland, compared with the highly managed lowland pastures. There is not a bag of fertiliser to be seen on Richard and Lizzie Vine's neat moorland farm, no pesticides or herbicide sprays, and by using a local abattoir the stress of travelling their final miles is reduced. Then the beef is dry aged for at least three weeks. "Soil, cattle and time are our only ingredients," says Richard. Unlike intensively reared beef which is fed a high cereal diet in order to finish them quickly and produce a series of uniform carcases.

This was a common theme across the county – farmer-grazier-butchers with an emphasis on quality, taking their time and producing

Richard Vines' Welsh Black cattle on the open moor above Chagford

sheep and cattle in an unhurried way, giving us, the consumer, every opportunity to end up with some of Britain's finest beef and lamb on our tables.

Richard is a member of the Dartmoor Farmers' Association which has been set up to promote and sell beef and lamb raised in the most traditional way on the moor. By providing a more specialist market for this meat, and the qualities that Dartmoor brings to it, it is a win-win situation helping to preserve this very special ancient landscape, with its small farms, often found in the most windswept and desolate locations.

Unimproved pasture gives these browsing creatures an incredibly varied diet, everything from rushes, seed heads, wild flowers and bilberries as well as grass. Sustainable hill farming maintains the environment for wildlife and recreation. But the balance has to be right.

5000 years of caring for the land, and farming with respect, has created this unique way of life. Uncultivated grassland, no fertilisers, no sprays, rough herbage, essential to the moor's ecology – also helps to promote slow growth, producing some of finest meat in the country – with improved flavour, and the all important marbling.

Quality and flavour – there is all the difference in the world between grass fed, native beef breeds and intensively reared continentals crossed on a dairy cow.

Oxen

What is often forgotten is that for over a thousand years cattle were primarily used as draught animals long before cart horses became all the rage. The Luttrell Psalter dating from c 1330 is illustrated with a team of two men and four oxen ploughing in the fields. Oxen, usually castrated male animals, formed an important part of the local economy and were also used to pull carts and perform any other farm work which required a bit of muscle. They were slow and steady and when they died, even though they were a bit tough, you could still eat them.

There is a wonderful description from William Marshall in 1796 of the quality of the singing that accompanied their work ploughing the fields:

"Oxen are universally worked in Yoke; yet are remarkably tractable; and step out with a pace which a Kentish clown would think a hardship to follow, with his high horse team.

▲
A team of oxen ploughing from
The Luttrell Psalter c 1330

The style of Driving an Ox team, here is observable; indeed cannot pass unnoticed by a stranger. The language, though in a great degree peculiar to the county, does not arrest the attention; but the tone or rather tune, in which it is delivered. It resembles with great exactness the chantings, or recitative of the Cathedral service. The plow boy chants the counter tenor, with unabated ardour through the day; the plowman throwing in, at intervals, his hoarser notes. It is understood that this chanting march, which may sometimes be heard to a considerable distance, encourages and animates the team, as the music of a marching army, or the song of rowers. Let this be as it may, I have never seen so much cheerfulness attending the operation of ploughing, anywhere, as in Devonshire."

▶ ▶
Two young Red Ruby bulls have a friendly tussle at Occombe Farm's Visitor Centre

Maybe one day, when the oil has run out and tractors have all been put away in museums, we shall see teams of red and black oxen ploughing in Devon again.

ANGEL MEAT AND CHICKEN ARKS

OVERLEAF
"Patrick" is a Whiteface Dartmoor
ram. He has now retired from the
show ring at the grand age of nine.
He is one of the best and his
progeny have won at county and
local shows. He will now stand at
stud on Fiona West's farm at
Swinedown on Houndtor 1200ft
above sea level

◀
*Sheep graze in the fields near
Walkhampton church on the
western edge of Dartmoor near
Tavistock*

*A surprise visitor abandons the
passenger trailer on a children's
tour of Little Comfort Farm, near
Braunton*

▼

SHEEP HAVE BEEN A VERY IMPORTANT PART of Devon's economy not just for meat but for wool. Descended from an original native breed, the Whiteface Dartmoor is described by its breed society as ideal for the modern consumer, of a good flavour and texture – known as Angel Meat.

Evidence shows that Dartmoor was probably first farmed around 4,000 BC. On Dartmoor there is plenty of evidence to show that Bronze Age man preferred the open high ground to the enclosed forests. There would have been hundreds of settlements on the moor, some in year round use, others just for the summer. Dartmoor has been described as a "summer pasturage for sheep and cattle" and in the late 19th century cattle would come from as far as Kent for summer grazing. The system of moving cattle and sheep onto the high moor for the summer months, sometimes known as transhumance, carried on until after the Second World War. Cattle would be taken from collection points and driven through the lanes to the various sections of the moor. This practice of sending the stock for the summer grazing freed up the lowlands for growing winter keep, hay, roots and oats. On Dartmoor this was reversed with farmers renting winter keep, bringing their animals down to lamb or calve then back up again onto the high moor commons. Off the moor land would be anywhere from Ipplepen, Marldon or even down to Thurlestone. Some were paid for at so much per head while commoners had free rights to graze certain areas during the summer. Animals became 'leered' or 'hefted' to certain areas.

Unlike similar systems in Wales, where this was known as the hafod, farmers would not stay up with their stock. Here on Dartmoor this was known as agistment. On Dartmoor it would be the moormen who would be responsible for the animals once they had arrived on the moor. Sometimes they were known as quarter men, each responsible for one of the four quarters: North, South, East and West. There was a system of pounds where the animals would be gathered after a drift. Pony drifts are still common in the autumn. It is an ancient and yet efficient system. Some of the pounds or enclosures are still in use today like Dunnabridge Pound. These pounds are sometimes prehistoric, like Grimspound and also enclosed settlements. They were linked to reeves, ancient boundaries that stretched across the moor for miles.

Sally Vincent's White Faced Dartmoor sheep have wonderful views over the River Dart above Dittisham

Others were very large like Erme Pound. These remains show that the moor has been used for thousands of years for summer grazing. Indeed it is this custom which has shaped most of Devon's droving lanes.

The open moorland is divided into 'commons' – separate areas where commoners have grazing rights and their rights are tied to surrounding farmlands. Formed in 1985, The Dartmoor Commoner's Council, governs the exercise of rights, vegetation management and animal husbandry. There are 23 parishes which have commoner's rights.

During the 14th century there were as many as 9,750 cattle enjoying the summer grazing on the moor. Modern traffic has made this system impractical, and in one of the last big movements, in 1944 more than 800 bullocks were driven from the southern end of the moor alone.

Cattle, however, for many years were not the most important livestock. It was sheep that provided the county's great wealth from the wool trade.

Exeter was one of the most important ports in the country, exporting to Holland, Germany and Spain, and for more than 30 years, into the start of the 18th century, Devon exports were the most important sector of England's textile trade. Defoe described Tiverton, another centre for wool, as "the greatest manufacturing town in the county."

So mutton was a rare treat when an animal was past its best, in terms of how we would now judge eating quality today. In 1808 Vancouver wrote of the native Dartmoor breed that "when put to good keeping . . . they always prove the very best of mutton, and never fail commanding a superior price". And Eliza Bray, in her 1832 description, writes of them as "the well known Oakhampton mutton", kept principally for the sake of their wool, but of superior flavour.

Fortunately a few of the traditional Devon wool breeds, the Grey Faced Dartmoor and the White Faced Dartmoor survive, mostly in the hands of specialists. At one time it was the Grey Faced on the west of the moor. On the east of the moor the White Face predominated. Originating from Exmoor, the Devon Closewool and the Exmoor Horn, have been bred for hardiness. Both have recently made a comeback for the quality of their meat. The Exmoor Horn in particular thanks to the Mutton Renaissance. There is also the Devon and Cornwall Longwool which is derived from the South Devon and Devon Longwool and this, as its name implies, is reared predominately for its fleece.

On Dartmoor the Scotch Blackface slowly replaced these breeds as it was hardier and could stay out all year if necessary. The first man credited with keeping them on the moor was John Gemmel, in 1877 at Teignhead Farm, who brought 1300 Blackfaced sheep down from Scotland. One of his tenants who also brought Blackfaced sheep down from Scotland was called, appropriately enough, James Lamb.

Visitors at Little Comfort Farm, near Braunton

Postbridge, in the centre of Dartmoor, reveals through some of its ancient remains that it was quite likely to have been farmed by settlers in the Bronze Age. High ground was the safest place for settlements and any cultivation would have been to feed the tinners, mining for tin.

It was the Saxons who introduced a more settled form of agriculture in the fifth century, although the concept of shared pastures and common fields came later like Braunton Great Field (see chapter 8).

In the post-Norman and medieval era it was the monasteries and great landowners who held most of the land, and this would have been a time of great planting of orchards and vineyards.

However the real landscape changes came in the 17th and 18th centuries, which led to the landscape pattern with which we are so familiar today. Only the vast and untameable wilderness of Dartmoor, parts of Exmoor and other uplands escaped the creation of small fields enclosed by high hedges and dry stone walls. Even on the fringes of Dartmoor, farms such as Holwell were cultivated until the early 20th century.

Devon has long had a history of producing excellent meat and dairy produce. Early meat production would have been one or two animals per family, most of which would be slaughtered in the autumn, then cured to provide much needed salt beef, salt pork and bacon during the winter and spring months. As farms and estates grew, so livestock production moved into a more commercial format.

The less well off would probably have to be content with a few backyard fowl, the occasional pig for the cottage who could afford one, and food that could be trapped or hunted, legally or otherwise.

But in the 15th and 16th centuries farming thrived either through food to supply the Navy in Plymouth or for provisioning the ships fishing as far away as Newfoundland. Raleigh and Drake would have taken shiploads of salt beef and salt pork when they started their epic journeys.

It was the coming of the railway in 1844 that transformed Devon's cattle, pig and dairy industry.

Sunday Roast

One of the most influential Devon families that started sending meat and dairy produce away to the growing urban markets, fed by the industrial revolution, was Lloyd Maunder, who by 1898 were selling direct to customers such as John James Sainsbury for his chain of "provisions shops".

Always progressive and forward looking, in the late 1950s Lloyd Maunder was the first company to pioneer broiler chicken production in this country, working with local farmers to produce cheap chicken that everyone could afford.

Before the Second War chicken had been a great delicacy, a treat, and was often in fact laying hens that had come to the end of their useful lives. Percy Maunder and his son John set up contracts with local farmers to produce these chickens. By the end of the 1950s they had achieved their

Lloyd Maunder butchers shop Kingsbridge
▼

Stamp collecting – Riverford beef

target of producing a "ten shilling" (50p) bird. The rest is not quite history because although Lloyd Maunder became a major producer and at one point had the most modern and efficient processing plant in Europe, the company also spotted the rising interest in free range and higher welfare birds. This led to other contracts with local farmers to set up small poultry production units that could fit in around their other farming commitments. For many livestock farmers in Devon, hit badly by the impact of the 2001 foot and mouth epidemic, this was an essential lifeline. It would not be putting it too bluntly to say that the relatively quick cash flow, compared with the time taken to produce beef cattle or sheep, has helped the Devon landscape to retain its patchwork of relatively small fields, bounded by wonderful hedges, small copses and woodland that is so easy to take for granted.

More recently, recognising that some consumers were looking for birds produced to higher welfare standards, the company introduced what has become a major part of its production – free range and organic outdoor birds. Ironically the backyard chicken has become a popular feature of many Devon small to medium sized farms, in addition to smallholdings and hobby farmers. This is in part a reaction to the growing desire to have ethically produced food with a trusted provenance, a "grow your own" response to the economic downturn of 2008 onwards. In truth I suspect that many of the lifestylers keeping a few pigs or chickens are probably not saving any money, but the quality of what they grow and eat will be infinitely better than anything shop bought, not to mention the pleasure enjoyed in the process.

After more than 100 years of promoting putting Devon produce on the national map and helping to give it a national reputation for excellence, in January 2008 Lloyd Maunder was taken over by the 2 Sisters Food Group, although the business remains the same. This expansion into more specialist poultry threw a lifeline to many small and medium-sized farms when times had been hard. Without this added income stream which brought a relatively quick return, many of these family farms would have disappeared in the last decade and been absorbed into bigger units where economies of scale are what matter. The Devon landscape would have been the poorer for it.

Another successful specialist poultry producer is Jason Wise of Ark Chicken. Jason Wise is a man with a mission – to bring us top class chickens and chicken products at an affordable price. Not for him the lure

Jason Wise – Ark Chicken, Roosters of Babylon, near Silverton, Exeter

of big contracts to supply the supermarkets. His parents had been part of the intensive chicken sector when he had been growing up but he was not satisfied with the welfare standards or the speed of production. So in 1999 he set up Ark Chicken in the Culm Valley, moving to Silverton in 2002.

Small groups of chickens range out of doors all day, sleeping or sheltering in specially designed arks dotted across the farm. His minimal scale means that Jason and his small team, led by chef and former lecturer Phil Oram, maximise every part of the birds they produce. In addition to selling whole and jointed chickens, they make stocks, soups, chicken pasties and pies, a fabulous range of chicken liver patés, and deal in game during the winter months.

He can be found at farmers' markets, or sells from the farm gate, although he does not call the appropriately named Chicken Shack a farm shop.

Creedy Carver's Peter and Sue Coleman of Merryfield Farm, near Crediton have built a reputation for high welfare, high quality chicken – both free-range and barn reared. Latterly joined by son, James, who rears

Free range chickens at Little Comfort Farm, Braunton
▼

ducks to the same demanding standards for them, they now supply outlets throughout Devon and the southern counties.

Another family who also turned their back on intensive chicken production was Peter and Henrietta Greig. Peter's father had run broiler units in Kent and when the couple married and settled, initially in North Yorkshire, they decided that this was not the sort of food that they wanted to feed to their young family.

They have been uncompromising about this and the way that they farm, butcher and sell meat ever since. Pipers Farm has grown from a small Devonshire farm to a business that relies on a network of small, traditional, family farms to rear poultry, pigs, beef and lamb in time-honoured, unstressed ways. This means with the highest possible animal welfare levels, using traditional breeds that take much longer to finish – a grass fed Devon bullock will not be mature enough to eat at its best before 36 months, says Peter. Compare that with a barley fed continental cross bullock, such as Charolais or Simmental, which would take no more than 18 months from farm to fork.

▲
Peter Greig of Pipers Farm with his dog, 'Fly'

So up on Exmoor, and along the Exe and Culm Valleys, dozens of farming families know that if they produce to the right standards, they have a ready market for their animals.

Peter Greig relies on traditional Saddleback pigs reared in small groups, run outdoors in the summer but in cosy indoor, straw-filled quarters for the winter. He eschews labels such as organic because his system is really a one-off hybrid that does not fit any of the tightly defined systems. What it does do is to produce the highest quality meat to his exacting and uncompromising standards. At the same time Pipers have the satisfaction of knowing that they are helping to sustain small scale family farms to remain viable.

Small scale family farming businesses are the ones that created the landscape and that doesn't get better than in Devon. Pipers animal feed is milled by a small, 100 year old local feed mill and animals are slaughtered at a small local abattoir, just 20 minutes away.

No compromise is the by-word for many of the county's other top meat producers. And to borrow one of Peter's straplines the result is "probably the best eating sensation in the world."

What also sets Pipers Farm apart from many others running similar mail order meat businesses, is that they also have a butchers' shop in the centre of Exeter, selling not only fresh cuts and cured meats such as their own bacon and hams, but also a range of ready meals, some more expensive than others. Cheap, Pipers Farm produce is not but, to use an over hackneyed phrase, "you get what you pay for". And Henrietta has recently introduced "meals in a mo" for time pressed careerists and working families, and the firm offers local deliveries to offices and homes in some parts of Exeter.

While the high street butcher may have become a threatened species over the last half century, Devon has its good share of proper butchers. From on-farm butchers and meat box businesses, such as Higher Hacknell Farm, which was probably one of the first organic producers in Devon to recognise the growing interest in buying organic meat by mail order – to independent high street stores such as Lloyd Maunder Westcountry Family butchers, which remains in control of Andrew Maunder, the fourth generation to work in the business that was founded more than 120 years ago.

The company has 13 stores in Devon and prides itself on sourcing its meat as locally as possible. So each week the individual shops have

Lloyd Maunder butchers shop, Kingsbridge

blackboards showing the name of the farm supplying that week's beef, pork or lamb. It has a dedicated sausage maker, turning out more than 17 different types of sausage sold in all its shops, and of course the highly skilled butchers take a great pride in turning out special cuts and butchering the meat to create some quite literally mouth-watering displays. Like many of their remaining contemporaries, they have recognised that traceability, quality and freshness are the key, along with properly hung, dry-aged meat. So beef is hung for a minimum of 21 days, lamb for 5 days.

However if you thought that the traditional butcher was a dying breed, replaced by direct sales either from farm shop and farm gate sales, or through mail order, think again.

Mark Gribble in Ivybridge has set up a new chain of butchers, supplying caterers and restaurateurs and retailing through three shops across south Devon in less than a decade. He is not surprisingly 'bullish' that the high street butcher has a future.

Although he is less concerned about basing his meat around traditional breeds, he knows that he must offer exceptional value for money.

He is quite clear that the way an animal is treated throughout the food chain is what creates a good eating experience.

"It's not necessarily the breed. It is about being raised naturally, on grass wherever possible, being given the time it needs to mature, then being handled properly at the abattoir, hung properly and butchered well. And finally it must be cooked well."

Again he recognises the importance of the link between the food on our plates and the lovely Devon countryside. Before I had time to start explaining the outline of this book he was telling me the story that I had hoped to hear.

A phenomenon that started in the mid 1980s is mail order meat. As Britain's food culture started to re-establish itself, individual farmer-butchers such as Peter Greig recognised a huge untapped market which led to mail order and meat box schemes. Now many farmers do this in many different ways, from the more formal Well Hung Meat Company, which is almost but not quite exclusively a meat box scheme – there is a small farm shop that you can call in at, perched on the southern edge of Dartmoor at the side of a busy main road – to smaller businesses that build up a loyal group of customers and find that they need to do little in the way of marketing and advertising.

Selling meat direct is often the key to successful marketing and in this way the farmer or butcher builds up that all important relationship with his customer. Often it is a two way process and the customer, who may well live many miles away in a town or inner city, will hopefully learn more about farming and the seasonal trends of agriculture.

3 /
GOOSE SANDWICHES AND HOG ROAST

◄
*Neil Woolcock in full swing at
the The Goosey Fair auction at
Tavistock's livestock market,
held every year on the second
Wednesday in October*

DEVON IS A VERY LARGE COUNTY and it is scattered with ancient market towns that were in themselves, until recently, self-contained and self-sufficient units. They often relied on weekly markets, but the really big events were the annual fairs that drew people and livestock from far and wide.

Tavistock Goosey Fair

One such colourful survival from medieval times is Tavistock Goosey Fair. In 1105 Henry I granted a Royal Charter to the monks of Tavistock to run a weekly Pannier Market which is still held on Fridays. A few years later in 1116 another charter made Tavistock a full market town and a three-day fair was also granted to mark the feast of Saint Rumon, patron saint of the Abbey. This was celebrated annually on 29th August. After the Dissolution of the Abbey in 1539 the fair was changed to Michaelmas, 29th September, the feast of St Michael, where it stayed till 1822, when it was shifted once again to the second Wednesday in October where it has remained ever since. Apart from geese, the fair also saw cattle, sheep and horses being sold. It was also a hiring fair where farm labourers could seek employment for the year. In the past people had goose and gander rights and would fatten them up on the common land. Rents and tithes were also paid in geese and they were used very much as local currency. Goose fat was much prized.

One person who knows Goosey Fair better than most is Neil Woolcock of Ward and Chowen who still auctions the geese up at the cattle market.

"The numbers of geese vary each year. Because of Defra rules and regulations there are fewer producers than there used to be many years ago. Sometimes we might have 30-40 geese, some years we might have 60 -100. Outlets for geese are now few and far between. Most of the geese are Emdens. They go from £14-£15 up to about £20 depending on the size and the potential for growth. Most geese are not for breeding but are bought to fatten up for the table at Christmas. Judging the weight – it is all in the eye and a lifetime's expertise."

"The likes of the celebrity chefs, they can do wonderful things with a goose when it is dead. They do prefer them oven ready rather than alive. Geese are very rarely driven in these days, but mostly now only for the press and television cameras. The geese tend to come in the backs of cars or in small trailers. They all have to comply with regulations."

"Goose lunches? You can still get goose sandwiches it is part of the tradition of Goose Fair. Normally the auction takes half to three quarters of an hour. Michael Brearly, our local vicar, he blessed the geese this year and hopefully he might have put in a good word for those buying the geese as well."

*Richard Mathers with a fine
goose*
▼

All the fun of the Fair in Tavistock

"Goose Fair is a rare survival of a traditional market. It is not the most commercial part of the market but it adds a valuable piece of colour to the type of market we have in Tavistock. Other people do very well."

Cattle and Sheep Auctions

Auctioneers are a very important link in the food chain. Not only do they facilitate the buying and selling of farms, they also facilitate the buying and selling of livestock. They understand how the community works and they have to keep their fingers on the pulse. Seasonal livestock markets and local slaughter houses are the life blood of the farming community and the backbone of the local economy. They are the link between the farms, the landscape and the butchers who provide the local meat which chefs so desperately need. But local meat has to be of high quality and the auctioneer can usually judge a good animal when he sees one. In Tavistock many cattle come off the moor after the summer's grazing and are sold as stores to fatten them up on better ground lower down. It is an ancient tradition.

The auctioneer, Neil Woolcock, takes up the story again:

"In the past we used to hold a cattle market on the same day as Goosey Fair but now we have it a few days earlier. It is one of our biggest store cattle sales of the year when we may have 500-600 of West Devon's finest store cattle – a lot of continental breeds these days as well as Galloways and South Devons. Indeed cattle come to us from as far as thirty miles away. We now hold it on the previous Tuesday. We do get a sprinkling of Red Rubies. Prices have been quite favourable in recent years, you could be looking at average price of £500-£550 but we have had bullocks up to £1000."

"Devon sheep? We do get a few Closewool sheep, these breeds are coming back. Keeping the old breeds going is a terribly important part of the agricultural history of the area, Grey Face Dartmoor, White Faced Dartmoor, Devon and Cornwall Longwool. It is great that our clients are still keeping them. We used to have St John's Fair, second Wednesday of September, the market then held about 200 pens all Grey Faced Dartmoor ewes. Lucky if we have ten pens now. They used to cross them with Suffolks. Now its mostly Scots Blackface and mules."

"We used to also have sheep sales in Dousland and cattle sales in Princetown, subject to the weather, they have quite a lot of weather in Princetown. When the railway closed in the 1950s the pony sales came down to Tavistock."

"I have been auctioneering for the last twenty years and my father, Russell Woolcock has been auctioneering for the last sixty years. He has been secretary of the Dartmoor Commoners Council for almost as long. The moor is divided into Four Quarters: East, West, North and South. The quarter men were appointed by the Duchy and looked out to the cattle. Each quarter now has five commoners. There were other ancient rights like Venville rights, as well as rights of turbary, estover and pannage."

"You have to know your farmers, you have to know your buyers, you have to know your stock. You have to know its value."

"My father saw farmers into their farms in the 1940s and 1950s and carried out their retirement sales forty-fifty years later. It is lovely seeing young farmers going into new farms and starting up a relationship with them. A lot of the farms round here are still passed from father to son. They put life and soul into the farm. It is lovely to see that continuity and investment. It is great for my father, he can see youngsters in their twenties in the market now, and he can remember their grandfathers at the same age."

"The local food movement has provided a wonderful opportunity for the farming community to diversify. It has provided them with other outlets for them to market their product. Because at the end of the day, the farmers in Devon have a fantastic product and they want to see it being

Auction ring in Holsworthy Market
▼

marketed to its fullest ability. What's lovely about the butcher's shops round here is that you can walk in and say 'Who's beef are you selling today?' and they can say 'Yup I am selling Patrick Toop's or Willy Dawe's beef.' I know them and I know where the beef came from and you can say that about all the stock round here. It is lovely."

Back to Basics: The good life –
Hog Roast and Bacon

In 2000 Roger and Jackie Milsom moved to Little Comfort Farm. Comfort is not in short supply despite the name. It is hidden away in a beautiful, peaceful and almost secret valley not far from the North Devon coast. They have two business streams, self-catering holiday cottages and organic farming, producing beef, lamb, mutton, pork, apple juice and free range eggs. Jackie also makes jams from the fruit grown in her garden. So far this sounds like the story of many other small farms, often run by "good lifers" or escapees from city life.

Jackie and Roger are different. Both from farming families and so totally aware of the difficulties of farming life, they are passionate about what they do. The difference is that they are in a unique position to merge the two businesses and fulfil their desire to communicate with their customers how the food on their plates is produced.

However this is not a sanitised version of farming or a farm theme park, there are no rabbits, apart from wild ones, or guinea pigs. There are Red Ruby cattle, a flock of Lleyn sheep, Gloucester Old Spot pigs and Silver Link laying hens. Holiday families are encouraged to join the daily farm

Gloucester Old Spot piglets at Little Comfort Farm

tours and to help feed the animals each morning.

"When they first arrive the children all rush about because it's countryside and fresh air. By the end of their stay their level of interest and understanding has moved into another stratosphere," explains Jackie, adding that more than half their customers return each year.

"One girl, who lives in a colliery area in the Midlands, has been coming since she was eight and is now 14. She won't leave the place, does all the egg packing and feeds all the lambs."

Peter Greig with a couple of his saddlebacks in the orchard at Pipers Farm

There are ready meals made using the farm's meat and vegetables, or visitors can buy pork, beef that has been properly hung for four weeks, mutton and lamb to cook immediately or to take home at the end of their stay. Breakfasts here instantly go up a notch with newly laid eggs and a bottle of Little Comfort apple juice. By the time this book is published, their meat may also be available by mail order, although the farm's output is so small that almost all of it is sold to visitors or to local customers.

Beef is grass fed and slowly matured for a "delicious depth of flavour" says the board in the office, also "hung for four weeks".

Historically, pigs were the natural cottagers' source of food, particularly as a valuable store of winter meat, preserved by salting and smoking. Indeed the cottagers' pig was a fairly common sight until the early 1960s. As with most farming livestock, various areas of the country had their own local breeds, such as the Wessex and Essex Saddlebacks and Gloucester Old Spot.

In Devon, the Devon Lop seems to have originated around Tavistock in the 15th century, where Tavistock Abbey then charged 2d (1p) per head pannage (the right to allow pigs to forage in woodlands for acorns and beech mast). In Cornwall called the Cornish White, it spread throughout the South West and was renamed the British Lop.

The Devon Black is thought to have been a Spanish black pig imported into Plymouth in the 1600s and crossed with the Lop. Today's recognised breed is the Large Black, originating from Devon, Cornish and East Anglian breeds.

With the drive for intensive, factory scale production many native breeds died out and the few that were left ran perilously close to extinction. Pioneers such as Anne Petch, (see chapter 15) encouraged by The Rare Breed Survival Trust, realised that the most flavoursome pork was produced from old fashioned breeds, reared in a traditional farming system. In 1979 she installed an on-farm butchery and, via her mail order service, achieved a national reputation for fresh pork, sausages, hams and bacon.

Increasing public awareness for food provenance has encouraged more and more farmers to diversify.

Debra Custance-Baker with two of her prize winning Large Black pigs at the Devon County Show 2009

Diversification should be fourth generation farmer Andrew Freemantle's middle name and presumably the judges who awarded Andrew the 2008 Devon Diversification Award thought so too.

Andrew runs the 70 acre Kenniford Farm at Clyst St Mary in partnership with his father Alan and helped by his mother Linda. Andrew is passionate about welfare – his free-range pigs are RSPCA Freedom Food approved – "I am proud to farm in a way which ensures my animals are treated humanely". At the same time, whilst many pig farmers are losing more than £20 per animal, he recognises the need to be profitable and achieves this by selling direct to the consumer. So, in May 2000 they opened the farm shop, an outlet for their own pork, sausages and bacon. After enjoying a hog roast at his own wedding reception, Andrew bought a roasting machine of his own and Kenniford Hog Roasts has grown from 16 in the first year to about 250 last summer. Next came their catering trailers, not only for the round of summer shows but others permanently stationed in

Ben Watson of Riverford Organic Farm, proudly showing his organic bacon

MOLE VALLEY FARMERS LTD

It might surprise you to know that during the last financial year, Mole Valley Farmers sold 61 tonnes of cheese, 120 tonnes of bacon and 50 tonnes of sausages! A far cry from its small beginnings. It also tells you a lot about farmers' high protein diets…

In 1960 a handful of North Devon farmers around South Molton got together to form a buying group. They saw that animal feed and farm equipment was much cheaper if they bought in bulk. Little did they imagine that 50 years later it would be the country's largest rural buying co-operative with a turnover in excess of £270 million. They now have 9 branches in the South West selling everything from farm buildings and animal feed to biscuits and yoghurt.

As Andrew Jackson, the Chief Executive, points out "The ethos today is still the same as it was in the 1960s – to supply farmers with goods and services to help their profitability. No one buys more competitively – the main reason for MVF being here. Also you don't have to be a farmer member to enjoy what Mole Valley has to offer – our non-farming customers make an important contribution, they appreciate quality products at keen prices".

The first food product on the shelves was bacon – to satisfy the demand for farms that did "B & B" and the range kept growing. "As a retail outlet", Andrew explains, "we are an important gateway for local and regional food because we have a very close affiliation

Mole Valley Farmers' car parks in South Molton, Cullompton and Newton Abbot. Recently extended, the Kenniford farm shop now serves as an outlet for other local suppliers. So what next....

At Lower Ashtown Farm, near South Molton, Mark Boundy has taken another route to market – rather than selling direct to the consumer himself, he rears for those who already have an established butchery or mail order business.

He set up his organic pig enterprise almost by accident. In 2000 he sold his dairy herd to a neighbour and soon after his young stepson asked for a pig for his birthday "I have always liked pigs – and it all started from there" says Mark. His herd now numbers 23 Saddleback cross sows and their litters, so he finishes approximately 250 porkers a year and has set up a regular supply chain to farm shop butcheries, such as Occombe Farm (see chapter 15). Why organic? Mark is very clear: "Because I know my pigs have a good life and are fit and well. It makes me happy to see them playing in the field – behaving naturally".

Preserving meat has always been a skilled art and for centuries curing and smoking was done, not to please the palate, but strictly to keep the meat edible for the cold winter's nights. In the days of sail, salt pork and beef fed the ship's company on their long voyages at sea. In fact, as late as 1938 Eric Newby reports that this was the staple diet of the tall ship Moshulu, because of its lack of refrigeration and long journeys between ports.

Over time different parts of the country developed different cures – dry salting or pickling in brine and adding a variety of flavourings such as honey, sugar, molasses, herbs and spices. Before sugar was widely available, wild honey was the sweetener of choice.

Smoking is popularly over oak, but other woods and aromatics can be added such as apple wood, or beech for colour. There are two distinct methods, cold smoking – to add flavour but not to cook the meat – and hot smoking, which not only imparts a rich flavour but cooks it as well.

Many of the butchers and farm shop butcheries included in this chapter also cure and smoke their own meat, in particular sides of bacon, hams and salt beef but also sausages and poultry. Riverford do it and also the Holt in Honiton who even smoke butter. Today this is not so much done as a preserving method but to add variety and an extra flavour dimension. For example, Pipers Farm cure and smoke all their own hams and bacon and at Christmas produce cooked, spiced beef. Peter Greig knows that this is a long, careful process and his customers know that it is worth the effort. Firstly it is cured in brine, and air dried. Then it is soaked overnight before being steeped in a mix of rich, dark muscovado sugar and aromatic spices for 24 hours before cooking and pressing; the result

Jilly Greed, at Rewe, near Exeter

gratifying both the eye and the palate. The appearance is a pleasing pink iridescence, with a pastrami like texture; the taste is soft full flavoured beef with aromatic spicy overtones.

Livestock farming thrived in parts of Devon during the 100 years war and then later with numerous cod fishing expeditions to Newfoundland and voyages to the Caribbean, provisioning or victualling as it was called in the Navy, became a vital part of Devon's economy. But the peace that finally broke out between Britain and France after 1815 pushed agriculture into a depression. Sally Vincent of Dittisham takes up the story "a study of the one inch ordinance map will show the numerous tracks leading down to the creeks of the Dart estuary. Many of the old stone wharves survive, notably at Old Mill Creek, Dittisham, Bramble Tor, Tuckenhay and Sharpham on the western shores and at Greenway, Galmpton, Stoke Gabriel and Dawsbarn on the eastern bank. Cider and country produce were loaded at these points, for shipment to London; whilst vast quantities of granite were brought down from the quays of Totnes, where, as the extensive wharves and warehouses reveal, a large proportion of the coastal trade leaving the Dart was handled."

Much agricultural produce was exported to other parts of Britain, and until the railways arrived this was almost exclusively by sea.

In Devon the development of pig farming went hand in hand with the development of commercial dairies. This dairy-pig cycle became very commonplace – it made sense to recycle the whey to fatten pigs, and remained an accepted way of doing things until very recently. Thanks to cheap imported pork and the decline of the dairy industry this simply became unviable.

A Way of Life – Water Meadows

Was it climate change that drove the farmers eking out a living in settlements such as Grimspound off the moor? There have been several key moments that have shaped the history of food production in Devon, and thence the landscape, and this was probably one. Another key point was the effects of the industrial revolution and the impact of cheaper imported foods, particularly corn, which led to the repeal of the corn laws. The great agricultural depressions of the 1840s and 1870s saw a mass exodus of farming families and farm workers. Many of them moved to the growing industrial cities further north, where the wages were better even if the living and working conditions were probably not. Some emigrated to the New World and the emerging colonies.

The water meadows at Rewe, near Exeter, have not been intensively managed for centuries. Instead Edwin and Jilly Greed's herd of South Devon, Blondes and mixed breed cattle become some of the richest,

Edwin and Jilly Greed's herd of South Devon, Blondes and mixed breed cattle in the water meadows at Rewe

tasting beef from feeding on this natural herbage. The Greeds know that this landscape needs special management, the flooding helping to create these lush, herb-rich pastures. Raising cattle for beef here is a centuries' old tradition, Jilly is the fourth generation to farm here. Sitting as it does on the flood plain of the River Exe and Culm, around 225 acres of this 500-acre farm floods regularly, so these lovely water meadows are carefully managed as much as a landscape feature as for grazing cattle. But Jilly has no doubt that this produces a special product.

"I cannot think of anything more traditional on our farm than this. It's the most perfect and natural way to produce quality beef. Year after year, generation after generation of these beautiful cows and calves graze the lush meadows, made fertile by the river itself, with the insects and birds all around them. Pure joy!"

4 /
CREAMING IT OFF

OVERLEAF
The Guernsey herd that supplies milk for The Devonshire Farmhouse range of clotted cream and ice cream, at their farm near Chagford on Dartmoor's northern edge

IN THE EARLY SPRING there is nothing quite like the sight of a herd of dairy cows going back out to grass after a long, cold winter. Tails are up, the air is cautiously sniffed, then they're off, skittering and racing around, reacquainting themselves with familiar territory.

If you are up on Dartmoor you might catch the unusual sight of the Vincent family's Guernsey herd – large, docile beasts ranging in colour from chestnut and white to almost pale creamy white. I suspect that seeing a dairy herd on Dartmoor is increasingly rare, even though this is not right up on the high moor. Even rarer is the fact that this is a Guernsey herd, not the conventional black and white cattle found almost everywhere else in the county. Holstein-Friesian dairy herds have become thought of as the standard, although many farmers are switching to hardier breeds such as red and white Ayrshires. In fact the Holstein is very much an imposter – really only taking over British dairy herds in the second half of the 20th century. Prior to that traditional dairy breeds such as the Dairy Shorthorn or the British Friesian were popular and in Devon, of course the South Devon which was very much a dual purpose cow.

The Vincent family has been farming at Higher Murchington, just outside Chagford for three generations. Duncan is responsible for producing the milk while his brother Ian turns this into a range of golden-coloured dairy produce. The bottled milk, which they sell locally through their own milk rounds and the Moorland Dairy in Chagford, is lightly pasteurised, not homogenised like most of the milk found in supermarkets and processed by the big dairy companies. Trading under the name Devonshire Farmhouse Ice Cream, they also make cream, clotted cream scalded and treated in the traditional way, and a range of ice creams (see chapter 13).

The Vincents' reaction to the "white water" syndrome that has taken over commercial dairy production, where the companies pour out millions of litres of undistinguished watery milk a day, is becoming more widespread in Devon. A handful of individual farmers have recognised that they may be the last generation to understand the real taste of milk, and that the white stuff in the supermarket polybottles has little taste, and is over-pasteurised to within an inch of its life, which creates an unnaturally long shelf life.

"In my opinion to have Guernsey milk without standardising it, not homogenising it, is just perfection, it has to be the best," says Ian.

Once drunk, these creamy milks have a taste that sticks in the memory. The trouble is that the majority of us do not recognise them for what they are, products that reflect the local terroir, the grasses, herbs and meadow flowers on which the cows graze for much of the year. Rather than milk that simply is fed by nothing but silage and cattle cake.

A perfect Devon farmscape looking west from Cadbury near Tiverton

Oliver Watson who oversees the Riverford Farm dairy herd

Today Devon's dairy farms are dominated by the black and white Holstein Friesians, including at Riverford Farm Dairy where Oliver Watson has been running an organic dairy herd for some 15 years, one of the early organic herds in the South West. The farm runs in parallel with his brother Guy's fruit and vegetable operation, ensuring a perfect partnership that keeps the land in good heart for both cattle and vegetables, creating a sustainable environment and using the manure produced each year by the 250 cows to build soil fertility without the use of artificial fertilisers. The rotation of the land between cows and vegetables means that clover leys are grown and harvested as forage. The land not used for vegetables is used for grazing and making silage for the cows' winter feed.

The organic dairy, which came into production in 2000, turns out unhomogenised, organic milk, cream, yoghurt and clotted cream. It started by just processing 300 litres each day, now 5,000 litres are produced and sold daily. The cows are milked in the morning and the milk is immediately processed and packed. What doesn't find its way into the Riverford products goes to local school canteens or the organic milk processor OMSCo, of which Oliver was a founder member.

A panorama of steep hills and pocket handkerchief fields near Riverford Farm, Totnes

It might be hard to visualise Devon as having anything other than sleek, glossy, highly productive dairy cows managing the landscape, helping to protect the network of small family farms, with their hedge-surrounded fields, copses and occasional water meadows, but we shouldn't overlook the advent of maize growing in the last couple of decades, and the post-war switch to silage instead of hay, which have brought a new shape to the landscape as well as new environmental problems. Yet step back a few thousand years and cattle were very much a beast of burden, used principally for ploughing and only secondly as a food source. They were small, tough and hardy, milkiness was not their purpose. Milk, cream and cheeses were found only in the monasteries and wealthy households – in medieval times for instance in the kitchens of manorial houses the plentiful spring and summer milk was preserved and used extensively in cooking, or made into butter.

For the rest of the population it was the sheep, later the foundation of Devon's thriving wool industry, which was the animal of choice for providing limited amounts of milk, some butter and cream. During the spring and summer months the ewes would be milked and any milk not used for immediate household consumption would be preserved by making butter and cheese.

It was only in the late 18th and early 19th century, when Devon lost her pre-eminence as one of England's leading wool counties, that sheep became a meat animal. But in the last 30 years there has been a revival in sheep's milk products. Most of this, with the exception of The Big Sheep in

Devonshire Farmhouse clotted cream is made the old fashioned way on their farm near Chagford

Butter from West Down Dairies, West Hill Farm, near Ilfracombe

MOLE VALLEY FARMERS

A neat synergy that occurs on many of these farms is their link to one of the region's most successful farmer-owned and run co-operatives, Mole Valley Farmers. Set up in 1960 by a group of North Devon farmers in South Molton, this supports and supplies many of the county's food producers through its 9 branches (4 in Devon, 2 in Cornwall, 3 in Somerset). So farmers such as Bernie Worth use the company's organic dairy feed, seed corn and grass seeds and he also sells his produce through some of the Mole Valley Farmers branches. As a retail co-operative it has also introduced a line of branded local products (see chapter 15).

North Devon (a sheepish tourist attraction), has been by specialised companies such as Naturemaid in North Devon, which produces ewe's and goats' milk and yoghurts on a small scale.

The shift to cows as the predominant source of milk started in the 16th century, one of the driving factors being the Enclosures Acts which, of course, favoured the large landowners and farmers. As farms expanded and techniques improved, any surplus milk would be turned into cream and butter and also sold at local markets. For several hundred years Devon had specialised in making butter, not from cream but from clotted cream, but in his survey of Devon at the beginning the 19th century Charles Vancouver noted that this had a very limited appeal outside the county.

"The greatest part of the butter made in this country is sent to London. The butter-factors at Honiton will not, on any consideration take butter made from the clouted or scalded cream. This process, therefore, notwithstanding that economy ought long since to have led to its discontinuance (unless on a small scale for potting or winter use) is entirely abandoned in the large dairies, as well as in most others that supply the larger markets in the country… This butter churned thus early from cream (ie fresh not scalded) before it has acquired any taint or sourness, is affirmed to possess a much better keeping quality than that produced from clouted cream."

Devon's dairy industry really took off after the Great Western Railway reached Exeter in 1844. This combined with technical advances and improved pasteurisation made it easy to send fresh milk to London. Not surprisingly the name Lloyd Maunder crops up here, with the family very influential in driving this forward. The company recognised the commercial opportunities for both farmers and dairies if new markets could be found in the capital, and other thriving city destinations, and set up the Witheridge and District Dairy Company. Other dairy factories sprang up all over the county, some concentrating on clotted cream or butter. Those on the edge of Dartmoor and Exmoor supplied local needs, while others nearer Plymouth had access to a growing market for fresh milk in the city and to supply the Navy.

Gradually a network of branch lines was built through east, south and mid Devon and the area around Torrington, to facilitate getting the milk to Tiverton junction, its departure point for London. The classic synergy between milk and pork production emerged early on in Devon as the first commercial milk processing factories were being set up. One of the biggest was in the Culm Valley. At the time the cycle of feeding the leftover whey to pigs was so essential that these factories were known as dairy piggeries.

"Whereas in the eighteenth and nineteenth centuries many farms would have several sows that were bred with the express view of salting the young porkers for domestic or local use. But as the railway improved and markets grew farmers increased the size of their herds and in Devon the development of pig farming went hand in hand with the growth of dairies," the history of Lloyd Maunder records.

One of the first factories in the Culm Valley was set up by three large dairy farmers, Edward Lutley, John Clist and Samuel Farrant after visiting a

Chocolate Heaven – One scoop or two?

CLOTTED CREAM

When was the first cream clotted? The answer is probably several millenia ago, as the clotted cream that we know is similar to kaymak, a food found all over the Middle East, Afghanistan, Iran and even India. Kaymak is a rich, clotted cream, traditionally made from water buffalo milk by a similar method to that found in Devon. Alan Davidson, in The Penguin Companion to Food, suggests that it may have been Phoenician traders who brought the method to Cornwall more than 2000 years ago.

Making clotted cream was a slow maturing process, the milk was allowed to settle overnight in milk pans, which were set over a lowish heat until a head formed on the milk. The pans went back to the dairy for a second night, and this method is said to have produced a thick, semi-solid, rich, clouted or clotted cream. Dorothy Hartley, in Food In England, wrote "a clout is a thick patch, presumably of leather, since you have old shoes unclouted – and the cream wrinkles up into thick leathery folds".

Much of that clotted cream was turned into butter, although it is clear that as milk products gained access to markets in London and beyond the county – the Devon butter made from clotted cream was not

▶
West Down Dairies near Braunton produce organic yoghurts, milk, butter and cream cheese

successful site in Derbyshire. Initially they had problems disposing of the skimmed milk, and could not replicate the twice-daily deliveries of the northern system. Their solution was to mix night and morning milk, which was sent to the factory each morning. The skimmed milk went to the dairy piggeries. A factory at Torrington took milk from all over North Devon and at one time was one of the largest in Europe. At the same time more farmers' wives could be seen selling butter and cream in Devon's markets, including the growing number of pannier markets that were being built to accommodate the overall agricultural expansion.

Less than a hundred years later that prosperity had been replaced with the agricultural depression of the 1930s, which left many farmers faced with throwing their milk away. Things were so bad that the Milk Marketing Board was set up in 1933, to guarantee a market and a fair price to all

Close encounter for herdsman Phil
Hill, Langage Farm

preferred. For local
consumption the old recipe
remained in use until the
middle of the 20th century,
according to food historian
Peter Brears.

"To convert the clotted
cream into butter, it was
poured into a freshly
scalded and rinsed shallow
wooden tub and agitated by
the flat of the hand of the
dairy maid, which had
similarly been washed in
very hot water and then in
cold. After anything from
half an hour to three hours,
the butter came, and was
washed with three or four
waters before being beaten
dry. This process gives a
rather harder butter, with a
superior flavour."

producers. By simply leaving the churns at the farm gate, for the first time
in hundreds of years farmers had lost control over marketing their own milk
and dairy produce.

More serious, although completely unforeseen at the time, are the long
term effects after the board was dismantled in 1994. These have left dairy
processing in the hands of a small number of large dairy companies.
Devon's strong tradition as a bountiful milk producing county has been
undermined by the dairy politics of the last decade and the industry, as
elsewhere in Britain, is a shadow of its former self. Only Milk Link has any
milk processing capacity of any size in Devon at its creamery at North
Tawton, making a range of cheeses, and at Crediton for cream and long life
milk. Two smaller farmer-owned and run co-operatives tried for a while to
process and sell fresh Devon milk to Devon outlets, but Peninsula Milk
Processors were taken over by Milk Link while Deliciously Devon, owned
by Torridge Vale, was swallowed up by Robert Wiseman.

Today most of the milk produced on Devon's larger dairy farms goes
out of the county to be processsed by the big players, Dairy Crest and
Robert Wiseman. On the plus side an indirect benefit of this has been the
revival of the number of dairy farmers who have taken matters, including
processing and marketing, into their own hands.

Jersey Cow, Langage Farm, Smithaleigh, near Plymouth

▶ ▶

Families such as Chris and Sue Batstone, at West Hill Farm near Ilfracombe in North Devon, once self-professed as hell bent on chasing efficiency of scale, had a complete change of heart at the end of the 1990s. Thinking that there must be a better way of earning a living than the 24/7 treadmill of endless milking of high yielding cattle, they decided to switch to organic farming methods and bottle and deliver their own milk. They also developed a range of wonderful creams, yoghurts and a sensational chocolate sauce. None of their products quite fitted conventional descriptions, for example crusty cream was a gorgeous golden yellow confection with a crust but not as dense as clotted cream. The Batstones sold some of the recipes and milk rounds to Bernie Worth, now trading as West Down Dairies.

Other dairy farmers who have taken back control of their milk include Dunns Dairies at Drewsteignton, Westons Farms near Bampton and Roadford Valley in North Devon. Although these principled farmers are determined to give their customers a taste of real milk, they are also aware that they have to offer skimmed or semi-skimmed options, which leaves plenty of surplus to be turned into yogurt and other dairy products.

Most of these, like the Vincents, do not homogenise their milk, allowing the cream to rise and settle at the top. Homogenisation smashes up the cream particles and distributes them through the milk. Interestingly there is an ongoing debate about the health implications of homogenised versus unhomogenised milk and rate of absorbtion of fat particles into the bloodstream.

A word too on fat contents. For decades there has been an anti-milk hysteria which completely overlooks that fact that a pint of full cream milk is only four per cent fat. Let me repeat that, four per cent. This puts semi-skimmed, 1.7 per cent, and skimmed (frankly why bother unless you have a pressing health issue, there are much easier ways of removing harmful fat from your diet) at 0.3 per cent firmly in the white water category.

Also often overlooked is the growing recognition of the health benefits of milk that is produced naturally, mainly from grass, rather then the increasing trend for what is known as zero grazed where cows barely go outside, or milk produced from herds fed on highly concentrated feeds based on maize, soya and corn. Initially it was throught that the grass-fed organic cattle produced higher levels of Omega 3, CLAs (conjugated linoleic acids) and vitamin E. This piece of research gave a boost to a struggling organic dairy sector. However this thinking has been extended to non-organic dairy cows, provided they are producing milk in a less pressured way, on as natural a diet as possible, that is mainly grass-fed.

Langage Farm, on an industrial estate just outside Plymouth, has built up a portfolio of dairy products from the Harvey family's original herd of

Free Range eggs, West Hill Farm,
near Ilfracombe

Jersey and Guernsey cows. The distinctive deep yellow colour of the milk and cream helping them to stand out on the shelves in a crowded retail environment. On their Domesday farm in 1980, they started by producing clotted cream to sell in the local shop. Today they employ nearly 50 people and have added to their range golden pouring cream, crème fraiche and soured cream. Using traditional farmhouse methods they offer a full flavoured cream cheese and also a hand cut cottage cheese; as well as ice creams, sorbets and yoghurt.

Traditionally the dairy was not just about milk, it included eggs too. Once almost every rural household would have had a few backyard chickens. But this died out after the Second World War as in their quest for cheap, plentiful food the supermarkets chased egg production into battery cages, thousands of hens living a miserable existence crammed into a dark, noisy environment. However the egg sector is undergoing something of a revival, aided by the idea of pretty, free ranging birds laying beautifully coloured "designer" eggs, which taste rich and deeply eggy, and a new vogue for duck eggs. Many chefs are recognising that eggs – poached, soft boiled or even fried – make the grade as an ingredient to match seasonal specials. One of the most obvious during the last couple of summers has been the combination of asparagus and eggs. A few smallholders, and small and medium sized family farms, are making good businesses out of producing free range eggs.

One particularly engaging story is Elsa's Eggs. In 2008, based on the northern edge of Dartmoor, ten-year-old Elsa was shortlisted for, and won, a top national award for her free range, organic duck eggs. She rears, feeds and tends to the laying birds herself. These are large white ducks, a hybrid egg-laying bird, similar to the popular Khaki Campbell. Helped by her four younger siblings, Alfred, Dora, and twins Percy and Harold, she also collects, grades and boxes the eggs. These have become so popular that they are sold through Abel and Cole's organic boxes, in a handful of local Waitrose stores and at the farm gate. Although the wind and rain sometimes blow sideways on this part of the moor, Elsa's parents Rona and Nevil Amiss, of Higher Fingle Farm, have been strict in enforcing the

Elsa examining her duck eggs for cracks before they are packed for market – Higher Fingle Farm, Crockernwell

principle that this should be run as a proper business. Having won the top prize Elsa reinvested the winnings in better housing, more ducks and a new design for her packaging. A hint of a foodie with a promising future.

The early years of the 21st century have been a difficult time for milk producers, and a growing number are opting out of the tyranny of selling to processors who are trapped in the stranglehold of their buyers, the supermarkets. This is all about price and price wars, yet milk is an essential everyday product and few of us stop to look at the price as we put it in our shopping baskets. The end result has been a massive contraction in the British dairy industry and a shortage of fresh milk, and milk for processing into other dairy products. So in Devon the best guarantee of supporting the industry is by buying from the small, local dairies that have opted out of this system and are bottling their own milk and selling it through farm shops, village stores, campsites and in some cases starting their own delivery rounds.

The county's dairy industry, big and small, is one of the key factors that maintains its distinctive and glorious pastureland. To keep Devon looking the way it is, we need to remember, time and time again, the mantra of buying local.

RIND
MAIDENS

WALK INTO ANY DEVON PUB at lunchtime and order a Ploughman's Lunch, what would you expect to be served? A piece of Devon Blue? Curworthy? Or Sharpham, golden, rich, and creamy? Many pubs have their own version using local cheeses, giving a taste of Devon's lush pastures on a plate, but many more still use the traditional Cheddar, which, although it had its origins in Somerset, has been produced in Devon for centuries.

At Home Farm, Newton St Cyres, there has been cheesemaking of some sort for more than 450 years. In the 21st century this is in the capable hands of the 17th generation of the Quicke family, who have owned this land and estate just outside Exeter for longer than anyone cares to remember. While they are also one of the oldest Devon Cheddar producers, they have only been making their present range of cheeses for some 30 years.

This remarkable revival was driven by Sir John Quicke's haunting memory of how in the 1920s, before the Milk Marketing Board was set up, his father used to send milk to Exeter only to find that there were no buyers. In the early 1970s, milk prices were falling and the farm's milk was going to another cheesemaker. Spurred on by the idea that they might be losing out, Sir John and Lady Quicke visited other local cheesemakers where they discovered that they were all doing better financially, "so it became obvious we ought to do it", Prue Quicke recalls. A new cheese room was built in 1972, and the first cheeses appeared a year later, but Sir John's work in London meant that it was left to his wife to find a cheesemaker and sell the cheeses. Even then they wanted to produce

*Mary Quicke's dairy herd –
Newton St Cyres*

*Showing it's age, a full round of
Cheddar matures in the Quickes
Cheese store*

The curd is sliced up in a huge stainless steel vat

"something unique, something akin to chateau-bottled wine instead of a commodity", she explains.

But that fine cheese almost failed to survive beyond the 1980s as none of the next generation of Quickes seemed interested in taking on the farm or cheesemaking when their parents retired. Eventually their daughter Mary allowed homesickness for Devon to facilitate her return from London. She spent a year learning how to make cheese in Cheshire, then worked in all aspects of the business. Today Quickes Traditional is one of the biggest Cheddar makers in the country, producing a range of prize-winning cows' milk cheeses, from vintage to smoked, along with Red Leicester, Double Gloucester and an award-winning hard goats' milk cheese.

"What makes a traditional Cheddar, as opposed to a rectangular block Cheddar wrapped in plastic, is quite simple", says Mary. Her cylindrical, cloth wrapped cheeses are made using traditional starters and, unlike many British cheesemakers, animal rennet. They are hand cheddared and matured in the cloth.

Milk, though is the key to any cheese, of whatever variety, and Mary has paid great attention to the breeding and feeding of her 500 dairy cows, so that they spend most of the year grazing outside. This helps to get the correct ratio of fat to protein and of course there is no argument that milk from grass makes far superior cheese to milk from cows fed on corn or manufactured feeds.

It takes three cheesemakers and up to 10 people to turn this milk into cheese, most of which is allowed to mature for anything from 11 to 15 months for mature Cheddar, 15 to 20 for extra mature and over two years for vintage mature, one of the Quickes' most successful cheeses. When

Hard graft – Hands On
The cheddaring process shows the curd being worked, drained, sliced and finally packed into cheese cloth lined drums for pressing

MAKING CHEDDAR

Quickes Traditional uses the previous day's milk, which is sent to the cheese dairy where most of it is pasteurised – the dairy makes a limited amount of unpasteurised cheese – and put into 1,000 gallon vats. When the milk has reached body temperature the starter is added, followed by the rennet, turning it into what we would recognise as junket. This is then cut into small pieces, becoming the curds and whey, which are scalded and then drained; the curds are then cheddared – cut, built up into blocks, turned and worked by hand. This is a key process for any cheese described as a traditional, artisan Cheddar. The whey is gradually drained off and the curds are milled and salted. Salt is essential, not just for flavour but for driving out moisture during the maturing process. The curds are packed into scrim-lined moulds and pressed. The next day they are turned out, dressed in a smoother muslin, washed with hot water to seal them and returned to the moulds for further pressing. This is repeated the following day, and it is not until day four that the cheeses finally go into the wooden shelved store to mature, "typically for a year" Mary Quicke says. Each cheese is turned regularly – every week in the early days and every 2 weeks as the cheese matures – to ensure uniform flavour and texture.

tasted, these prize-winning Cheddars have a complexity and length of flavour which Mary describes as "creamy, complex, unfolding, pleasing all the way".

Mary's passion for cheese is infectious. Her ambition is to make "world class cheese and for excellence in farming". She seems to have fulfilled that ambition as her cheeses can be found on sale in locations as diverse as America and Australia, the post office in Port Stanley in the Falklands, as well as in many supermarkets, cheese specialists and delicatessens throughout the UK.

What a contrast between this and the very beginnings of cheesemaking. The early nomadic herders discovered how to make the first curd cheeses with milk held in a small container, perhaps with a local herb added to help the milk to coagulate. These would have been eaten very young. It was the Romans who showed how surplus milk could be preserved and different cheeses made, introducing more sophisticated cheese making techniques, including the use of animal rennet or herbs, such as Ladies Bedstraw or wild thistle, to start the cheese making process.

Rennet produces a different kind of fermentation from simply separating curds and whey, and the early cheesemakers discovered that this could make what we know as hard cheeses with long keeping qualities. Most modern cheeses are made with vegetarian rennet, but a few cheesemakers still believe that animal rennet is better, giving a complex, more rounded flavour to the cheese. In Devon only Rachel Stephens at Curworthy and Quickes Traditional use animal rennet. The remainder of Devon's artisan cheesemakers have opted for the vegetarian version.

For most of the rural poor, servants, tenant farmers and their workers, ewes' milk was the main source of milk for cheesemaking. Their cheeses tended to have a low fat content making them thin and hard, although they did have longevity. In medieval times there were "green", soft, and hard cheeses, and a cheese known as 'spermyse'. This was a curd cheese with added herbs; "green" meant "young" rather than green in colour, much like the fresh, soft cheeses that have become popular since the end of the 1990s, pressed enough to hold their shape but still moist and fresh. Some may even have been wrapped in herbs like modern day Cornish Yarg which is wrapped in nettles.

For hundreds of years the dairies in the great houses, abbeys and monasteries would make their own cheese as an additional way of preserving surplus milk, either to be stored for the winter, or to be sold, depending on how much was available. In the 17th century at Leyhill in Payhembury in East Devon, Sir John Willoughby's household accounts recorded a fine income from cheese and butter. In 1644 more than

800lbs (363½kg) of cheese and 87lbs (39½kg) of butter were sold in the second half of the year. There were two types of cheese: cheese made from whole milk, which sold at 2d or 2½d (1p) per lb, or scald milk cheese. This was made from milk that was warmed and the cream skimmed off. What was left was made into cheese, which was apparently mostly consumed by the servants. It sold for about half the price of the whole milk cheese.

Later East Devon became well known for what we would call Cheddar, although the rest of the county resolutely stuck to making butter and clotted cream with any surplus milk (see chapter 4). More than 20 years of war with France, from 1793-1815, gave farmers a ready market for anything they could produce, but after Waterloo in 1815, cheese, poultry, butter and corn were once more imported from Normandy, resulting in a new agricultural depression with many small farmers leaving the land.

Two other events in the mid 19th century reinforced the decline in farmhouse cheesemaking and the change of emphasis from preserving surplus milk to selling fresh milk. These were Louis Pasteur's discovery of pasteurisation techniques in the 1860s, and Brunel's Great Western Railway reaching Exeter in 1844, which opened up provincial markets for fresh milk. Dairy factories sprang up all over Devon (see chapter 4).

DEVON CHEESES

CURWORTHY

Belstone (c)

Chipple (c, with spring onions)

Curworthy (c)

Devon Oke (c)

Meldon (c)

MIDDLE CAMPSCOTT FARM

Campscott (e, o)

Campscott Cumin (e, o)

Campscott Speciality summer (e, o, only occasionally available)

Campscott Goat (o)

NORSWORTHY DAIRY GOATS

Chelwood Ash (g, u, soft, ash-coated)

Chelwood (g, u, soft)

Gunstone (g, u, hard)

Norsworthy (g, u, semi-soft, washed curd)

Posbury (g, u, flavour added)

Tillerton (g, u, mould-ripened)

OAKDOWN FARM

Oakdown goat

QUICKES

Double Gloucester (c)

Red Leicester (c)

Oak Smoked Cheddar (c)

Traditional Cheddar mature (c)

Traditional cheddar with herbs (c)

Unpasteurised cheddar (c)

Vintage cheddar (c)

Hard Goat's Cheese (g)

A further blow to Devon's cheese traditions came with the First World War, which brought about the end of much farmhouse cheesemaking and a loss of vital skills. Things did not improve in the agricultural depression of the 1930s. The Milk Marketing Board was set up to give all dairy farmers an outlet for their milk and any cheese they made. In theory this guaranteed a price and a market, but in practice this was the start of the demise of the traditional territorial hard cheeses, including Cheddar. However the South West clung on to its farmhouse cheesemakers and just before the Second World War there were still 514 farms making Cheddar and Caerphilly in Devon, Dorset, Somerset and Wiltshire. The final blow came during the Second World War. Rationing included cheese, virtually all of which was produced by the big national cheese factories as the "National Cheese" a bland, hard cheese. There was no milk and no concessions for the traditional territorial cheeses – Stilton, Caerphilly and so on. Only a few dedicated artisan cheesemakers struggled on, and by 1948 there were just 57 registered farms making Cheddar. By the time rationing ended in 1954 the English farmhouse cheese industry was a shadow of its former self and 20 years later there were just two Cheddar cheesemakers in Devon, including the Quickes at Newton St Cyres.

The influence of the supermarkets in the 1970s and 1980s further depressed any efforts to revive proper cheese making. They were driven by the convenience of pre-cut and pre-wrapped cheeses that customers could select themselves, and most of the cheese available was block Cheddar of varying strengths. It was what Patrick Rance describes as "the destruction" of our English cheese heritage".

So it was against this background in the 1970s that specialist cheesemakers started to do their own thing, although as Sir John and Lady Quicke found, acquiring licences and permissions was made as difficult as possible. They were not alone. Another Devon pioneer at that time was Robin Congdon, at Ticklemore Cheese, who revived the art of milking sheep. Initially he made soft ewes' milk cheeses and yoghurt which he sold in London. However a partnership with Maurice Ash and the Dartington Hall Trust led to a range of innovative cheeses in different styles. He has now cut back to three classic blue varieties – Beenleigh Blue, a ewe's milk cheese; Harbourne Blue, made from goat's milk, and Devon Blue, a classic blue cow's milk cheese deliciously moist and creamy.

By the time milk quotas were introduced in 1984 only 0.45 per cent of British milk was being made into traditional cheese on farms. Nevertheless it was during this decade that other enthusiastic men and women started building up Devon's reputation for unique artisan cheeses. In 1988, when Patrick Rance re-printed The Great British Cheese Book, Devon had 17 craft cheesemakers of varying sizes – farmhouse no longer

Sharpham's Herd Manager Dave Curtis
▼

being the correct description because although the cheeses were undoubtedly made on farms, the word had by then been misappropriated by the big creameries and used to describe any cheese made in large volumes.

Of the original 17 cheesemakers, six remain today – Quickes Traditional, Vulscombe, Sharpham, Curworthy, Langage Farm and Lower Sharpham Barton (Ticklemore) – although some have changed location and cheesemakers have come and gone. They have been joined by a raft of new producers of many shapes and sizes, making around 60 artisan Devon cheeses from cows', ewes' and goats' milk. Styles have developed significantly too. Where once there might have been Cheddar and perhaps soft goats' milk cheeses, the range stretches from pungent, rind-washed cheeses to soft, mould-ripened such as Elmhirst, made with Jersey milk and added cream.

Elmhirst is one of the stars of the Sharpham estate in South Devon, where Debbie Mumford and Mark Sharman produce a range of hand-made cheeses mostly from their own organically produced Jersey cows' milk. This, says Mark, is what makes them unique, given that the traditional view is that the fat globules in Channel Island milk are too big to make soft cheeses. "It is a difficult milk to make cheese out of, but the reward is in the flavour." He's right, they are rich, creamy and taste quite different from similar products made from standard cows' milk.

Sharpham, a mould-ripened coulommiers-style cheese, the first of this type to be made in Britain, was dreamed up by Maurice Ash and his Polish cheesemaker in 1981, working in a converted stable in the 18th century coach yard of Sharpham House. Ash's intention was to get away from producing for the commodity market and to create jobs by making artisan cheese. The recipe came from France and was adapted to fit his vision of supporting the rural community. A few years later Debbie Mumford came to Sharpham from Ticklemore, and now makes five cheeses in a purpose-built dairy, which deliberately avoids being highly mechanised. "That's not what we're about from a human or a product point of view," Mark says.

Sharpham – unlike any French Brie and after nearly 30 years still the best seller – Elmhirst and two versions of Devon Rustic are unpasteurised and made with milk that comes straight from the Jersey herd. "We like that close

TRUCKLES

Westerley cumin (c)

Westerley (c, hard)

Maisy (c, fresh with herbs and garlic)

WEST HILL FARM

Buckland - (c, o, rind-washed)

Pickwell - (c, waxed semi-hard)

Halsinger (c, fresh unripened)

COUNTRY CHEESES - *these cheeses are made by Devon cheesemakers for Country Cheeses*

Bakesey Meadow (g, u, mould-ripened)

Celeste (c)

Chemmy (g, u, soft log)

Devon Sage (c, hard with sage)

Devon Smoake (c, oak smoked Devon Oke)

Smoke by the Water (c, smoked, limited availability)

Sweet Charlotte (c, Emmental type)

Trehill (c, hard with garlic)

Vergin (c, Curworthy with preserved ginger)

Withybrook (g, u, pyramid, ash coated)

c = cows' milk

g = goat

e = ewe

u = unpasteurised

o = organic

▶
A Jersey from the herd at Sharpham

connection to what we produce," he explains. "The Jersey milk is the key, because it has such a distinctive flavour." Ticklemore is made for Robin Congdon with local goats' milk.

One of the reasons why Devon makes great cheeses, Mark adds, is because "we can grow great grass and can produce great milk. It's logical that cheese should be made here rather than shipping milk out of the county".

What Devon may lack in artisan fresh milk and cream producers, it more than compensates for with its cheeses. New styles are emerging all the time, many of them encouraged by enthusiasts like Gary and Elise

Nicky Davis separating the whey from the curds in a vat of Sharpham Soft Cheese

Kate Davis cutting the curds in a vat of Sharpham Soft Cheese

Carl Elesmore and Nicky Davis filling the moulds for Sharpham Soft Cheese

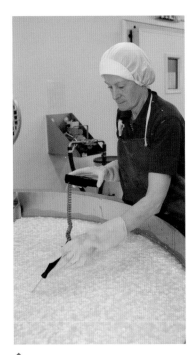

Kate Davis checking the
temperature in a vat of Sharpham
Rustic cheese curds

▶
Nicky Davis fills a colander with
Sharpham Rustic cheese curds

Sterilizing plastic colanders used to shape Sharpham Rustic Cheese

Debbie Mumford labelling the cheeses

Jungheim, who set up Country Cheeses in 1994. Although the shop is almost entirely dedicated to Westcountry cheeses, the odd foreigner, such as Stilton and Flower Marie – from East Sussex, "it is so good there's nothing else like it so we sell it" – have crept into the chiller cabinets, which are otherwise stacked with a range of more than 100 South West, artisan cheeses, around 30 per cent of these made in Devon. The display includes large cloth-bound Cheddars and other territorials such as Double Gloucester, sitting next to pungent rind-washed cheeses; there are blue cheeses of every hue and texture made from every milk imaginable; ewes' milk cheeses – soft and hard – similar goats' cheeses, ash-coated pyramids, and of course soft, runny mould-ripened cheeses, all in perfect, peak condition, ready to eat. Even the most disciplined shopper would find it hard not to be tempted into buying more cheese than they had planned.

Why the focus on Westcountry cheeses? "We wanted to pick it up ourselves and see where it had come from," Elise explains. "I want to support local producers like Rachel Stephens who is employing people, she's using local milk and supporting the local environment in this lovely place, and we help that by selling her cheeses. Otherwise we'd end up with a few big factories instead of lots of little dairies."

Passionate about cheese and small-scale, craft cheesemaking, the Jungheims spend a lot of time working with the producers. True affineurs, they will only buy the cheeses they think best and then spend time making sure they reach their customers in prime condition. Thanks to their commitment and excellent trading relationships with the producers, they have a range of cheeses made specifically and only for them, including seven from Devon.

Sharpham's Rustic cheese.
Maturing quietly in the cold room

It was Gary's mother who started a cheese stall in Tavistock's pannier market when she found that Rachel Stephens' Curworthy, one of the most local cheeses, could not be bought in the town. When Gary's mother fell ill, the couple took over and continued running it for three or four years, before opening their first shop just a few yards away. Now they also have stores in Topsham and Totnes.

Gary's view is that while the old-established cheesemakers are "very intuitive", many of the newcomers take a more scientific approach. "It's the intuitive ones I'm attracted to like a magnet," he says, adding that many factors affect a cheese, anything from the grass, animal husbandry and the cows to the weather, the starter culture, conditions in the dairy, how long it is matured, and each individual cheesemaker. "It's closer to wine in many respects than any other food, the passion, the same sense of terroir."

Both Gary and Elise are adamant that unpasteurised cheeses are far better. "You can make really good cheese from pasteurised milk but you can make a really sublime cheese with unpasteurised milk."

This couple has also been one of the driving forces behind encouraging chefs to respect their cheeseboards and make them showcases for local cheeses.

"We've seen a big change," says Elise. "People are deciding to be

Real cheese connoisseurs –
Gary and Elise Jungheim at
their shop Country Cheeses in
Tavistock Market

proud about what's here."

They have spotted that the local and speciality food issue has become as much about people and lifestyles as it is about the product. In many cases customers want to buy a bit of that dream or image, and they clearly believe it is their duty to ensure that when their customers buy Devon cheeses that dream is fulfilled. Their mission to educate consumers on the delights and strengths of the region's cheeses culminates in the Real Cheese Fair, held each August in Tavistock, where cheesaholics can meet the cheesemakers, taste and discuss the cheeses.

The Jungheims have set a specialised standard that is hard to beat, but around the county there are plenty of other options for tasting and buying Devon's finest cheeses. Holsworthy also has a fine cheese shop, Market Cheeses, while Barnstaple's Butcher's Row offers the West Country Cheese

Some of the Devon cheeses stocked by Gary & Elise

Co, which stocks more than 100 farmhouse cheeses, and most other delicatessens and farm shops have a good range of Devon cheeses. Look for them in farm shops and farmers' markets, often a testing ground for new cheeses or for cheeses produced in small quantities that are not widely available. Otherwise for an on-line cheese buying experience with a difference, it is worth trying the Cheese Shed. Based, quite literally in a shed in Bovey Tracey, Ian Wellens works with a local delicatessen to send out mail order cheese boxes – an easy way to get the best local cheese in optimum condition delivered to your door.

There are a couple of big creameries in Devon, turning out large volumes of consistently standard cheeses, but these lack the sense of terroir and variations that come with the seasons. Taw Valley at North Tawton makes a range of block cheeses including Cheddar, Red Leicester and Double Gloucester. Parkham Farms, near Bideford, makes up to 4,500 tonnes of block Cheddar each year, using milk from their own herd and

CHEESE STYLES

Fresh: The youngest, usually made to be eaten within a few days, mild, lactic, often lemony, no rind. Example: Ridgewell, Oakham Farm.

Soft White, or Mould-Ripened: The curds are deliberately left moist, and are lightly pressed before coming into contact with penicillin candidum, which creates the familiar white coating. Examples: Sharpham, Bakesey Meadow.

Semi-soft: Some have coloured rinds, ranging from brownish-orange to thick grey-brown. Pressed lightly, some have washed curds, whilst others are rind washed to create pungent cheeses. Examples: Buckland, Norsworthy.

Hard cheeses: Usually made by cutting and pressing the curds, often wrapped in cloth, as with Cheddar, and then left to mature. Examples: Devon Oke, Quickes Vintage Cheddar.

Blue: Unpressed, the blueing is caused by adding a penicillin mould to the milk, later allowing air into the cheese by piercing with metal rods. This helps the blueing to spread through the cheese. Example: Devon Blue.

from around 30 other local dairy farms. On a slightly smaller scale Langage Farm, near Ivybridge, makes cottage and cream cheeses, both their own brand and for the organic Holy Cow range.

In the great revival of British cheeses that has taken place since the mid 1980s, Devon has played a major role adding to the more than 850 different cheeses made in these islands, now outnumbering French artisan production. What would General de Gaulle have said I wonder? Mon dieu? He only had 246 different cheeses to deal with. No wonder our government cannot govern effectively these days.

One of the fascinating things about these cheesemakers and sellers is that many have come to it as a second career. They range from former architects to Dutch school teachers, jazz musicians and mining engineers. What they share is a fascination with the alchemy between milk, pasture, weather and dairy that creates such a variable yet fascinating artisan product, giving Devon and the Westcountry a new identity and sense of purpose.

◄

Derek Stratton in his cheese shop in Holsworthy

▶

Country Cheeses, Topsham

6/ GLITTERING HARVEST – NET GAIN

O N A COLD BRIGHT MARCH MORNING there is a queue outside Beer Fisheries. Tucked into the lee of a cliff on the East Devon coast, what is little more than a shed hacked out of the rocks is selling the freshest of fish, landed literally just a stone's throw away on the curved, pebbly beach at Beer.

Unprepossessing it might be, but the quality of the fish caught by the Newton family's three day boats is superb. Less than 24 hours between being hauled from the sea and reaching the slab. Outside the tiny shop trays are full of freshly cooked crab and lobster – prepared a few feet away in the adjacent store, as soon as they arrive. Here another family member is painstakingly hand picking more crabs to be sold as fresh crabmeat. Inside on the counter are gleaming sea-fresh pollack, mackerel, skate wings, whelks, Dover sole, plaice, scallops and sea bass, all landed earlier that day, a small sample of the rich diversity of fish species found off the Devon coast. Virtually all that the Newtons catch goes straight to the shop, which is open all year round.

This is still a family business, spanning four generations over more than 40 years, who between them bring the catch in, process the fish, cook and prepare the shellfish, and sell it. The Newtons are the last family to earn

The youngest member of the
Newton family of fishermen at Beer

Beach fishery

Lillie May – fishing boats
and beach huts – Beer

their living directly from the sea by fishing from Beer, one of the few remaining fleets in Britain where the boats are launched straight off the beach; beach fisheries are rare these days. There is one at Cadgwith in Cornwall and another at Hastings in East Sussex. It is a sad reflection of the state of Devon's fishing industry that of the handful of small boats at Beer only two make a full-time living from fishing. The rest either fish part-time or are used for angling or deep sea fishing trips.

As you walk down the slipway from the main village street the fact that this is very much a working beach, with few concessions made to summer visitors, is inescapable. Day trippers and residents share the beach with the boats, winches, piles of crab and lobster pots next to tangled nets, floats, more ropes and jerrycans.

One half of the shore is littered with "Danger – Winch" warning signs to alert tourists to the tightly strung cables attached to the beached boats. A row of white painted beach huts sits on both sides of the beach, there are a couple of beach cafes – definitely only open during the summer season, so now firmly shut up against the elements – advertising tea, coffee, ice creams and crab sandwiches.

Beer may seem like a curiosity now but once dozens of tiny harbours on the north and south coasts, and any sheltered bay and beach, would have sent out fishing boats to make a living. Each coastal community had

Walking the plank

DEVON FISH

Anchovies (occasional)
Angler (monk) fish
Black bream
Brill
Cod
Cuttlefish
Dabs
Dover Sole
Grey mullet
Gurnard
Haddock
Hake
Herring
Huss
John Dory
Lemon sole
Ling
Mackerel
Megrim sole
Octopus
Plaice
Pollock
Pout
Ray
Red mullet
Sardines
Sea Bass
Squid
Sprats (occasional)
Torbay sole
Turbot
Whiting
Wrasse

SHELLFISH

Brown Crab
Clams
Cockles
Lobster
Mussels - farmed and
naturally grown
Oysters - farmed Pacific
Scallops
Spider Crab
Whelks

▸
Brixham – early morning in the Fish Market

its own unique fishery entirely dictated by local conditions. Steep cliffs made many parts inaccessible, while sandy beaches and coves could only accommodate smaller boats rather than those destined to sail long distances.

The pressures of fish quotas, the Common Fisheries Policy (CFP) and EU regulations mean that the number of vessels is dwindling, working from a much reduced number of locations. The bulk of Devon's commercial fishing fleet can be found in Brixham and Plymouth, with Appledore, Exmouth, Kingswear, Dartmouth, Teignmouth and Ilfracombe as minor players. Exmouth in its heyday, at the turn of the 20th century, was well

known for its herring fishery, sending up to 40 tonnes of herring a day to Billingsgate when the fish were running in early spring. Now, like Teignmouth, fewer than a dozen boats fish regularly from this harbour.

The total value of fish landed in Devon is around £40 million a year, passing through Brixham, Plymouth and Appledore with Brixham taking the lion's share at around £20 million, making it England's leading fishing port. Brixham supports around 20 beam trawlers – the port is said to be where beam trawling first caught on from Dutch boats – and 40 smaller, day boats including trawlers, netters and boats that pot for shellfish; vessels from other south coast ports, from Newlyn to Shoreham, will land here too. A few boats go after pelagic fish – herring, mackerel and pilchards, better known as a sardine.

"Some put them on as Lyme Bay sardines and they fly out," says Rick Smith, managing director of Brixham Trawler Agents (BTA), a cooperative owned by fishermen, trawler owners, processors and a few private individuals. "Sell them as pilchards and no one wants them."

Anyone for Red Gurnard?
Fish education in progress

Quality is the key, he explains. Skippers are staying at sea for less time so the fish is fresher when landed. They have shortened the time of trawls and are using more ice to ensure that the fish arrives in the best possible condition.

"They've realised that it's a highly prized food and needs more attention," he says.

The BTA sorts and auctions the catch, provides fuel, ice and general support services to the fleet. Smith is proud that his systems make every piece of fish landed fully traceable, "from boat to throat". Although there is

Brixham harbour

Brixham – boxed in

a growing awareness of fish as a healthy food, sustainability and ensuring healthy stocks for the future is as important an issue for the fishermen as it is for well-informed consumers.

If you are lucky enough to be at the fish market during the auction it is easy to see the rich diversity of fish caught along the Devon coast. Early in the morning a group of men in white coats is moving swiftly down a series of boxes containing fish landed the previous evening, each box with a ticket naming the boat that caught it. The auction is sharp and swift, as wholesalers and processors, fishmongers and a man and his van are keen to buy anything from sparkling fresh mackerel to John Dory, scallops and cuttlefish. Occasionally unusual Mediterranean fish can be spotted, and sprats and anchovies make sporadic seasonal appearances. On a good day more than 40 different species will be for sale. In autumn 2009 there were significant catches of anchovy as well.

Much of the fish, around 60-70 per cent, is exported, particularly cuttlefish, a major catch for Brixham, which has thriving markets in Italy, Spain and Japan. Despite this Devon's fishing industry contributes £11 million annually to the local economy through on-shore processing and other ancillary employment.

Brixham has been one of England's premier ports for hundreds of years, with a history stretching back to the Domesday Book. From the middle of the 18th century it sent fresh fish to London, and in 1850 had the largest fishing fleet in the country of 130 boats. Brixham skippers had no qualms about following the fish if that meant sailing as far as Fleetwood or Grimsby.

Historically fishing boats have always been relatively migrant over the centuries and Devon fishermen were no exception. They would follow the great shoals of herring and mackerel around the coast, and were among the pioneers of the Newfoundland cod fishery. Before the restrictions of the Common Fisheries Policy (CFP) they would choose to catch and land wherever they could make the best profit, even up into the North Sea. So they could have been found anywhere from Dublin to Aberdeen or Lowestoft. From the North Devon coast it was easy to send fish to Bristol and Bath.

The Devon fleet has a broad cross-section of boats. The majority, small day boats less than 10 metres long, usually fish close to the shore within the six mile territorial waters limit. Whereas the larger, over 10 metre, boats are as migrant as ever, following the fish when and where quotas permit.

Starting young
▼

Appledore, an equally historic port on the North Devon coast, also claims a broad spectrum of species but over the years has gained a reputation in particular for rays (of which there are several varieties, and should not to be confused with skate, although often misleadingly sold as "skate") lobster and squid, which is growing in popularity in Britain.

Although fewer than 20 boats use the Appledore facilities, these can include vessels from Padstow, Bideford and Ilfracombe. Not for nothing is this bit of the coast known as the Iron Coast, so unwelcoming is it, offering little shelter between Padstow and Clovelly. These boats have gained a reputation for quality and this is what earns their skippers premium prices, often at Billingsgate market. Unlike Brixham and Plymouth much of the Appledore fish goes to UK markets, only around 30 per cent going abroad.

Quality was the watchword I heard everywhere. "The days of selling a bit of fish that isn't right are over," says Tony Rutherford of Bideford Fisheries, who handles all the fish landed here. "If you won't eat it yourself don't sell it."

Despite the political wranglings in Brussels about fishing quotas, discards and changes to the

CFP, Brixham, Plymouth and Appledore appear quietly confident about their future, although it is no longer easy to predict how many boats will be fishing each year. In Brixham a £16.6 million development is due for completion in 2011. Appledore opened new landing and processing facilities in 2009, costing £3.7 million, making them some of the region's most high-tech fishing facilities.

The impact of celebrity chefs is helping to promote Devon's fish and Brixham has a new champion in the form of Mitch Tonks. In addition to his seafood restaurant in nearby Dartmouth, Tonks is actively involved with the Brixham harbour project and has endless plans to find ways of encouraging us to eat more fish.

Dartmouth is another south coast port that once played a vital role in Devon's commercial trade. Today it is probably best known for its annual regatta and as the home of the Britannia Royal Naval College, the training centre for Naval officers. Combined with its neighbour Kingswear on the opposite bank, it is still the main landing place for the large quantities of crab caught off this part of the south coast. But more than 700 years ago it was one of South Devon's premier ports. It was the centre of Devon's pilchard fishing industry and it was from Dartmouth, Plymouth and Teignmouth that some of the earliest voyages to the cod fisheries in Newfoundland departed. Sir Walter Raleigh described the Newfoundland fishery as "the mainstay and support of the West". Anything between 250 and 400 ships were estimated to have been involved in the fishery at its height, along with between 6,000 and 10,000 men. The Dartmouth fleet was probably one fifth, 20%, of these. So important was this fishery that at times of war crew on ships sailing to Newfoundland were exempt from being press-ganged into the Navy.

The riverfront at Dartmouth

It was a long and arduous trade with ships leaving in early spring and returning at the end of the summer, having sold their haul of salt cod in Spain, France, Portugal and sometimes Italy. Off the back of this trade in salted cod, many boats returned with cargoes of Portuguese wine. They also traded in stock fish, unsalted cod which had been dried out in the

"The Exchange" – Dartmouth
An ornate house front constructed in 1635

open air on wooden frames and later in special drying sheds. It was often rock hard and had to be reconstituted with water then beaten into submission!

Fishing had become such a lucrative export trade for Devon boats that by the 17th century ships had tanks fitted that kept the fish alive. Turbot and lobsters would be held in rock pools until a consignment was ready to sail from Teignmouth to the capital. By the mid 18th century trade from Plymouth was thriving, sending sole, turbot, sturgeon and salmon to London, Bristol and Bath. Hake went to Portsmouth while mackerel, herrings, crab, lobster and crayfish were exported to the Channel Islands.

One person who visited Dartmouth on his travels was Daniel Defoe and he left us this vivid description of a sudden, vast shoal of pilchards entering Dartmouth harbour in 1722:

"The opening into Dartmouth harbour is not broad, but the channel deep enough for the biggest ships in the Royal Navy; the sides of the entrance are high mounded rocks, without which just at the first narrowing of the passage, stands a good strong fort without a platform of guns, which commands the port...

I had the curiosity here with the assistance of a merchant of the town to go out to the mouth of the haven in a boat to see the entrance, and castle, or fort which commands it; and coming back with the tide of flood, I observed some small fish to skip, and play upon the surface of the water, upon which ask'd my friend what fish they were; immediately one of the rowers or seamen starts up in the boat and throwing his arms abroad, as if he had been bewitched, cryes out as loud as he could baul, a scool, a scool. The word was taken to the shore as hastily as it would have been on land if he had cried fire; and by the time we had reached the keys, the town was all in a kind of uproar.

The matter was that a great shoal, or as they call it a scool of pilchards came swimming with the tide of flood directly, out of the sea into the harbour. My friend whose boat we were in told me this was a surprise which he would have been very glad of, if he could have had but a day or two's warning, for he might have taken 200 tun of them, and the like was the case of other merchants in the town, for in short no body was ready for them except a small fishing boat, or two which were out in the middle of the harbour, and at two or three hawls, took about forty thousand of them. We sent our servant to the key to buy some, who for a halfpenny bought us seventeen, and if he would have taken them, might have had as many more for the same money: with these we went to dinner; the cook at the inn broiled them for us which is their way of dressing them, with pepper and salt which cost us a farthing; so that two of us and a servant dined, and at a tavern too, for three farthings, dressing and all..."

Our friend treated us the next day with a dish of large lobsters, and I being curious to know the value of such things, and having freedom enough with him to enquire; I found that for 6d or 8d they bought as good lobsters there as would have cost in London 3s to 3s 6d each.

In observing the coming of those pilchards, as above, we found that out at sea, in the offing, beyond the mouth of the harbour, there was a whole army of porpuses, which as they told us pursued the pilchards and tis probable drove them into the harbour, as above. The scool it seems drove up the river a great way even as high as Totness bridge, as we heard afterwards; so that the country people who had boats and nets, catch'd as many as they knew what to do with, and perhaps lived upon pilchards for several days; but as to the merchants and trade, their coming was so sudden, that it was of no advantage to them."

At much the same time that Dartmouth was earning its reputation for salt cod, Clovelly was also a thriving fishing village, specialising in herring and mackerel in the autumn, long-lining for cod in the winter and potting for lobsters in the summer. In the 1630s sixty boats fished for herring from this tiny harbour. The catch went mostly to Bideford, although some might go across the Bristol Channel to Wales, with the boats returning with a cargo of coal. At one point a large fleet of herring boats was based in Clovelly for the late autumn season, as it was the only safe harbour along this stretch of the coast. Because the boats only fished for a couple of hours, using sustainable drift nets, their fish gained a reputation for freshness and flavour. The Clovelly Herring became a cheap winter food, many of them salted or brined to preserve them.

Fishermen gossip over their boats at Clovelly after landing herring for the Herring Festival

Clovelly is a copybook example of the decline of Devon's fishing industry. Today a handful of boats fish for various species, but only two specifically pursue herring – traditionally known as the "silver darlings" because of their bright silver scales and relatively small size – which normally appear on that part of the coast in the late autumn. The Clovelly herring is celebrated each year at the Clovelly Herring Festival.

One of its champions is Dan Garnett, former lifeboatman, fish merchant and now a self-proclaimed "barrow boy with a blackberry". A first generation fisherman, when he moved to Clovelly in 1979 five boats were catching herring, and he started drift netting for them in a small rowing boat.

"I'd go out on the tide after the silver darlings; it's got to be the most sustainable way of fishing. We used to get reasonable amounts but numbers are very variable now." He soon realised that there was great potential to market them as something unique and started selling for all the Clovelly boats. This led to wholesaling other Appledore fish to local hotels and restaurants. He combined this with 15 years as a fishmonger, which is where he can be found now, promoting fish with a genuine passion from his unmissable barrow, five days a week across North Devon.

Dan Garnett a Clovelly fisherman and fish merchant is a passionate advocate of sustainable fishing

So where else can you buy this cornucopia of top quality, fresh fish?

Another satisfied customer – Dan Garnett

Nick Legg

The Fish Deli, Ashburton

The answer is not as simple as you might imagine, as Devon does not have the number of fishmongers you might well expect to find serving such a diverse fishery. But the fishmongers that thrive, do so because of the quality of their fish and the service they offer.

Many such as the Fish Deli in Ashburton are not to be found in coastal towns. Run by former chef Nick Legg and his wife Michele, what might have been a moment of moorland madness opening so far inland has proved to be anything but. The wet fish counter is a feast for fish lovers' eyes, with a display of dazzlingly fresh fish, scales intact, eyes bright, landed only a few hours earlier at Dartmouth, Brixham or from the small boats at Kingswear – from the affordable to the luxury end, anything from sea bass to River Teign mussels, lemon sole, mackerel, squid, line-caught pollock, hand-dived scallops or sea trout. Keen to promote fish from sustainable sources, the walls are covered with blackboards proclaiming Nick's message of "sharing a passion for local fish sourced from local day boats

The Fish Shed at Darts Farm,
Topsham

and selected with marine conservation in mind".

The mood inside the shop is infectious and it is hard to avoid leaving empty handed. Nick has a series of "fish for a fiver" recipes to show his customers that a fish meal for four need not be expensive. "I'm trying to encourage people to think 'I want fish to eat' and that it is not difficult and not boring. If they can look at my blackboard and think 'I can go in and say I want fish for a fiver' it makes it easier for them to buy a product that many of them are not used to." If you are feeling pushed for time he has a range of fish dishes to take away and reheat, such as fish cakes, luxury fish pie or bouillabaisse. As the name suggests, it is a fish delicatessen so is well stocked with other fishy foods, most of them locally produced. It is easy to see why this shop, opened in 2004, has such a huge following.

One of Plymouth's best fishmongers is acknowledged to be Lloyd and Anne Down, while there are two good fishmongers in Barnstaple's Butchers' Row and Mark Lobb based just outside Dartmouth. Jacksons in Newton Abbot (see chapter 7) is also something of a local institution.

Some farm shops, particularly those close to the coast, have recognised that the growing interest in fresh, Devon fish is another attraction for customers, and have introduced their own wet fish counters. An example is the Fish Shed at Darts Farm. At the Churston Traditional Farm Shop the fish comes straight from Brixham, only a couple of miles away, each morning. The Fish and Shellfish Store at the Greendale Farm Shop sells sustainably sourced mussels and oysters, fresh fish and shellfish, all from Exmouth boats, landed less than five miles away. This arrangement means the fish come direct from the harbour, cutting out the middlemen and guaranteeing the fishermen a market and fair price all year round.

Both Devon coasts have a reputation for the quality of their shellfish, lobster from the north, crab in the south. But all is not well in this sector. According to shell fisherman Chris Venmore, secretary of the South Devon and Channel Shellfishermen, there are too many boats, including a number based elsewhere, setting too many pots, and prices are poor.

Nevertheless for the consumer it is reassuring to know that this is one of the most sustainable ways of catching shellfish as they can continue feeding and moving around once in the pots. Any undersized crab and lobster – there are minimum landing sizes for both – and any hens with obvious signs of eggs, all go back into the sea live.

For some of the best Devon shellfish, visit Nick and Anita Hutchings at Britannia of Beesands, on Start Bay between Torcross and Hallsands. They have a unique business covering all aspects from net to plate. Nick still fishes most days, and he and Anita market shellfish and fresh fish for a number of other local boats. Recognising that consistency of supply is everything, particularly during bad weather, Nick has built holding tanks to keep shellfish alive and in tip top condition. On dry land they have a fish counter, offer a mail order service and have a café where you can enjoy locally caught fish, shellfish, and lots of other seafood goodies.

Fish and Chips The Fish Shed, Darts Farm, Topsham

Another source is Walrus Fisheries in North Devon, which has a unique relationship with Mortehoe Shellfish, a café/restaurant that has become something of a local legend. This genuine family affair was started by Julie and Winston Huelin more than 30 years ago and in a truly boat-to-plate operation two generations are involved in catching, cooking and presenting the freshest seafood to their customers. While Julie and her three daughters cook shellfish and other fish dishes in a simple, unpretentious way, her son Geoff has taken over from his father catching lobster and crab along the North Devon coast. Julie insists on only the freshest fish and shellfish, served at a small number of tables in her front room, or the garden if the weather is fine. "Our aim is to give you the undisguised genuine taste of seafood. If you order a lobster or a crab – that is exactly what you will get, mainly because we can't cook anything fancy," she says. What doesn't find its way from the Walrus to the café in Mortehoe is sold live to local hotels and restaurants, or to private customers within a short distance of Ilfracombe. If you

want something to take away that is effort-free, Mortehoe Shellfish sells cooked shellfish and other fish dishes to order. The family also has a shellfish van that tours the area during the summer.

Fishing remains the most dangerous peacetime occupation, pitted against the unpredictability of tides and weather. It is the last truly hunter-gatherer operation in our food chain. Of course it is helped by modern electronics and navigation systems, nets and fishing gear designed to minimise catching undersized and juvenile fish. But it is the same technology that can cause problems too – it means that, in theory, the Marine and Fisheries Agency (MFA) should know where any boat is at any time.

▸

Lobster Quadrille with band attached

Despite fierce criticism from the media and green groups, for many years Devon fishermen have put measures in place to manage their stocks – off the north coast there is a ray box, a clearly defined area where fishing is banned from December to the end of May to protect juvenile rays; the South Devon crab box off Salcombe, on the south coast, is a potting gear zone only, where no trawling is permitted. Interestingly in January 2010 Lundy became England's first Marine Conservation Zone (MCZ) and will cover the same area as the former Marine Nature Reserve. In 2003 a No Take Zone was declared off Lundy and this seems to have worked very well.

What the future holds is uncertain. There is an inherent dilemma here. While the Devon coast produces a broad range of species of top quality fish, caught by fishermen who care about giving their customers the best product, they are trapped by the twin pressures of economics versus earnings. The number of registered boats is dwindling slowly – in 2005 there were 399 but at the end of 2008 that had fallen to 354. Not all of these will be at sea full-time; some will not be fishing at all while others will be part-time, their skippers and crew supplementing their income with onshore jobs.

Imagine what Brixham and Plymouth, Beer and Appledore would be like without their fishing fleets? It is the fishing communities that make the Devon coast so special, and they need a healthy fishing industry if they are to survive. Seafood, like many other commodities, is no longer a cheap food, although some species are less expensive than others – herring and sardines are affordable by all, whereas turbot and lobster come in the luxury category. If we want picture book fishing villages, populated by local people rather than used as holiday lets, we must be prepared to put our hands in our pockets and pay the going rate.

The famous and very ancient Pilchard Inn on Burgh Island

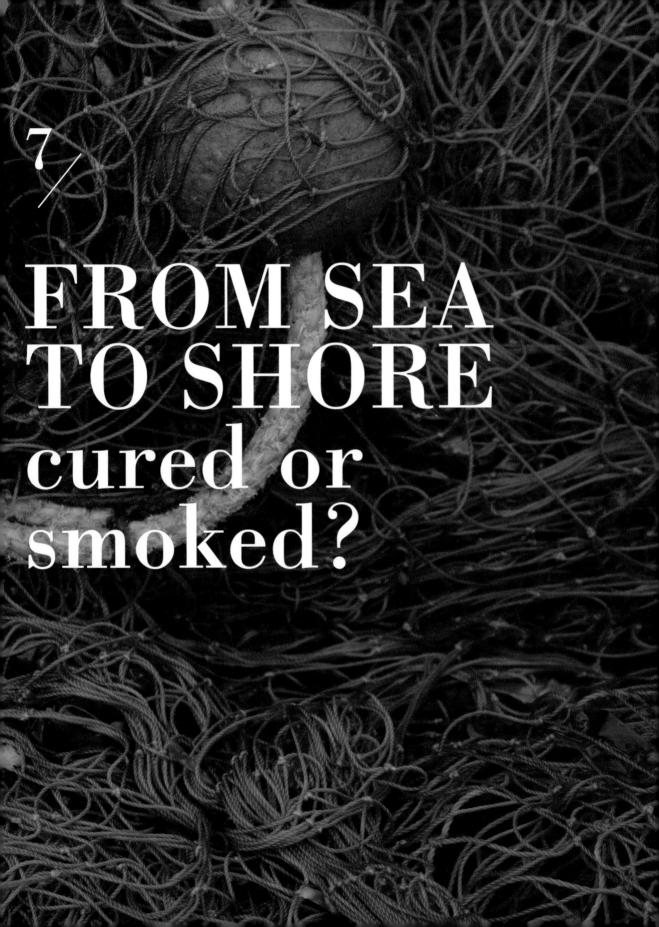

FROM SEA TO SHORE

cured or smoked?

A SMALL GROUP of people stand on the banks of the River Teign just at the point where it enters the sea, some wearing oilskins and waders. Among them is award-winning chef Tim Bouget, whose restaurant Ode is literally only a few yards away from the shore. Like the others he is in search of the ultimate culinary prize, the now rare and elusive wild salmon or its close rival the sea trout, also known in Devon as salmon peel. They are watching a small boat rapidly

Paying out the net

moving in a wide arc on the River Teign, paying out a net as it goes. Swooping round it returns to the shore. Breathless from his exertion rowing this heavy boat, the oarsman jumps out and, joining one of the men in waders who has been patiently standing and watching, they take up the free end of the net. The two men trudge upstream back to the starting point, at the same time quickly hauling in the net. The catch is carefully removed. Two wild salmon, a disappointing haul of what is regarded as the king of fish, not just for its rarity but its flavour and texture.

Although Wes Highgate is no longer a licence holder he is authorised to help the last two remaining official permit holders on the River Teign, the last fishermen netting salmon for a few short weeks in June and July and sea trout, which can be caught from March until the end of July.

Salmon fishing is in their blood. Wes is one of several generations that have continued this traditional way of fishing on the river, though he admits it has never provided a full-time living. "Salmon fishing is something that gets hold of you," he says. His fascination with these beautiful and challenging fish comes through in every sentence. "They all have their own characteristics, the way they feed, the way they move."

This ancient fishing method is similar, although on a smaller scale, to seining for pilchards. Seining comes from the French word for purse, and

DEVON SALMON

Official records from MAFF show that the Devon salmon population was still healthy after the Second World War. Figures for 1949 show the salmon catches:

Dart – 1,711

Taw and Torridge – 4,500

Exe – 3,957

Tamar and Plym – 2,209

Teign – 1,271

Axe – 83

Avon – 10

These of course were official figures so the actual catch would have been much higher.

was widely used by Devon fishermen from medieval times. As the tide is turning two teams of three or four start near the mouth of the river, targeting the deep pools where the salmon lie. Each shoot repeats the process following the salmon as they swim upstream. This ancient skill just survives but is heavily regulated and monitored. All the fish landed must be tagged and recorded before being sold.

River netting for salmon and salmon peel is the interface between salt and fresh water fishing. For hundreds of years the Devon rivers were rich in salmon, sea trout and brown trout, second only in reputation to Scotland's classic salmon and trout rivers. In 1900 five thousand salmon were caught and landed by rod and net fishermen on the Dart alone. In 2006 that had dwindled to 200 fish for the whole of Devon and most of them released back into the river. In 1984 only one fish was taken on the Torridge, which 30 years earlier had been classed as one of England's finest salmon rivers.

Salmon returning up river to spawn is one of nature's most natural breeding cycles, but it has also become one of the most contentious in the fishing world. The decline of these fish has been well documented, and the

Wes Highgate " it was this long"

blame oscillates between soil erosion, industrial pollution, agri-chemicals and fertilisers, fisherman and anglers, depending on who you talk to. One thing is certain, who or whatever is to blame, Devon's rivers are a shadow of their once glorious past.

The Environment Agency has paid many of the remaining traditional netsmen in Devon to put away their nets for up to ten years, reducing a group of around 50 to just 12 as part of a strategic approach to restoring stocks. It is a rare treat to get a glimpse of some of last netsmen on the Teign or the Dart, hoping to catch wild salmon as they return to spawn in the gravely river beds where they were born. Here the male and female salmon thrash around in very shallow waters, the eggs are fertilised and then covered up in small mounds of gravel with their tails. These are called redds and are hard to spot.

Devon is a county of many rivers. The Dart, Taw, Tavy, East and West Ockment, Avon, Erme, Plym, Lyd and Teign all rise on Dartmoor; the Taw and Torridge meet at Appledore. The Sid, Axe and Otter run south through deep valleys into Lyme Bay, where they are joined by the Culm, the Yarty and the Coly. The county's longest river, the Exe, starts its journey to the sea in Somerset, rising near Simonsbath on Exmoor.

The early hunter-gatherers would have fished these rivers, trapping or spearing fresh water fish such as perch, roach, salmon and chub. Ironically research published in 2009 suggested that it was over-fishing these species that turned the early fishermen towards the sea, to harvest what is effectively Britain's last wild food, which itself, for certain species, is now deemed to be under pressure.

Daniel Defoe on his travels in 1722 leaves us a wonderful description of fishing with dogs for salmon fishing with dogs in tidal salmon traps at Totnes. at Totnes.

"About 22 miles from Excester we got to Totness, on the river Dart. This is a very good town of some trade, but has more gentlemen in it than tradesmen of note; they have a very fine stone-bridge here over the river, which being

seven or eight mile of the sea is very large, and the tide flow 10 or 12 feet at the bridge. Here we had the diversion of seeing them catch fish, with the assistance of a dog. The case is this, on the south side of the river, and on a slip, or narrow cut or channel made on purpose for a mill, there stands a corn-mill; the mill tayl, of floor for the water below the wheels is wharft up on either side with stone, above the high water mark, and for about 20-30 ft in length below it, on that part of the river towards the sea; at the end of this wharfing is a grating of wood, the cross-bars of which stand bearing inward, sharp at the end, and pointing inward towards one another, as the wyers of a mouse-trap.

When the tide flows up, the fish can with ease go in between the points of these cross-bars, but the mill being shut down they can go no further upwards; and when the water ebbs again, they are left behind, not being able to pass the points of the grating, as above, outwards; which like a mouse-trap keeps them in, so that they are at the bottom within about a foot, or a full foot and a half water. We were carryd hither at low water, where we saw about 50-60 small salmon, about 17 to 20 inches long, which the country people call salmon peal, and to catch these, the person who went with us, who was our landlord at a great inn next to the bridge (Seven Stars Hotel) put in a net on a hoop, at the end of a pole, the pole going across the hoop, which we call in this country a shove net: the net being fixed at one end of the place they put in a dog, who was taught his trade before hand, at the other end of the place, and he drives all the fish into the net, so that only holding the net still in its place, the man took up two or three and thirty salmon peal at the first time.

Of these we took six for our dinner, for which they ask'd a shilling viz twopence a piece and such a fish not at all bigger and not so fresh, I have seen 6s 6d each given at a London fish-market, whither they are some time brought from Chichester by land carriage."

With the exception of smoked wild salmon – and there is some still to be found if you know where to look and ask the right people – the real McCoy when it comes to farmed fish in Devon is smoked trout, which can be found at several trout farms situated on some of Devon's fast flowing rivers.

Dieter Wirtz has been quietly farming rainbow trout at Plaistow Mills for more than two decades. These are exceptional fish, some going for restocking fishing lakes and rivers, some sold fresh for the table, some smoked and processed.

As a former master chef Dieter knows a thing or two about good food, so takes his smoking very seriously. The fish are either hot or cold smoked over beech and oak. Cold smoked trout may be his speciality but he takes the view that each batch should be treated individually "we smoke it until it is ready," he says simply, adding that he combines modern technology with old fashioned smoking techniques. The cold smoked trout is outstanding, to my mind a taste that cannot be compared with mass-produced smoked salmon. The texture is dryer, denser and less fatty. The reason? "The biggest thing is the leat water," Dieter says, suggesting that the fast flowing waters makes them swim harder, unlike the flabby lazy fish reared in large cages on conventional salmon farms. This gives the trout a firm flesh and he believes, is a healthier environment for the fish. You can take pot luck and turn up at his delightfully unmodernised mill to buy his trout, otherwise most of it goes to restaurants, fishmongers and farm shops.

▶
Dieter Wirtz's fillets of smoked trout emerge from the smoker.

SOME HISTORY

Many people have strong views about fish farms but there is an argument that aquaculture may be the only way that we will be able to eat fish in the future. Devon's many rivers, with their good supply of freely flowing water, makes them ideal for this. Along with farms producing coarse fish and brown trout (*Salmo Trutta*) for restocking rivers and fishing lakes, a small number of fish farms grow rainbow trout (now known as *Onchorynchus mykiss*) for the table, some of them also smoking or processing it themselves.

Most of them use traditional cold smoking methods, preparing and curing the fish by hand before hanging in the smoker over oak or beech chips. For hot smoked trout the fish are cleaned, left whole and brined for a couple of hours. Then they are hung in the smoker, usually over oak or beech shavings, although Mike's Smokehouse at Loddiswell near Kingsbridge uses manuka sawdust which comes from New Zealand and gives a quite distinctive flavour. For hot smoking the temperature is gradually brought up to a maximum of 80°C to cook the fish. A few hours later when they are done, they are filleted and packed.

Cold smoking is a gentler art, working at around 30°C. This does not "cook" the fish in the same way as hot smoking, but continues the traditional form of curing, using salt rather than brine, that goes back hundreds of years. Some also make smoked trout patés or sell just-out-of-the-water fresh fish.

These fish farms are on a much smaller scale, a tiny cottage industry when compared with the massive commercial Scottish salmon farms that have given fish farming its poor reputation. Devon's fish farmers believe that their trout are healthier than farmed salmon, thanks to the conditions they are reared in – where the fish are not too crowded and the water remains clear and clean – compared with the hundreds of cages of fish found on often non-tidal lochs in Scotland. One Devon producer was quite confident there should be no detectable difference between the water down river and the water above the farm.

Someone like Dieter Wirtz will produce around 25 tonnes of fish a year, while the Scottish salmon industry, and it surely is industrial in scale, exports around 12 million fish a year, excluding domestic consumption.

Terrific trout are not the only fish farmed in Devon. Aquaculture extends to oysters and mussels around both north and south coasts and in tidal river estuaries, all of them small-scale, highly sustainable as plankton eating molluscs that that don't require artificial feeds or medication.

Oysters, are one of the oldest, native species of mollusc found around Devon. Harvested at low tide from many of the county's river estuaries, for hundreds of years they were so abundant and so cheap that they were as widely consumed by the poor as by the wealthy.

The River Tamar was teeming with them and the River Exe was also rich in mussels, eels, salmon and mullet, while fish tithes paid in Sidmouth and Otterton came to around £15 a year. The south coast fisheries were among the most profitable in the region, and by the 1420s the fishermen dredging the Exe Estuary for oysters and mussels would have paid the Earl of Devon for the privilege.

In the 21st century it is the Pacific oyster, sometimes also known as the rock oyster, (*crassostrea gigas*) rather than native oysters (*ostrea edulis*) that are farmed around the Devon coast.

Richard Marsh is standing up to his knees in water, methodically turning bags of oysters. He works his way up the rows of racks on the banks of the River Avon. Timing is everything as these are only exposed at low tide. The bags are turned every two weeks from August to October, once a month during the winter.

Richard Marsh and his father Peter at Bigbury Bay Oysters must run one of the most scenic oyster farms in the world. Sitting on the banks of the river Avon, a little upstream from Bigbury Bay, the views both upstream and downstream are breathtaking. It is in this idyllic and peaceful setting, that they produce around 15-20 tonnes of Pacific oysters a year, giving a whole new meaning to mucking about on the river…

Oysters have probably grown naturally here and on many of Devon's other rivers, such as the Dart, Teign and Exe, for hundreds of years. What sets these apart is the combination of fresh and tidal water. Native oysters, which mostly thrive in saline conditions, are of course much more seasonal, bearing out the old adage that you should only eat oysters when there is an R in the month. Pacifics on the other hand, are in season all year round, although Peter Marsh reckons that January and February are when they are at their best. So while some chefs like to make an occasion out of serving native oysters, oyster bars and others like the year-round consistency that comes with the Pacific. The two types are easily distinguished – natives are rounder and flatter and the Pacifics are more elongated and deeper. The slower they grow, says Richard the sweeter and nuttier the taste.

His enthusiasm can convert even the most uncertain about eating oysters. At any food festival there will be crowds around the Bigbury Bay Oysters' stand, either those already in the know or oyster virgins about to experience a revelation learning how best to enjoy an oyster – tip don't swallow it whole, instead press it gently against the roof of your mouth until it has almost all dissolved. Then chew and swallow the firmer meat. The taste is a revelation and lingers long and sweet. "There are two other aspects to tasting," says Richard. "An oyster cleanses your palate and makes you feel you are alive." No wonder they go with champagne.

Peter Marsh

Richard Marsh of the Bigbury Bay Oyster Company along the banks of the River Avon

It is less than a decade since Richard and his father took over the oyster farm. The first thing that was needed was clear water – an essential that was lacking although Peter, a keen environmentalist, recognised was the key to the rest of the business. He spent several years working with other organisations to restore the water quality. Native oysters will thrive in saline conditions, whereas Richard and Peter Marsh believe the faster growing pacific oysters do better in fresh water. As it is tidal the Avon provides the best of both worlds. While these bivalves require the best quality water, they themselves have a minimal environmental impact – they feed by filtering phytoplankton from the sea water and require no medication unlike farmed fish.

Unlike many of the other oysters raised in Britain which are exported to France, the majority of Bigbury Bay oysters are sold to British markets, most direct to chefs and oyster bars. Depurated in water under ultra violet light for 42 hours to purify them, they can be found a few yards up the road from the river at The Oyster Shack at Aveton Gifford, they are served by Rick Stein and sold in London's Borough Market.

Oysters aren't the only farmed shellfish that Devon can be proud of. Both coasts are renowned for naturally grown mussels. In North Devon Brian Hill is the man in the know, and is the third generation of his family to harvest mussels from the shoreline around the Torridge and Taw estuary.

Richard Marsh prepares oysters for
an alfresco experience

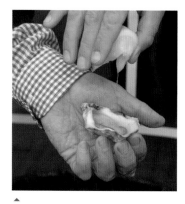

A squeeze of lemon

Ilfracombe harbour

He has been picking the biggest sweetest mussels from the river bed since 1957. However the good quality of the water in these rivers means that they are also excellent locations for oyster and mussel farming.

Brian is not the only mussel farmer who dredges wild mussels from the seashore and the beds of the river estuaries. Barry Sessions of River Teign Shellfish, Lustleigh, also does the same on the River Teign.

But more active mussel farming also takes place at sea, just off Brixham and Exmouth where the mussels are grown on ropes. These plankton feeders are some of the most sustainable shellfish, causing no pollution.

Brixham Sea Farms Ltd were the first in the UK to grow mussels in open sea conditions. Sited between Fishcombe and Elberry Coves, to the west of Brixham harbour, this organic Torbay farm is certain that "the exceptional quality of mussels produced is due to the low stocking density and abundant food source from this open sea environment". They farm a naturally occurring hybrid of the native (or blue) mussel (Mytilus Edulis) and the Mediterranean (Mytilus Galloprovincialis), ideally suited to Torbay's higher water temperatures and environment. Their depuration plant is on the River Dart at Galmpton. Fish farms are not just about fresh fish – but also mussels and oysters. In Devon this means Bigbury Bay oysters, Exmouth Mussels Ltd or River Exe Shellfish, river Teign Shellfish. Also cockles, clams, winkles in small quantities.

In North Devon some mussels are dredged from the rivers Taw and Torridge, then put through the usual depuration process.

For hundreds of years fish was a dietary staple in coastal communities, particularly when there were shortages of other basic foods such as grain. the only ways of preserving fish were by smoking, drying and salting. Apart

The 'Mussel Man', Brian Hill

from wind drying, smoking was one of the early methods of preserving fish. This was later followed by curing with salt, and it was said that in parts of the county there were no trees within five miles of the coast because all the timber was used as fuel for the salt pans. According to the Domesday Book, Devon had 22 saltpans including some at Seaton that were still active in 1145. The names of some of the coastal villages give a clue to the fact that salt was once produced there, for instance Salcombe and Budleigh Salterton, where salt pans were recorded from the 13th century. In 1724 Daniel Defoe also visited Barnstaple where he recorded ships sailing to Liverpool bringing back cargoes of rock salt which was then dissolved in sea water to produce "salt upon salt", which was used for curing herrings. Demand for salt, either for curing for herring and pilchards or for the lucrative salt cod trade, was so high that it was also imported from France. The salt tax, introduced in 1698, made imported salt cheaper.

Herrings were gutted then barrelled up in rows with layers of salt. Because of great emphasis in the middle ages on fasting, and not eating meat, salted herrings became an important part of the diet, particularly for the peasantry and for the poor crammed together in the towns.

Every coastal village would have its 'pilchard palace' where pilchards would be salted, pressed and preserved, either to feed local families or to be exported.

Mussels

There are several theories as to why the pilchard industry declined. One suggests that the introduction of the railways and refrigeration eliminated the need to preserve fish in the short term. But in the last decade pilchards have found new popularity rebranded as sardines (a sardine is an immature pilchard) and are flying off the fishmongers' slabs. A "Lyme Bay sardine" conjures up a quite different image from memories of pilchards in tomato sauce and school dinners.

Smoking

Used for centuries as a preserving method for long term storage, with the availability of refrigeration and efficient transport, today's smoking concentrates more on texture and flavour.

Apart from the few wild salmon caught by local netsmen, the rest of the salmon likely to be found in Devon is imported from fish farms in Scotland and elsewhere. But if you can't have smoked Devon salmon, you can find plenty of other smoked Devon fish.

At Jacksons in Newton Abbot, which combines a fishmonger's, fish and chip shop and a smokehouse, smoking fish for a range of customers has become a major part of this family business, that started more than 75 years ago.

Matthew Endacott is the third generation to buy his fresh fish direct from Brixham market each day, and is already having no difficulty encouraging his son and daughter to help out at times. He is happy to smoke almost anything, within reason, including bespoke smoking for customers who bring in their own catch. "Some of these work better than others, we've done crab, tomatoes, mushrooms, garlic, sea salt. . ." The slab at the front of the shop includes smoked cod's roe, smoked conger eel, smoked mackerel, salmon, hot smoked trout, kiln roasted salmon and Jacksons' own cured kippers, along with a good selection of wet fish and local crabs, lobster and mussels. He might also smoke other varieties, such as pollack.

Smoking is always done over oak chips and the time taken depends on the weather. Cold smoking, he explains, is more difficult in warmer weather as the ambient temperature makes it harder to control the temperature in the kilns. Similarly the time of year influences when some fish are at their best for smoking – herring from the late summer but not at the end of the year, mackerel from mid-summer, both needing a certain degree of oiliness to smoke well.

When it comes to salmon he has to buy Scottish farmed salmon, but he is quick to explain that the end product is how smoked salmon once was, before it became universally available and affordable to a wider cross-section of customers. "We smoke the traditional way, we don't inject brine but dry cure with salt," he explains.

Mike Smylie The peripatetic
Kipperman puts in an appearance at
the Clovelly Herring Festival and
smokes the local catch over a
traditional oak chip fire

However he adds that kiln roasted, or hot smoked salmon, outsells cold smoked salmon, even though his has a quite different taste and texture from the mass-produced version found on every supermarket shelf.

It is an interesting reflection that in present times smoked salmon, once thought of as an expensive, luxury food, is now found in abundance in every supermarket, while fish and chips, once thought of as a working class food, as well as becoming a truly British food icon, is no longer as cheap as chips. In fact Matthew believes that his fish and chips are still good value. "Seasonal fish with chips and a hot drink for £3.95, you can't get a decent burger, chips and a drink for that."

And finally – smoking may have been banned in pubs, but at the Holt, in Honiton, Angus McCaig's tiny smokery is going from strength to strength. Angus, who runs the kitchens assisted by his wife Kate (see chapter 16), while his brother Joe is the front of house face, started smoking local fish and meat as a hobby. This has developed into Smoking Jacket Foods – which has become a vehicle for smoking a wide range of local produce, including smoked salmon, shell on prawns, free-range duck breast and chillis. Found at farmers' markets and local shops, as well as in the Holt's kitchens, this is the modern face of smoked foods.

They even smoke butter with maple.

8 /

HAND PICKED

PICKED FOR PERFECTION. At Tavistock Farmers' Market in West Devon a queue of eager customers is lining up at the Olive Organics stall. Shoppers here know that when they buy any of the salads, herbs and vegetables that Elizabeth and Jeremy Rickeard will have had that phrase in mind. Everything selected for sale will be in optimum condition for that day's market. There are bags of salad leaves, fennel, sugar snap peas, several varieties of lettuce, new potatoes and herbs, chosen from more than 100 different crops grown on their 4.5 acre smallholding on the Bere peninsula in the Tamar Valley. These also include, depending on the time of year, broad beans, rhubarb chard, courgettes and several different types of tomatoes. All chosen, says Elizabeth, for "flavour and quality, as opposed to high yield, uniformity, and stackability" the factors needed when growing for the supermarkets.

For the Rickeards growing organically is "not just about the chemicals that we don't use and what we don't do, it's also about what we do do. It's about the way we try to look after the soil and the environment, aiming for a sustainable, balanced ecosystem, that provides the best possible conditions for plant growth."

So popular are their products that this is always one of the first stalls to sell out at the regular farmers' market. So loyal are their customers that if they are unable to turn up themselves the Rickeards know exactly which salads and vegetables they would normally buy and can send their friends and relations home with precisely the right product.

Once the whole of the Tamar Valley, including the Bere peninsula, was a highly productive, thriving market garden area, supplying London and other cities with fresh produce, particularly soft fruit, taking natural advantage of its mild, almost frost-free climate which put it several weeks ahead of its competitors elsewhere in the country. There had been a horticultural industry in the valley for hundreds of years supplying local markets, but it was when Brunel's Great Western railway reached Plymouth in 1849 that the transformation of the valley began. It was Thomas Lawrie who discovered that this could be "the earliest outdoor strawberry growing in England". On a visit to Covent Garden in 1862 he found "that there were no outdoor strawberries offered, whilst the crop at home was nearly finished before we left". The next year he started sending strawberries to Covent Garden where he received 2s 6d (12.5p) a pound for a product

Elizabeth Rickeard picking peas in Bere Alston ready for Tavistock Farmer's Market

◄

Braunton Great Field showing the curved strip boundaries created by generations of ploughing with oxen

Peas in a pod

Beans in the rain

that would have sold in Devonport for 6d (2.5p). The end of season fruit went to jam factories in Plymouth and Bristol.

It is hard to believe that thousands of workers toiled in these steep and difficult valleys producing such a wide range of crops, but for many it was the only alternative when many mines, including the Devon Great Consols tin and copper mine, started to collapse in the 1890s. By this time the "gardens" were at their most productive. Large quantities of daffodils, rhubarb, cherries, plums, raspberries and gooseberries, were sent direct by train from Bere Alston and Bere Ferrers to cities such as London, Glasgow and Birmingham. During the First World War the emphasis switched to essential crops such as potatoes and other vegetables.

The post-war years changed all that, as the steep, labour intensive slopes were unsuitable for mechanisation and unable to step up production as agriculture and horticulture in the rest of the country were being encouraged to do. Then came the Beeching cuts in 1962/3 to hundreds of miles of branch railways, the advent of air freight and the rising influence of the supermarkets demanding "just in time" deliveries of products that are grown for their ability to travel and their shelf life. Today only a handful of growers remain on both banks of the Tamar, those on the

Guy Watson and the Riverford
Farm hoe gang

Devon side concentrating mainly on horticultural crops for local markets. Most, but not all, of those left still have stalls and honesty boxes at their gates, offering the homecoming worker fresh soft fruit, vegetables or salads. Some of the steepest land has reverted to scrubby woodland and the flatter land has been turned over to more general agricultural production.

At the other end of the scale, in the South Hams, is Riverford Organic Vegetables that has grown from "a man and his wheelbarrow" to a multi-award winning, organic vegetable box business.

Guy Watson is the youngest of five Watson siblings (see also chapters 3 and 15). After working in London and America as a marketing consultant, in 1985 he started with three acres of his family farm and a dream to "put fresh vegetables on the family table at a price everyone can afford". His dream is now the biggest organic vegetable box scheme in Britain. Riverford Organic Vegetables boasts more than 400 acres of organic produce, growing more than 100 different vegetables from mizuna to chives, strawberries, rocket, potatoes and swede, with around 300 employees and a multi-million pound turnover, delivering to more than 30,000 Devon households a week.

"When it started in 1985 I didn't have any idea that it would end up on this scale," he says. "I don't think I had any particular aspirations and I knew I wanted to run my own business because I was not very good at being an employee. I knew I had to be outside – ironically I spend most of my time in the office now – I knew that I couldn't be forever selling new things to new people, it had to be a repeat business. And I didn't have a lot of money."

Initially he supplied local shops and his brother Ben's farm shop that had just opened. Then when he realised that he did not want to deal with the supermarkets, started the vegetable box scheme in 1993. He was inspired in this by Tim and Jan Deane, who had been box pioneers two years earlier. Initially he made all the deliveries himself, then set up franchises that he knew would be better run by others. What Guy Watson did was to understand the dynamics and how to commercialise an idea with huge potential.

Organic farming was not chosen for any quasi-hippy, alternative lifestyle reasons, more that of a realisation of the dangers of agri-chemicals, and a recognition of an emerging market that is still growing. "It wasn't particularly that I wanted to save the world but I felt that this was a huge health issue. Just for me personally, as a youth I used to spray the corn on the farm very badly and I'd make myself sick."

However as the rush to buy local organic produce with known provenance grew exponentially, it was clear that Riverford could not meet demand. So in 1997 Guy helped to set up the South Devon Organic Producers Co-operative. For the co-op's 12 members, mostly local small and medium-sized family farms, this has brought an added bonus and guaranteed income stream as, with a few exceptions, Riverford undertakes to sell or market the majority of their organic crops.

For a man running such a green businesses on such a scale the challenge of carbon footprints and efficiencies tax him greatly. As the business continued to grow, Guy became increasingly uncomfortable with the food miles travelled and wanted to refocus on local growing and delivery. The result has been setting up a network of four "sister" farms in Hampshire, Yorkshire, East Anglia and Cheshire, based on the Riverford model, which deliver the same range and service within a 50-mile radius,

Local produce in the Riverford Farm Shop
▼

Beetroot

between them making around 20,000 deliveries each week.

"I'm trying to find the smallest way of doing it and have the most local, and therefore the best connection with customers but be able to do things in the most professional manner. This is where I think some small box schemes (I know some of them do a great job) fall down a little bit."

Not all the 1200 acres on the farm that lies between Buckfastleigh and Totnes are cultivated for vegetables simultaneously – they are worked in rotation with Riverford Farm Dairy, which was certified organic in 1995, (see chapter 4). So the pastures are rotated as grassland and grazing and probably only 400 acres will be growing vegetables at any one time.

The Riverford box system has developed into an all-singing, all-dancing choice of organic produce, working with the other elements of the family business to provide meat, and dairy produce and groceries, giving customers the ability to choose exactly what they want in their weekly or fortnightly box. Interestingly the Riverford boxes belie the myth that organic produce is expensive. Guy Watson's boxes consistently undersell their supermarket equivalents, often up to 20 per cent cheaper.

Others prefer the simplicity of smaller box schemes, such as Linscombe Farm, near Crediton, Rod and Bens, or Shillingford Organics, based just outside Exeter; but these too are finding that with more choice available in the market place they also have to offer something a bit special.

If Riverford is a one-off then so is the Braunton Great Field in North Devon, which was laid out by the Saxons in the 8th century AD. It is one of two remaining medieval strip farming systems in England, and still

Giant stems of rhubarb from the fields at Darts Farm, Topsham

sensitively farmed to maintain its very special structure. It was a classic open field system that was communally farmed for hundreds of years, each family having the right to grow crops and graze their animals. The arable land was unenclosed; livestock were grazed on the village commons and briefly on the Great Field after harvest and all farmers had access to meadowlands that were used for grazing and hay. By the middle of the 16th century communal farming had given way to individually-managed strips, which were allocated so that each of the owners or tenants had their fair share of the fertile and less fertile land. In medieval times land was divided into long, rectangular strips of one acre, ten times as long as they were broad. Then sub-divided into ten narrow strips one furlong (220 yards) in length and one chain (22 yards) wide, separated by narrow, grass balks known as landsherds. Each farmer would hold a number of strips.

An acre strip was permanently fixed by Edward I in 1305. It was based on the amount of land that a man with 2 oxen could plough in one day. Interestingly horse races are still run in furlongs and the length of a cricket pitch is still one chain ie 22 yards.

In Braunton each strip was named, names such as Venpit, Hayditch or Copper Corner reflecting their local characteristics. History suggests that The Great Field was very fertile land, and at one time Braunton was sending away surplus produce to other local towns by sea. In 1842 the records show that there were 448 strips, by 1994 that had dropped to 86 unenclosed strips, and in the 21st century encroachment around the edges means that the Great Field has probably dwindled to less than 20

Spring furrow – Braunton Great Field
▼

per cent of its original size. It is still farmed, mostly by descendants of some of the original owners, although some of it would appear to have been amalgamated into larger blocks.

One man who can claim more than 600 years of growing tradition on the Great Field is David Hartnoll. He believes that his ancestors were probably farming their share of it in the 14th century and local records show the family renting, then owning, a farm in North Street in Braunton in 1625. It is just over 20 years since they moved to their current location on the edge of the village. Part of the farm, around 90 acres, is on the Braunton Great Field. Despite the narrow strip layout presenting a few problems, farming this unique area is not difficult he says.

From early May to mid June he spends virtually every daylight hour cutting asparagus. He also rears beef and lamb, grows arable crops, potatoes and vegetables, mostly for sale at local shops and farmers' markets. Over the years the asparagus has become a significant part of his farming business, although it only accounts for around 10 of the 700 acres he farms. Most of this is sold to hotels, restaurants and wholesalers in this part of Devon.

"It's a long crop to establish," he says, "but it's become one of the few English vegetables that holds its value in season."

Asparagus may be a tiny part of the county's horticultural output, but it illustrates how a small number of specialist growers have recognised the thriving market for quality vegetables, salad leaves and herbs. It seems that more small producers are happy to make a living from a few acres and some polytunnels, many of them growing specifically for local pubs and

David Hartnoll grows asparagus on Braunton Great Field

restaurants, others for farm shops, farmers' markets and local retailers. For many of us, apart from those able to grow their own, these are the products we dreamed of finding during the last decade but found the reality was usually tired, limp and disappointing, or only sold in specialist, hard to find ethnic shops tucked away in urban back street locations.

For the growers, none of this comes easily. Working on this scale means long hours cultivating their crops for relatively small returns. By opting to do something different their satisfaction comes from their customers who appreciate the quality of their crops. A happy coincidence or a sign of changing times when chefs and restaurateurs spot the benefits of the freshest, local produce, delivered daily?

Carolyn and Paul Bellinger, just outside Ottery St Mary might be described as typical. Their smallholding on part of Carolyn's former family farm is just one example, supplying salad leaves and seasonal vegetables, edible flowers, tomatoes, leeks, globe artichokes, spinach, courgettes, herbs, squash, potatoes, cucumbers, strawberries and raspberries to the Jack in the Green, just six miles away, and a handful of other local pubs. Each year Matt Mason, head chef at the Jack in the Green, sits down with the couple to discuss the cropping to maximise the best range of different products that he will be looking for during the year. They also sell at selected farmers' markets in East Devon and at the farm gate.

A cornucopia of unusual fruits, herbs and vegetables from Carolyn and Paul Bellinger's Market Garden in Ottery St Mary

The fruit garden has a range of soft fruit, from gooseberries to red and black currants, tayberries and blackberries. The polytunnels are full of the heady smells of tomatoes and the wonderful perfume of basil hangs in the air, not one but at least four types; in addition to the sweet basil there are Thai, purple and lime basil growing here. Carolyn crushes a couple of leaves between her fingers producing a sweet lime fragrance and taste.

Beetroot comes in a range of wild and wacky colours, golden and striped, while beans can be anything from yellow to black.

"We set out with the intention of growing heritage and unusual varieties, we knew we had to add value in some way," she says. "It was the way to make our produce stand out and offer something different from the supermarkets."

To complete the mix the couple have replanted an orchard, and also have chickens, ducks and pigs, all of which end up on the table.

One year they experimented with coloured potatoes such as Highland Burgundy Red, Vitelotte and Shetland Black, as well as traditional Arran Pilot, Duke of York and Pentland Javelin - types that have disappeared from our supermarket shelves because of their

refusal to conform to the demands of potatoes that will store for ever, can be washed and travel around the country and reappear in a store somewhere near you next spring. The Bellingers' potatoes are there to be eaten in season, freshly dug.

Although historians disagree about exactly who was responsible for introducing the potato, there is no doubt that Sir Walter Raleigh, along with Sir Francis Drake, two of Devon's best known buccaneers, played an important role introducing what has become a major part of the western diet. The first potatoes brought to England were likely to have been the sweet potato, while the conventional potato as we know it followed later, coming to Europe from South America in 1580. Drake is thought to have brought first roots from Columbia, but on his homeward voyage he landed on the Virginian coast which may have led to a misunderstanding of provenance. What is clear is that the early colonists to this part of America included Thomas Harriot, a key figure on Raleigh's first expedition to Virginia and that he brought back some tubers that were planted on Raleigh's Irish estate at Youghal, near Cork. There is no doubt that this decision helped to speed up their acceptability and lay to rest superstitions that the tubers were poisonous.

Nevertheless the potato took a long time to catch on as an important crop for Devon. In 1808 Charles Vancouver, in his General View of the Agriculture of the County of Devon, reports that during the 18th century the most progressive farmers used them as cattle feed or boiled and mixed with barley as pig feed. It took a few more years, and a series of poor cereal harvests, to encourage serious production as a field crop, and before families started to include them in their diet. For the poorest there would otherwise have been a very limited choice of vegetables, based mainly on turnips, carrots, cabbage and parsnips.

At the other extreme from the 18th century onwards, Devon's major landowning families, such as the Courtenays, Rolles and Aclands, would have been trying to out-compete each other for the range and exoticness of the fruit and vegetables that they could grow in their walled gardens and glass houses. The taste for unusual vegetables included cardoons, asparagus, globe artichokes, mushrooms and broccoli, while hot houses nurtured peaches, vines, nectarines, figs, melons, even citrus fruit. Lord Rolle, for example, proudly built an orangery at the end of the 18th century at Bicton Park in East Devon, while John and Theresa Parker of Saltram House, near Plymouth, built an orangery, peach and grape houses. They imported orange trees from Genoa to Falmouth, which were taken to Saltram by coach.

In the 21st century it is foreign travel and the influence of celebrity chefs that have titillated our appetites for more exotic fruit and vegetables.

◀
The first of the seasons new potatoes ready for box scheme customers at Riverford Farm's packing depot

FOOD FAIRS

Devon seems to have a penchant for fruity festivals. Each June the Combe Martin Strawberry Fayre celebrates the long tradition of growing the fruit on the warm, fertile and sheltered valley slopes around the village. The tables groaning with freshly picked fruit include some from the handful of remaining local growers and some from elsewhere, but it is the Combe Martin berries that sell out first. This coastal village, with its unique two-mile long high street, might seem an unlikely location to celebrate the strawberry, but until the 1950s growers were producing fruit and vegetables that were sold in Ilfracombe and Lynton. So numerous were the growers that at one stage this North Devon village held an annual strawberry feast for the Barnstaple workhouse. Further south Galmpton, in Torbay, has recently revived its Gooseberry Pie Fair, in which a giant gooseberry pie arrives at Churston station by steam train and then processes to the Manor Inn. This tradition dates back to 1873 although it has been discontinued and revived several times. Each July the village of Marldon has an Apple Pie Fair, a revival of a Victorian tradition inspired by local apple grower George Hill, while Newton Abbot has an annual Cheese and Onion Fayre and Buckfastleigh its Lamb Pie day each July and Pear Pie day in the autumn.

▶ ▶

The Combe Martin Strawberry Fair gets under way with locally grown strawberries fetching 30% more than 'foreign' ones from over the border in Somerset

So growers are producing leaves such as cavolo nero, pak choi or rainbow chard, vegetables that once would have been only found in gardens of real enthusiasts. With one eye on global warming and the future, Mark Diacono has planted olives, almonds, apricots and persimmon on his East Devon farm. At the same time the "eat seasonally, buy local" message that has spread across the county like a rash since the 2001 foot and mouth outbreak means that many growers are trying their hand at old favourites such as purple sprouting broccoli and curly kale, vegetables that for years had been taken for granted and in some cases almost disappeared. But much of this lies in the hand of smaller, specialist growers who have spotted a gap in the market.

It may feel as if fruit and vegetable growing in Devon is heavily biased in favour of organic systems, and while there is no doubt about the dominance of Riverford Organic Vegetables, it is true that the South West has more organic farmers and growers than any other part of England, thought to be around 43 per cent. However there are plenty of growers in Devon turning out considerable acreages of potatoes, swedes – one third of the nation's swedes is grown in Devon – parsnips, cauliflowers and other brassicas, particularly in the county's milder coastal areas. Nevertheless the impact of the supermarkets, working with limited numbers of packhouses and suppliers, means that conventional vegetable growing on any scale is in decline.

Since the demise of the Tamar Valley market gardens, Devon has no soft fruit production on any appreciable scale, but there are several growers who persist, despite the damp, maritime climate, mostly through pick your own operations. This means they can select varieties for taste and flavour as they are not selling into large commercial markets and do not have to meet the expectations of the multiple retailers. Most try to offer a wide range of soft fruits, and other vegetables or plants and flowers, such as Boyces of Manstree near Exeter, which also has a successful vineyard and nursery, Lukes Fruit Farm at Tamerton Foliot, Lifton Strawberry Fields and the Ashford Inn Fruit Farm in North Devon.

Some of these, such as Shute Fruit and Produce, have a range of fruit and vegetables on offer throughout the season, starting in June with strawberries, broad beans and new potatoes, then moving on to runner beans, pumpkins and Indian corn in October. Other crops include French beans, sugar snap peas and squashes, all carefully selected for their flavour and herbs such as dill, coriander and several types of basil.

Situated on the banks of the River Teign, it is hard to think of a better setting, on a warm summer or autumn day, picking raspberries or courgettes. Not for nothing do owners David Lamboll and Lori Reich describe it as their "slice of heaven in Devon".

FAIR MAID TO PLOUGHMAN
Devon Cider, Mazzards and Dittisham plums

A cider apple orchard in blossom
at Whimple which once belonged
to the late Raymond Burroughs
and before that belonged to
Whiteways Cider

DEVON CIDER WAS ONCE FAMOUS throughout the land and is often considered to be slightly sweeter than its counterpart in Somerset. Cider means apples and a hundred years ago Devon abounded in orchards. In spring the valleys would become a sea of blossom and in autumn the farmyards would be filled to bursting with mounds of ripe apples waiting to be crushed and pressed out. It is perhaps difficult now to imagine the scale of orcharding a hundred years ago and the visual impact on the landscape.

In 1894 there were 26,000 acres of orchard in Devon and these orchards stretched from Hartland and Exmoor in the north right down to the South Hams almost to the tip of Start Point. In some areas every farm

Devon cider press with
windlass by Clare Leighton
c 1930

had an orchard and every farmer made cider. Some had old presses of their own but others made cider communally in the village pound house. It was an ancient autumn ritual when the presses ran with juice and the whole village would have taken part. For months on end Devon would have been laced with the aromatic smells of ripe apple and rotting pomace.

Cider apples and dessert apples often have intriguing and peculiar names which give a clue to their origin, and Devon is no exception. Here you can find Fair Maid of Devon, Farmer's Glory and Devonshire Quarrendon. Some apples have specific links to places such as Bewley Down Pippin from near Membury, Upton Pine, Killerton Sharp, Killerton

Apple and binder twine, Gray's Cider Farm, Halstow

Raking windfalls at Grays Cider Farm, Halstow

At Heron Valley their prize herd of South Devons cattle get stuck into some healthy pomace

Sweet and Tale Sweet. Halstow Natural is only found on a few farms in the Tedburn St Mary area. Some make good apple juice like Brown's apple from Staverton near Totnes. Other names relate to their appearance or taste such as Spotted Dick, Crimson Victoria, Golden Bittersweet and Sweet Alford. Some apples are even named after people who raised them such as Reverend McCormick, vicar at Broadclyst, Tremlett's Bitter, Lucombe's Pine or Tom Putt from Gittisham near Honiton. Immortality in the cider world is hard won. But in the case of the Tom Putt it is richly deserved because Tom Putt is a dual purpose apple being both a cider apple and a

cooking apple. It became so popular that it was often called the Cottage Apple 'A rosy apple that grew in every garden and every orchard.'

Today if you go inside the church at Gittisham you can see the tombs of the Putt family. It was Tom Putt (1722-1787) a barrister who first raised the apple. He gave a graft of the apple tree to his nephew also called Thomas Putt (1757-1844) who was rector of Trent near Yeovil which was then in Somerset and now in Dorset. Very confusing for apple buffs. So Tom Putt is a dual purpose apple in both senses of the word. Just up the road from Gittisham church, at the end of a long winding drive, is the Elizabethan Manor of Combe House, residence of the Putt family since 1614. They owned the estate for 232 years. Ken Hunt, who now runs Combe House as a hotel with his wife Ruth, has planted a few Tom Putt trees in their garden and even makes cider from them.

But the cider making tradition in Devon is much older than Tom Putt. Devon's cider makers are part of a living tradition that came across in medieval times from Normandy and Brittany. Many of the earliest records come from monasteries. Tavistock Abbey for instance produced cider on its

All Doer (CG)
Allspice (CG)
Barum Beauty (CG)
Beech Bearer (CG)
Beef Apple (CG)
Bewley Down Pippin
Jackson's, Crimson King
John Toucher's (CG)
Bickington Grey
Billy Down Pippin
Billy White (CG)
Blue Sweet (MM)
Bowden's Seedling (CG)
(poss Jonathan, US)
Brown's Apple
Butterbox (CG)
Cerit (CG)
Coleman's Seedling
Court Royal/ Sweet
Blenheim
Improved Pound (CG)
Crediton Fair (CG)
Crimson Bramley (mm)
Crimson Costard (CG)
Crimson Victoria
Dawe (CG)
Devon Crimson Queen/
(mm)
Queenie
Devonshire Court Pendu
(CG)
Devonshire Quarrenden
Devonshire Queen (CG)
Devonshire Red (DA)
Devonshire Striped (CG)
Devonshire White Sour
(CG)
Docker's Devonshire (CG)
Don's Delight
Dufflin (CG)
Ellis' Bitter
Endsleigh Beauty (CG)
Fair Maid of Devon
Farmers Glory (Devon)
French Longstem (CG)
Golden Ball (CG)
Golden Bittersweet
Goring (CG)
Great Britain (CG)
Green Bittersweet (CG)
Halstow Natural
Hangy Down (DA)
Herefordshire Pippin (MM)

Plymstock estate in the 14th and 15th centuries and shipped the cider by sailing barge up the Tamar to Morwellham and then overland to the abbey for consumption at the dinner table. The cider would have been transported in large barrels called pipes which held approximately 120 gallons. In the 1790s Buckland Abbey also had one of the oldest known orchards in the country, dating back to c1600 and was probably much older than that.

Every monastery would have had several orchards and cider presses were rented out as a means of earning an income. Tithes and rents were often paid in cider.

Cider was also taken on long sea voyages to counteract the affects of scurvy as well as a way of washing down the salt cod and salt beef which was often their staple diet on board. In 1620, the same year the Pilgrim Fathers left Plymouth for Massachusetts, nervously clutching their bibles, another expedition left Exmouth for New Found Land armed with 'twenty six tunnes of beer and Devon Sider'. The Devon connections with Newfoundland go back to the time of Humphrey Gilbert (1589-1583) who came from the Compton and Greenway estate at Galmpton on the River Dart. Today there are still orchards in the Avalon peninsular in Newfoundland.

The Devon cider presses were often very large and therefore the 'cheeses', the mounds of chopped apple carefully layered and wrapped with straw, were renowned for their size. John Newburgh writing in 1664 says that 'In Devonshire where their wrings are so hugely great that a hogshead or two runs out commonly before the apples suffer any considerable pressure'. And they valued this apple juice as they did with the first honey that dripped out of the comb. And called it 'life' honey. Honey and orchards are inextricably linked particularly as it is the bees that help pollinate the apple trees. Bee keepers are still sometimes paid to keep their hives in the orchards in the spring.

Devon's great commentator on cider in the first part of the 18th century was Hugh Stafford of Pynes, a large house just a mile or two north of Exeter. In his book A Treatise on Cidermaking published in 1753, Hugh Stafford mentions at length the history of the Royal Wilding or Red Hill Crab which was found growing wild in a small quillet in the St Thomas's region of the city. Other Devon cider apples that he mentions are The White Sour, an 'early ripening small yellow apple', The Cowley Bridge Crab, which is 'dirty purple and green,' but a single tree can yield as much as 5 hogsheads per tree, the Backamore from Plimpton Mary, 'beautifully streaked with dark red and has a bloom on it like a plumb; it makes an excellent, strong and palatable cyder', but none has the endearing qualities of the Mediate which comes from Ermington, near Modbury. 'Of this apple is made that sort of

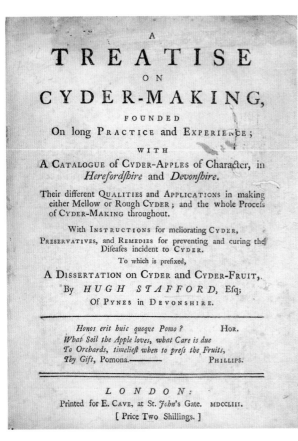

Hugh Stafford's Treatise on Cidermaking in Devon 1753

Hollow Core (CG)
Ice Apple (DA)
Improved Keswick
Johnny Andrews (CG)
Johnny Voun (CG)
Killerton Sharp
Killerton Sweet
King Manning (CG)
Kingston Bitter
Langworthy/ Sour Natural,
Wyatts Seedling
Limberland/ Limberlimb
Listener/ Summer Listener
Winter Listener
Listener (CG)
Long Bite (CG)
Longstem (DA)
Lucombes Pine

liquor which in Devonshire is called Hewbramble or Bramble cider; alluding to its roughness, which causes a sensation as if a bramble had been thrust down the throat and suddenly snatched back again.' Obviously very high in tannin but useful for blending. Stafford then mentions an Irish apple called the CockoGee which means Goose turd in Irish… said to have been brought back by Counsellor Pyne of Exeter who had care of Sir William Courtenay's estates in Ireland. 'The Cyder is the colour of sherry.'

Charles Vancouver writing in 1808 on Agriculture of Devon comments that so much cider was produced in the South Hams that annual exports by sea from Salcombe alone amounted to between 700 to 1500 hogsheads in a good year. He also comments on the difficulty of naming apples from one district to another. Saying 'The variety of names applicable to the same fruit in this and other districts, and even in adjacent villages, precludes all chance of being understood at a distance when speaking of any apple that maybe the favourite in such places.' He also comments that they use isinglass to fine the cider. 'To complete the fining of cider a pound of isinglass first soaked for ten or twelve hours in cold water is afterwards dissolved in about 5 gallons of cider and well incorporated with a whisk: about a quart of this is sufficient for a hogshead of cider.'

As to soils he has this to say : 'Long experience has shewn that the same fruit growing upon a moist loam or clay bottom will produce a vastly superior cider to that growing upon an understratum of shear sand or gravel,'

'The average price for cider last year at the pound's mouth ie at the press was 50/- a hogshead. Or even two guineas and a half.' He comments that he has seen no mistletoe in the county.

But cider was not just restricted to the more fertile areas of Devon in the east and south, it was an essential part of farming on Dartmoor. As recently as 1960 there were nearly 800 orchards within the boundary of Dartmoor National Park. Many of these orchards would have been small but it was a significant part of the annual crop. No farmer could attract good labour without good cider. Sheep shearing is thirsty work at the best of times. And a farmer who could not provide good cider was often put to the bottom of the list. Indeed cider was the agricultural barometer and farmers were judged accordingly. Cider apples will grow up to 800 ft and in some

Lucombes Seedling/ Kirton Fair,
Newquay Prizetaker
Major (CG)
Michaelmas Stubbard (CG)
No Pip (CG)
Northcott Superb (DA)
Northwood/ Woodbine
Oaken Pin/ Taylor
Paignton Marigold (CG)
Payhembury (CG)
Pear Apple (CG)
Pear Pine (CG)
Peter Lock
Pigs Nose
Pine Apple Russet of Devon (CG)
Plum Vite (CG)
Plympton Pippin
Pocket Apple/ (CG)
Hangdown, Horner's Handydown
Poltimore Seedling
Pound (CG)
Pynes Pearman (CG)
Quarry Apple (CG)
Queens (CG)
Quench (CG)
Rawlings (CG)
Red Jersey/ (CG)
Loran Drain, Loyal Drain, Loyal Drong
Red Ribbed Greening/ (MM)
Cornish Pine
Red Robin (CG)
Red Ruby (DA)
Redstreak/ Bovey Redstreak
Kernel Redstreak,
Redstreak (mm)
Reine des Pommes (CG)
Reverend McCormick
Reynold's Peach (CG)
Royal Wilding
Saw Pit (CG)
Sercombe's Natural (CG)
Slack Ma Girdle (CG)
Sops in Wine/ (CG)
Pendragon
Sour Bay (DA)
Spicey Pippin (CG)

instance 1,000 ft. Many of the quarries on the edge of Dartmoor were used to making the bases for cider presses and the larger circular troughs used for pressing the apples with a horse going round in circles.

Such was the scale of the orcharding and the demand for the Devon cider that some farmers left the land and concentrated full time on cider making and selling it far afield. The most famous Devon cider maker was called Whiteways whose business was started in Whimple to the east of Exeter by Henry Whiteway in 1891. Whiteways grew rapidly and went for quality only taking apples from reliable farmers. They also had an eye to export. They understood the value of advertising and marketing. Whiteways were soon sending Cyder to the D'Oyly Carte Opera House, as well as Eton and Harrow. He had broken out of East Devon into polite London Society whose cyder drinkers included Edward VIII, Conan Doyle and W.G. Grace. They had agents in Manchester and London and in the 1920s even branched out into cider making in Nova Scotia in Canada, when Whiteways bought a stake in the Annapolis Valley Cyder Co. Whiteways ciders were advertised as being 'the pure juice of Devon apples without the addition of any chemicals" Whiteways were also well known for their non-alcoholic drink Cydrax which kept the Temperance League at bay. Cydrax was later joined by Peardrax and these were exported to Moslem countries.

Whiteways also diversified into making British wine, ginger wine and British Sherry...and were eventually amalgamated with Showerings of Shepton Mallet. Sadly the Cyder works in Whimple was shut down in 1989 two years short of their centenary. Interestingly two ex-employees were so devastated that the tradition of cider making was being axed in Whimple that they set up their own cider works a few miles down the road at Darts Farm in Clyst St George. This is now Green Valley Cider run by Chris Coles and Nick Pring and uses many apples from the same orchards that once supplied Whiteways.

▶
Arthur and Harold Stephens, Bere
Ferrers © Chris Chapman 2004
Arthur died two days after the
photograph was taken

Many older people will also remember the names of other medium to large scale cider makers like Henley's of Abbotskerswell, Horrell's of Stoke Canon, John Symons & Co, who up until the 1940s made cider on the Plains in the middle of Totnes, with apples coming by steam train, river barge, as well as lorry, horse and cart. There was also F C Hill of Staverton and Inch's Cider at Winkleigh started by Sam Inch in 1916. Inch's kept going till they were bought out in 1998 by Bulmer's for £23 Million. Here again the ex-employees felt let down so they started making cider on the same site. This is now the Winkleigh Cider Company run by David Bridgeman.

One farm cider company that has outlasted them all is Grays of Tedburn St Mary who started making cider in the 1660s. Ben Gray says that 'they started delivering to Moretonhampstead and beyond after the Napoleonic War'. He has a long cob cider barn and many barrels. Some of the apples are from just that valley and were developed in his grandfather's time like Goring, Halstow Natural, Johnny Andrews and Sercombes Natural.

Another cider maker of note was Horace Lancaster of Felldownhead near Milton Abbot who ran Countryman Cider. His maxim was simple "Bread is the Staff of life but Cider is Life itself." He started exporting cider by the lorry load to Aberdeen in the early 1970s when they struck oil.

Some other family cider makers still in business are: Hancocks near South Molton, Ostlers near Barnstaple and Palmershayes near Tiverton. But there has been a healthy input of new cidermakers like Luscombe Cider

Five year old Devon Cider Brandy
from Real Drink, Stoke Gabriel

near Buckfastleigh, Bollhayes Cider at Dunkeswell, Milltop Cider near
Newton Abbot, Sandford Orchards near Crediton, Westlake near
Beaworthy. Real Drink at Stoke Gabriel now produce their own Devon
Cider Brandy which is heady stuff and was only released in autumn 2009.
Ashridge Cider at Staverton near Totnes make bottle fermented sparkling
cider using 'methode champenoise', putting the sparkle back into Devon.

One interesting family firm run entirely by women is Heron Valley in
Loddiswell near Kingsbridge. Natasha Bradley recently took over running
the cider farm from her parents who started the business in 1997. Natasha
now re-employs her parents and four sisters. She is the middle one. They
are tucked away in a side valley at a farm called Crannacombe which
means in Anglo Saxon, Heron Valley, hence the name of the business.
They also run South Devon cattle on the land and have planted more
orchards. The apples that they use are Fair Maid of Devon, Foxwhelp, Pig's
Snout, Dabinett, Sheep's Nose, Hangy Down Clusters and many more
which they buy in. They use modern presses and take great care with
keeping the apple and equipment clean. Natasha is keen on marketing and
she has found over 300 outlets for her Devon cider. Some is bottled and
the rest is on draught for the pubs. The public now want a clean refreshing
cider apple taste, they want slight carbonation and not too sweet or too dry.
Interestingly the public is now developing a taste for tannin which gives real
cider the depth and complexity which is normally associated with a good
Bordeaux. Cider made from dessert apples is by contrast often weak and
insipid.

Devon also has several cider and orchard related customs. Wassail is
common in Devon and is held around twelfth night, ie the 5th/6th January
Some use the old twelfth night which is around 17th January. Here men

Feeding cider apples into the mill
Gray's Cider Farm Halstow

Gentlemen of the Press – Ben Gray keeps an eye on his 'modern' hydraulic cider press

gather in orchards with three handled cider mugs and shotguns. They used to send a boy up into the top branches of the largest apple tree with a piece of toast soaked in cider to offer it to the small birds, wrens and blue tits that are seen as the spirit of the orchards. Then there is much singing and music, noise and banging of pots and pans and the shot guns are let off to scare away the evil spirits or as some say to wake the trees up from their slumber. One such modern wassail takes place at Stoke Gabriel and involves morris dancers, mummers and story tellers.

The next event in the orchard year is May Day and at Lustleigh Community Orchard on the edge of Dartmoor they hold a May Queen ceremony where a young girl is chosen each year and she walks round the village beneath a wonderful bower laden with flowers. Eventually she is crowned with a garland of flowers in the orchard and sits upon a large rock which acts as a granite throne. The ancient ceremony was re-started in

Ben Gray building a cheese layer by layer

Judges at the Devon County Show hard at work...

1905 by Cecil Torr and apart from a few years around the Second World War has carried on more or less ever since. It is always held on the first Saturday in May each year. As always it is an auspicious ceremony to ensure a heavy crop of apples and to get the blossom to set.

The last hurdle for orchards is to weather the late May frosts and such a problem was this in some parts of Devon, that they have ample stories to go with it. The critical time is around the Frankin nights, May 17th, 18th and 19th. One severe frost at that time could wipe out a whole year's apples and a whole year's cider, which would be devastating to a village. One report by P Hutchinson from the Devonshire Notes & Queries 1861 records the story thus:

> **Francimas, St Frankin Days, St Franklin Nights** are where the frost blights apple trees :- **St Dunstan** bought up a quantity of barley, and therewith made beer; the **devil**, knowing the saint would naturally desire to get a good sale for the article which he had just brewed, went to him, and said "that if he (the saint) would sell himself to him (the devil) the latter would go and blight all the apple trees, so that there should be no cider, and, consequently, a greater demand for beer." St Dunstan accepted the offer, but stipulated that the trees should be blighted on three days, which fell on **May 17,18, 19.**

This shows the great rivalry between saint and devil, or is it the links between Christianity and brewing as opposed to cider and the pagan beliefs? As well as the perennial problem of late hard frosts.

What is interesting is the way in which cider is made. For some it is a simple operation to collect the apples and crush them with a press. This can still be seen at Brimblecombe's Cider near Dunsford. Now the press can be an old wooden one, or an old hydraulic press.

Stillwood from Green Valley Cider

Half the secret of cider making is the way in which the cider is blended and kept. Often the cider barns are cool and dark. Many are made of cob and thatch, ideal for keeping the temperature even. So often farmhouse cider called scrumpy can be sharp and acidic. The skill of the cider maker is often keeping his cider in good condition. Many now bottle their cider which makes it easier to transport and this has led to a quiet revolution where bottled cider is now perfectly acceptable on a restaurant table. Cider has now become a respectable drink, consumed from the top to bottom of society. No longer is it just drunk at student parties, young farmer's clubs or drunk secretly by teenagers in bus shelters. Good cider can be fantastic and the bottle fermented sparkling ciders better than many cheap champagnes.

The renaissance and replanting of orchards in Devon is one of the really positive things to re-emerge from the last twenty years and this has been achieved by a handful of enthusiastic artisan producers. Devon is once more producing high quality cider and long may it continue to do so.

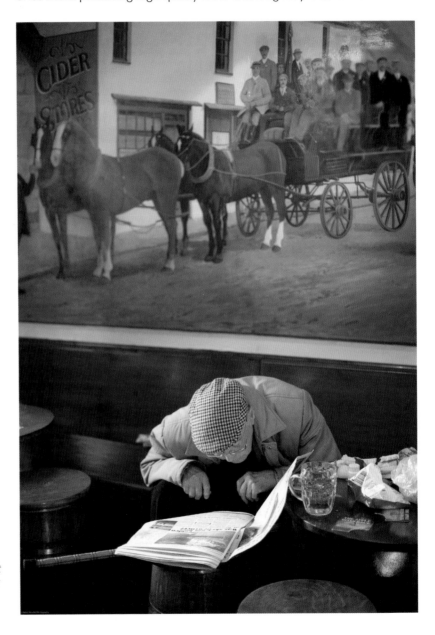

▶
A regular brings his own sandwich kit for a lunchtime pint in Ye Olde Cyder Bar, Newton Abbot and reads the Western Morning News

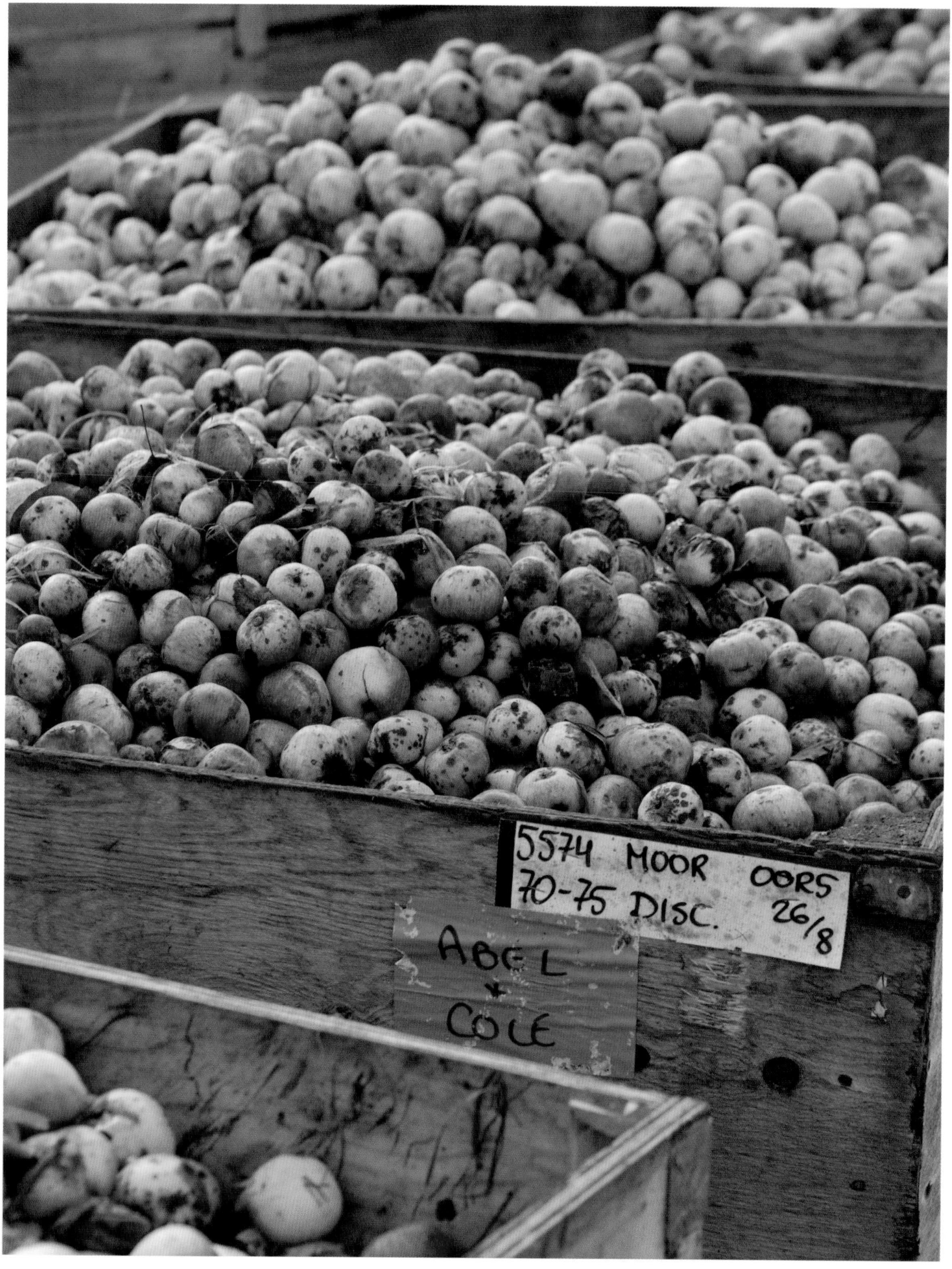
5574 MOOR OORS
70-75 DISC. 26/8
ABEL
+
COLE

As far as apple juice is concerned there are a good selection of producers. In East Devon Four Elms Fruit farm at Harpford near Sidmouth is run by Richard and Sue Smedley. They are by far the largest apple growers in Devon with 65 acres split between Newton Poppleford and Harpford. They sell bottled apple juice: Cox and Bramley, Discovery, Egremont Russet and Braeburn as well as the apples themselves in local Waitrose stores.

At Burlescombe on the Devon/Somerset Border, near the M5, is Redhill Farm run by Felicity and Andrew Shakespear. They have 28 acres of orchard. It was here that Everard O'Donnell planted his mother orchard in 1989 with more than 350 varieties of apple. Today they produce excellent apple juice which is sold in Wellington and Crediton. In the South Hams, there is Heron Valley, Luscombe and Real Drink. They all make and

Fair Maid of Devon...Natasha Bradley heads an all woman team at Heron Valley

sell apple juice. Interestingly Real Drink from Stoke Gabriel make single orchard apple juice, which means that with every bottle you can tell which orchard it came from. At Mill Top, Combeinteignhead, Sue and Richard Merrin also make cider and sell apple juice. They have a new outlet at the Butter Market in Newton Abbot where they also sell home brew kits. In the North Devon near Beaworthy, George Travis of West Lake produces about 15 varieties of apple juice including Luccombe Pine. He has even been known to produce a perry and a carbonated cider called Cidre Anglais.

As far as perry is concerned very little is now made in Devon but one of the best bottles made in Devon in recent times was a fourteen year old sparkling bottle of fermented perry made by Alex Hill near Clayhidon on the Blackdowns. It had the aroma of apricots and 'smoked' when it was opened. Perry pear trees are almost unknown in Devon today. They can grow to over sixty feet in height and in blossom are magnificent.

But Devon is not just famous for its apples, it is also famous for its cherry gardens or greens. Not only in North Devon, where the dark mazzard cherry was once grown commercially but also in the Tamar Valley. There was even a Cherry Garden Street in what is now Devonport. The sight of cherry orchards in full blossom must have been a fantastic sight indeed and the cherries rich, sweet and dark were much prized in the towns. There are stories of women up tall ladders in long skirts in the Tamar Valley singing to each other as they picked the cherries. Also regrators, or fruit merchants, from Plymouth and Devonport would go up the Tamar on sailing barges with gangs of women to pick the apples and other soft fruit to take back to the markets. They were happy times and it was an account of this, has been left by Rachel Evans in her book on Tavistock and its vicinity, published in 1846.

Chris Coles of Green Valley Cider – Darts Farm, Topsham
▼

◀
Bung Ho

This extract from *Home Scenes or Tavistock and its Vicinity* by Rachel Evans 1846 highlights not only the delights of Bere Ferrers and the cherry picking in the Tamar valley but also the proximity of Plymouth and the Naval dockyard.

"The fruitful parish of Bere Ferris is situated on the Devonshire side of the beach commanded by Pentillie castle. The shore is diversified by bold heights, broken by little valleys, which run in the direction of the river. Here are grown in abundance delicious small black cherries, which are carried to the Plymouth and Tavistock markets and thence dispersed to various parts of the country. A pleasant excursion it is to visit the parish of Bere, cherry eating in the proper season. The rich clusters of fruit almost drop into your mouth as you drive along the road in the neighbourhood of the orchards. These orchards are generally let out to "*regrators*" or fruit-sellers, who take possession of the trees for a season. I have known gentlemen let out an avenue of trees for the comparatively enormous sum of ninety pounds. Some farmers prefer having fruit pickers, who perform all the labour, and besides their meals, have so much a day. Last summer we encountered a party of these rural labourers, who were enjoying a plentiful repast in what might be truly termed a "Devonshire paradise"★ They were seated beneath some plum trees, which hung down with their rich purple bloom. Whole acres of ground around were filled with various fruits; gooseberries, currants, raspberries, cherries, pears, apples and damson plums seemed to vie with each other in their temptations to the stranger's palate. Certainly "Eve's kale-yard", of which Robert Burns so happily speaks, could not have presented greater luxuries than this extensive garden of forbidden fruit. And there were the pickers, carelessly laughing and chatting, heedless of the treasures spread so bountifully around them, until aroused to all necessary vigilance, by the bark of their

★ A facetious stranger observed, that "if it were only for its cream and butter, Devonshire might be termed an earthly paradise." We should add that its fruits equally entitle it to so proud a term.

watchful dogs. I must gratefully speak of the kindness of the owner, who on a hot Junue day, sent to entreat us to help ourselves to whatever we chose. Three times a week, boats are laden at an early hour of the morning with fruiterers and their baskets, who thus convey their produce to the Plymouth and Devonport markets. It was once my (lucky?) chance to return up the river in one of these market boats. I was amused to see the nonchalance of the women, who seemed to take no more notice of the progress of the boat, than if they were seated in a luxurious drawing-room by the fireside. They had no sooner chosen their places than all took from their capacious pockets, some work or knitting, and making their empty baskets serve as tables, commenced plying their needles with as much diligence as if their bread depended on their present labours. In the meantime their tongues were not idle; they discussed in a jargon peculiar to themselves, all the gossip of the neighbourhood, together with the adventures of the market. If the wind veered, they changed their positions, sat lower in the boat, and raised their krails higher. I never witnessed an instance of more perfect contentment. Besides the amusement of watching the my companions, I enjoyed the beauty of a calm summer's evening, Numerous pleasure boats, which, during the summer months, glide continually along the Tamar, passed us:- one with a band of music on board, long filled the air with melody; then the regular fall of oars announced the approach of the gig of a man-of-war. The grand hulks themselves, those huge Leviathans of art, were passed as we quitted Hamoaze: gently heaving their bulky sides with the play of the waves, they rise out of the water like some vast monsters of the deep. Well may England be proud of these artisans who rear such fabrics to set at defiance the world. Let him who takes an interest in his country's good, visit the dockyards of her navy…

TAMAR CHERRY VARIETIES

This lists all the cherries that may have been grown in the Tamar Valley over the last 200 years. Only a handful of varieties are grown today.

Best Black
Birchenhayes Early
Brandy Mazzards
Bullion
Burcombe
Drooping Willow
Early Burcombe
Early Red
Fice
Green Stemmed Rumbullion
Grylls
Halton Black
Herod Red
James Bullion
Jan James
May Duke
Morellos
Rumbullion
Smutts
Sweet Mazzards
Upright
White Heart

Mazzard harvest

It was the Second World War that brought an end to commercial cherry production - partly because at harvest time it was very labour intensive and workers were badly needed for harvesting more essential crops such as corn and potatoes. At the same time many orchards were grubbed up, a trend that has continued remorselessly ever since. During the war years this was to free up the land to grow basic foods, but in the 1970s, after Britain joined the Common Market, grants were available to continue vandalising and destroying orchards in the pursuit of higher profits, favouring subsidies available for rearing cattle, sheep and growing arable crops. In the last half of the 20th century Devon has lost more than 95 per cent of its orchards.

So today Mazzards are found only sporadically around Barnstaple in North Devon, a few remaining in hedgerows, odd ones found in apple orchards or standing alone in fields, in private collections or in community orchards. The best place to see these small, dark cherries is probably the Landkey Millennium Green, not far from Barnstaple. An orchard of the five varieties of Mazzard, Bottler, Dun, Greenstem Black, Hannaford and Small Black, was planted as part of a millennium project in 1999 and 2000.

The slow growing trees, which used to grow up to 50 feet tall and took up to 25 years to become fully productive, would have needed special 40ft ladders for the harvest, have been planted for their intrinsic landscape value as well as to continue a historic tradition, although the crop is mostly taken by the birds. In the spring sunshine it makes a wonderful sight, a reminder of how large parts of the North Devon countryside once looked. The small, dark, almost black cherries have a distinctive flavour and a deep purple juice. They were used mostly for desserts and some went into fruit wines, but many think they are best in a pie served with thick, golden Devon cream. In 1645, when Prince Charles visited the Countess of Tawstock, she paid 4s (20p) for 'masards'. Records show that in 1782 there was a mazzard press at Newport, near Barnstaple where the surplus cherries were probably made into fruit wine and liquor. They have a long, although somewhat unclear history, but in 1806 the Rev Richard Polwhele wrote that the parish of Goodleigh near Barnstaple was "for ages famous for its gardens of black and red cherries; the black are the largest and most luscious".

Once upon a time there were cherry feasts, just as there were at the other end of the county in the Tamar Valley which once had a similar proud cherry tradition. Again only remnants of orchards survive, limited to the area in and around the valley. There is one cherry orchard at Slew near Horsebridge but this a rare survivor. Burcombes were also a popular variety.

The decline of the Mazzard was driven by other factors such as natural predation by birds and squirrels, difficulty in marketing the fruit and the

better profitability of other forms of farming. It was a very short season of maybe 3 weeks and early imports from France and Spain did not help. Modern supermarkets cannot handle such short seasons, they want strawberries all year round. But there is a local food renaissance and a move back to local self-sufficiency, that has led to the revival of interest in the fruit. The hard work of a few enthusiasts led to the planting of the Landkey Millennium Green, two acres with around 65 trees. Michael Gee has been instrumental in getting Mazzards back on the map again.

At the other end of the county in the Dart Estuary is another rare survival.

In spring the hedgerows and gardens around Dittisham are transformed by the delicate white flowers of the Dittisham plum. Sometimes also known as the Dittisham Ploughman plum, it is specific to this picturesque village that nestles on the west bank of the River Dart. Its origins are not entirely clear. There are several differing theories as to how they came to Devon, but ancient tithe maps show that more than 100 years ago all the East facing slopes in this steep sided village and the surrounding valleys would have been planted with cider apples, while the

Michael Gee of Orchards Live in his Mazzard orchard at Landkey, North Devon

Dittisham plum blossom

southerly and west facing fields would have had Dittisham plums and dessert apples.

Sadly no commercial orchards remain, but there are plenty of trees growing wild in the hedgerows or in private ownership to provide a brief, seasonal and local glut. At the height of the summer, almost every house has a stall outside selling bags of these deep red plums. The can be eaten raw or cooked, used in pies, jams, ice creams, sorbets, chutneys and probably fruit wines.

Paul Vincent of Dittisham says that they are very dangerous because in August you pick one every time you pass a tree and then spend too much time in the small room or the dunny regretting your enthusiasm.

Devon therefore has a rich and varied orchard history and a fine climate for growing fruit. Maybe in a few years time it will be olives, almonds and tangerines. Anyone for Dartmouth Marmalade?

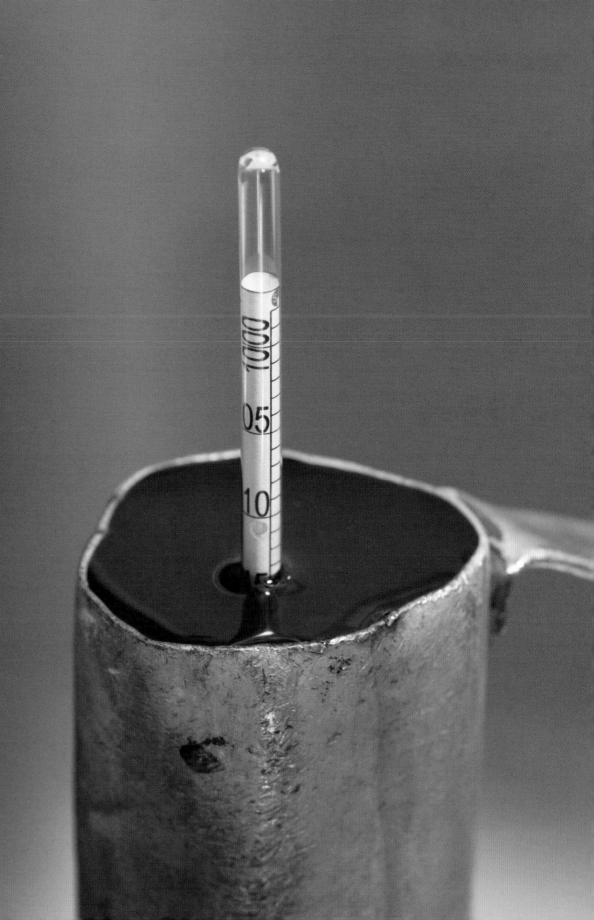

10/

A GOOD
MASH

O N A HOT SUMMER'S DAY when you have been out walking on Dartmoor and you come down into an old Devon pub like the Royal Oak at Meavy and order a pint of chilled beer to quench your thirst, spare a thought for Scott of the Antarctic. He was a local lad born a few miles away in Devonport. But more than that his father, John Scott, ran a brewery in Hoegate Street in Plymouth near the Barbican. In fact the brewery was bought in 1824 at auction for £4782 by his grandfather, Edward Scott, and his uncle – paid for out of prize money they had received during the Napoleonic wars. They ran the brewery for almost seventy years and even built one or two pubs in Plymouth including the Britannia Inn which still exists today at Milehouse. The Scotts lived at Outland House nearby. So there is more to brewing in Plymouth than meets the eye. How Robert Falcon Scott must have craved a pint of his father's Devon beer as he pulled that sledge back from the South Pole. Sadly Scott didn't make it but his story lives on.

The secret of brewing is not just in the water but in the skill of the brewer, the quality of the malting barley and the fragrance of the hops. In Newton Abbot, Tucker's Maltings is only one of a handful of firms that still continues the ancient craft of using malting floors. The firm has been in existence since 1831 when it was founded by Edwin Tucker in Ashburton. They were not only maltsters but seed merchants, which made good commercial sense. It was Edwin Tucker's eldest son John Tucker who

Tuckers Maltings and Teignworthy Brewery, Newton Abbot

Malted barley pours into a hopper at Otter Brewery

selected the site in Newton Abbot near the railway station and oversaw the construction of new buildings in 1900. They cost the grand sum of £8,000 and were officially opened on 5th November 1900 just in time for Guy Fawkes Night. Today the robust three story buildings are still in use with grain hoists, malting floors and louvres to control the ventilation. Often the pleasant smell of malting barley and brewing pervades that part of town. It is the only working malthouse left in the West Country and you can take factory tours in the summer months.

The malting floor at Tuckers Maltings. The dampened barley is spread out and allowed to germinate and partially sprout which increases the sugar or fructose content

The malting of barley is one of the oldest food processes known to man and references have been found to it in Sumeria dating from 2500 BC. The quality of the barley is paramount and Tuckers get their barley from Devon and Cornwall. The starches in barley are far more soluble than those in wheat, which is why barley is mainly used for beer and wheat for bread making.

Tuckers Maltings tour with Richard Wheeler

"My name is Richard Wheeler. I was born and bred in Newton Abbot. I have worked here in these buildings since 1959 which is over fifty years now. I was Managing Director of Tuckers and have now retired, but I am still Chairman of the Company. Our barley is grown under contract in the South West, mainly Devon and Cornwall, but occasionally Somerset, Dorset and Wiltshire. Malting Barley is the top grade barley unlike feed barley. It is very important that you have the right variety for malting and that it is grown in the right conditions and an awful lot of that is to do with the land that you are growing it on.

Barley hopper at Tuckers Maltings in Newton Abbot

▾

The West Country is not looked upon as a main malting area which is traditionally in East Anglia and Yorkshire but there are areas down here that are very suitable in Devon and Cornwall, particularly around the coast. A lot of that depends on the soil, light sandy soil, not the heavy clays. We have got growers who have got those right conditions. Some is winter barley and some is spring barley.

Maris Otter has been around for donkey's years and that is regarded very highly as a top quality malting barley. The problem is that it does not have the same yields but the quality of the barley is excellent. That is a winter barley. There are those brewers who have always brewed with marris otter and that is what they want. Maris otter is always regarded as a very forgiving malt, you get very few problems with it, It will brew consistently well and is good for a small producer.

For the last 10-15 years all the newer varieties are spring barleys, like Optic and Westminster, Tipple and Quench. These newer spring varieties,

are getting much higher extracts in maltose, the higher the sugar content, the more pints of beer the brewer is getting per ton of malt – which comes back to straight economics.

The grain when it comes in is tipped off the back of a lorry and then slowly dried in a drum with a fan drawing the warm air through. This Bobey drier was built in Bury St Edmunds and installed in 1952 and is regarded as The Rolls Royce of driers, very slow but like a tumble drier. It is very important that the barley is dried carefully and slowly otherwise you could damage the germination. We take it down to 12% moisture content and have to store it for up to twelve months till the next crop comes in. It comes up on a conveyor. No more West of England hessian sacks, some of which were 2 cwt and difficult to handle.

Barley needs a rest period, it needs dormancy, then we run it through into the next building where the main malting process starts. We liaise with the grower much more these days and we do sampling on the farm. Some farmers also dry the barley and store it till we need it. Many do a very good job.

These buildings were built in 1900 and the machine for screening and cleaning the barley, made by Nalder and Nalder, also dates from 1900 and is still in use everyday. Once dried and then cleaned the barley is steeped

Spreading the barley evenly across the malting floor at Tuckers Maltings in Newton Abbot

in large tanks. Five tons at a time steeped in 1500 gallons. It stays there for about 12 hours then it is drained, then twelve hours later it is steeped again. This is to get the grain to germinate. After about 60 hours when it begins to chit or the roots just start to show it is time to let it down onto the germination floors below. It is then spread with maltster barrows into small mounds that are then spread evenly with a shovel, till it is about 4 inches deep. It is then raked regularly, three or four times a day and turned so that it all germinates evenly and doesn't overheat. Each floor will hold about ten tons of barley and in Tuckers there are five floors working in rotation.

When it is ready and the shoots are about three quarters of the way

The visitor centre shop at Tuckers Maltings in Newton Abbot carries a wide range of unusual and specialist beers

up the grain the germination process is stopped by kilning. Ten tons of barley yields about 8 tons of malt. It is then cleaned, the roots knocked off and then bagged up. The roots go for animal feed. It is a very natural process and an ancient one. We are still at the mercy of the weather. The last couple of years have been very wet. I have every sympathy with the grower.

Here at Tuckers we survive because we are now operating in a niche market. The godsend is the local microbreweries. We use barley grown in Devon and Cornwall which is where the beer is brewed and then served up in local pubs. The whole things works in a circle and of course there is less haulage. We even have a beer festival here at Tuckers every year at the end of April. People are very loyal to their beers."

Tuckers supply more than 30 of the West Country's breweries with malt including many in Devon. Today micro-breweries are sprouting up as if there is no tomorrow.

One Devon brewery however is actually housed in the same building as the Maltings, so the malt has only yards to travel. Teignworthy Brewery run by John Lawton was founded in 1994. John was a graduate of Seale Hayne, the local agricultural college, and was so disappointed with the quality of mass produced beer that he started making his own. He now brews 100 barrels a week which is 28,000 pints. Hops come from the Teme Valley in Worcestershire. His regular brews are Reel Ale, Spring Tide, Old Moggie and Beachcomber. Some special ales are named after his children Amy, Harvey, Martha and are available on the children's birthdays. He also produces a whole host of other ales such as Neap Tide, Gun Dog and Scrum Down. The sight of his most potent and darkly strong brew R.I.P. Russian Imperial Porter in the making is memorable. He saves this for the Tuckers Malting's Beer Festival which is held at the end of April each year. R.I.P. is 10.5% porter. He also produces Edwin Tucker Walnut Brown and India Pale Ale for his maltsters. A very convenient arrangement indeed.

One of the many Devon breweries that also uses Tuckers malted barley is itself tucked away in the depths of the Blackdowns Hills not far from Honiton. More than most, brewers tend to keep their skills within the family as the Scotts did. It is all in the genes and the brewing gene can be dominant for generations. The McCaigs at Otter Brewery are a very good example where beer seems to flow through their veins with remarkable ease.

The brewery was set up in 1990 by David and Mary Ann McCaig, both of whom have long family connections with brewing stretching back for three generations. After 17 years working for Whitbread in Liverpool, David moved the family to Devon where initially he set up a joinery business. But at heart he wanted to get back to traditional brewing, making a craft real ale, at the opposite end of the spectrum from the industrialised, factory-scale brewing represented by brewing giants such as his former employer. So they chose a remote location near the scenic village of Luppitt.

"This was before the whole regionality thing," explains Patrick, one of four McCaig sons, and the fourth generation to continue the brewing tradition. "Local beers were not well perceived. But we have grown and grown and were doing it anyway as the issue of regionality started to come to the fore."

Although no longer responsible for the daily grind of overseeing the business, David and his wife Mary Ann, are still very involved with the brewery on a daily basis. David is still head brewer, working with technical brewer Keith Bennett, while Mary Ann feeds the 25 staff each lunch time

▲
Patrick McCaig of Otter Brewery, Luppitt

◀
Ale in full flood

and does "anything else that needs doing". The family's four sons are actively involved with or working for the business. Patrick is in charge of marketing, while Joe and Angus can be found a few miles away at the family's pub in Honiton, aptly named The Holt. Fred has recently rejoined the company to develop their sales in the Hampshire area.

The brewery is based on the family's farm, drawing its water from a spring near the head of the River Otter, hence the name. Conscious of the location in the heart of an Area of Outstanding Natural Beauty and within a Site of Special Scientific Interest, and with a strong steer from Mary Ann, the McCaigs have opted to run as sustainable a business as possible. Hence the waste malt goes to a local cattle farmer, the yeast remains to a neighbouring pig producer, while the effluent is filtered by reed beds and ponds on land below the brewery. The waste hops make good garden compost.

New cellars have been built to high eco-standards, including using clay blocks and a sedum roof which helps it to blend into the landscape. Although it will store the 15,000 brewers barrels – equating to more than half a million pints of beer – produced each year, the build spec means it does not require a chiller. There are plans to install a woodchip boiler in the boiler house where the beer is made. To reduce the company's carbon

Hops
▼

Hydrometer

footprint further the brewery's vans will eventually run on biofuel, "but only when we can get it locally", Patrick adds. In 2007 the brewery was the overall winner in the Greener Devon category of the Devon Environmental Awards.

Inside the brewery proper there is what feels like acres and acres of stainless steel and it is here in the fermenting room that the beer quietly does its own thing, fermenting slowly into some of the region's finest real ales. All in all, the process from mash to beer takes around a week – though for Otter Head it can take up to eight days. "We believe the slow fermentation allows the flavours to develop fully," Patrick explains. The mash refers to the malted barley that is steeped again in warm water in the mash tun.

Five beers are brewed here: Otter Bitter, Otter Bright, Otter Ale, Otter Head and Otter Amber. The ale is dark, malty, fruity and bitter – the antithesis of mass-produced, chemically induced and artificially flavoured beer. But UK-grown hops are in short supply and are the most difficult ingredient to get right. "For certain flavours we have to go to Slovenia, because UK hops don't deliver what we need," Patrick explains.

Otter beers are sold through pubs, delivering to between four and five hundred premises each week. Patrick is optimistic "The big brewers have

Sampling the brew

no interest in real ale, the whole drinking market is declining, but because of the resurgence of interest in regional and local food and drink, we are growing in a declining market." A fine achievement.

"At the end of the day we love doing it. When I go into a pub and hear someone order a pint of Otter I still listen and watch them drink it. I get an immense sense of pride out of it." Far from being hill billys, Otter has won

Gold at the Great Taste Awards for two years running and, as if that was not enough, down the road in Honiton, the Holt (see chapter 16) won Best Gastro Pub of the Year in the South West in 2009.

Another brave and enterprising brewer operating in an unusual and remote location is Simon Loveless. Living proof that if you have the right product your business can thrive at 1,400 ft surrounded by bleak moorland in the very heart of Dartmoor within spitting distance of a well known prison. It is in fact the highest brewery in the country. During 2009, when the world appeared to be in danger of financial meltdown, Britain was in the grip of one of the worst recessions for decades and pubs were going out of business faster than during the great depression, Simon's small brewery in Princetown increased its sales by 35 per cent.

Founded in 1994 in a small garage behind the Prince of Wales pub, The Dartmoor Brewery has now established itself as one of the most successful micro-breweries in Britain. It now occupies state-of-the-art premises on land purchased from the Duchy of Cornwall on the site of the former railway station which was closed in 1956.

The undoubted star of the brewery is its award-winning Jail Ale, taking its name from the infamous prison which overlooks the community and which was initially built to house prisoners from the Napoleonic wars. The full-bodied mild brown beer accounts for two thirds of the company's sales with Dartmoor IPA (Inmates Pale Ale) also scoring well in the popularity stakes.

Sipping a pint of Jail Ale for a spot of "quality control" head brewer and Managing Director Simon Loveless described it as "well balanced, moreish, with a sweet after-taste, a bit like chocolate".

It's a formula which certainly seems to have struck a chord with real ale lovers the world over. The beer even has its own appreciation society on the social networking site Facebook and has proved so popular that some landlords have even been known to refuse to stock it any more – because it outsells everything else in the cellar with the result that stocks of other beers go off and have to be ditched.

Simon describes Dartmoor IPA as a "classic pale ale – dry, hoppy and refreshing – deliciously thirst quenching" and both beers are supplied to inns and hotels mostly in Devon but thanks to public demand are also now being stocked at hostelries in other parts of the Westcountry. "We have regular customers who drive from all over the country to collect their orders and load up the boots of their cars or their vans," said Simon. "We have

Simon Loveless in the brand new Dartmoor Brewery in Princetown where he makes Jail Ale

now taken on a full-time sales rep who has contacts across Cornwall and we can only see the business expanding as a result."

"We are the most successful we have ever been and the demand continues to be huge. The sales figures speak for themselves because we are growing against the trend."

"The many visitors who come to this part of the world on their holidays taste the ales and once tasted they can't get enough of them. It's a quality

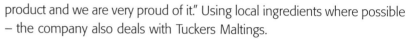

All regulars get a warm welcome at The Tom Cobley pub

product and we are very proud of it." Using local ingredients where possible – the company also deals with Tuckers Maltings.

Simon studied microbiology in Plymouth and Manchester and planned an industrial career but found himself working at a brewery in the South East as a chemist. Over the years he developed a fascination for the industry, gaining hands-on experience in all of its aspects with both Gibbs Mew in Salisbury and the Hop Back Brewery. Having been well and truly smitten with beer, Simon then wanted to start his own business. His initial plan was to go to France and set up in the French equivalent of Silicone Valley, where there are plenty of ex-pats. It was then that Simon formed a partnership with someone who was able to add much needed capital to his limited resources. That partner already owned pubs and hotels in Devon, one of them the Prince of Wales, and so France's loss became Dartmoor's gain.

Living locally Simon loves the lifestyle that running the brewery offers him. His wife handles administration and is one of the other seven employees at the handsome new brewery opened in 2005.

"We can walk to work and live in a beautiful part of the world," he said. "We love the village and know the people. We started out with two and a half people and now we have the capacity to produce more than 720 nine gallon casks a week with room to grow still further. That is purely down to the popularity and the quality of the product we produce."

But Devon ale needs Devon pubs. And there are some excellent pubs to choose from. Breweries need pubs and pubs need customers. One of the most interesting in Devon is the Royal Oak, mentioned earlier, not just because it overlooks the village green in Meavy and you can tether your horse outside (and countless farmers have done so over the centuries), but because it is owned not by a brewery or a landlord or a chain but by the village itself. It is a rare survival of the old system of church houses, where the church benefited directly from the quaffing of ale. Originally built in the 12th century the Royal Oak at Meavy is Devon's oldest community owned pub by a long chalk. It was later rebuilt and used by church wardens for church feasts and brewing ales that were sold to boost church funds and to help local poor. The annual church feasts would also have included the Meavy Oak Fair, which has been taking place for more than 100 years. Described in 1868 as a "fair for cattle and pleasure", more than 140 years later there are no cattle but plenty of pleasure. The oak tree itself was old in the time of Good Queen Bess and was known as a dancing tree where platforms were constructed in its branches and riotous dances took place away from the prying eyes of the vicar.

The Tithe Appointment for 1839 lists the pub as owned by parishioners. As a community-owned pub – since 1963 the parish council has owned it – one of the publicans' duties is to continue to raise funds for this village on the fringes of Dartmoor.

Another fine pub is The Tom Cobley Tavern at Spreyton, its licence dates back to 1589, and the village is the one from which the legendary Uncle Tom Cobley and all set off for Widecombe Fair on Tom Pearce's old grey mare. Uncle Tom did exist and is buried in the local churchyard,

The Bridge Inn at Topsham

though some say it is his nephew. His expedition is reckoned to have taken place around 1802. No doubt Bill Brewer, Jan Stewer, Peter Gurney, Peter Davy, Dan'l Whiddon, Harry Hawke, Old Uncle Tom Cobley and all, got a good head of steam up in the pub before they set of for Widecombe. The Tavern is now run by Roger and Carol Cudlip and in 2006 CAMRA voted The Tom Cobley as the Best Pub in Britain. They stock 22 real ales.

Widecombe Fair still remains a fine event and is held each year at the end of October. A well known local sheep breeder Colin Pearse still shows his Whitefaced Dartmoor Sheep and there is also a cattle show, pony competitions, terrier racing, bale rolling, sheep shearing, and fine ale to be had.

Coming off the moor, on the other side of the Rive Exe, where the River Clyst winds its way seaward, lies another excellent pub. The Bridge Inn at Topsham has barely changed since landlady Caroline Cheffers-Heard's great-grandfather bought it in 1897. But its history goes back even further as it may well have also been a Church House Inn, where the masons would have been the men working on Exeter Cathedral. This unique time machine has very few of the fancy trappings found in contemporary 21st century pubs. There is no bar, so beer comes directly

The Royal Oak Inn, Meavy which is owned by Burrator Parish Council. The ancient oak tree can just be seen to the left of the picture
▾

from the barrels, changing all the time, but all local real ales. There would be little space for a bar in the two small rooms, one once the tiny family parlour and what passes for a public bar where drinkers sit side by side enjoying one of up to 10 real ales on offer. A few token bottles of lager are available but served reluctantly. Cider comes just a few hundred yards from nearby Green Valley Cyder based at Darts Farm. There is no piped music, no chips and burgers, no juke boxes, although you might strike lucky with a ploughman's or a pasty. The so-called family room, at the back of the pub, is actually 15th century. Like many other historic pubs, the Bridge once had a brewhouse and brewed its own beer, above this are the remnants of a hop drying floor.

▶
The Bridge Inn in Topsham has the distinction of being the only pub in Great Britain that Her Majesty has ever visited. There are no beer pulls with pints, ½ pints (and when the beers are very strong ⅓ of a pint glasses) being filled by gravity from casks in a back room

Time warp or not, this is a genuine pub, with its roots firmly planted in its local community. It stands out because of what it is not, not just as a reminder of how pubs were in the last 100 years or so before they became almost inalterably overtaken by the modern pub culture.

Devon has several pubs that are unique – the Turf Inn beside the River Exe, the only pub in the country that can be reached only on foot, bicycle or by boat. There are others with quaint names like The Elephant's Nest at Mary Tavy, and the Who'd Have Thought It, Milton Combe. In Kentisbeare the Wyndham Arms has been renovated and revived by a voluntary community effort. The 14th century Yarcombe Inn, formerly owned by the well known Devon pirate and explorer, Sir Francis Drake, is now run by the community and even the vicar is allowed to pull a pint… after the sermon no doubt. The Tradesman's Arms at Scorriton has been bought by a group of friends, regulars at the pub, after it was repossessed and closed, while the Millbrook Inn, near Kingsbridge, was bought by a consortium of locals,

The Drewe Arms in Drewsteignton

who have made it clear that community involvement is at the top of their list of requirements. Then there is the Hoops Inn near Clovelly, the Waterman's Arms at Ashprington and the Drewe arms at Drewsteignton, famously run by Mabel Mudge who took over in 1919 and only retired in 1994 at the age of 99. Reputedly she was the oldest landlady in Britain which shows that beer is good for you.

But the recipe for success for pubs these days is not just the quality of the ale, the pub has to be the heart of the community and it also has to serve good locally sourced food. In this respect The Jack in the Green at Rockbeare has been a trailblazer in Devon for many years, with a detailed,

Waterman's Arms, at the head of Bow Creek, Ashprington

regularly updated website to reinforce that this is not just a few words on the menu. Owner Paul Parnell and head chef Matt Mason really do walk the walk. Dining pub and gastro pub are relatively new terms but convey the sense of quality which combines the quality of a restaurant with the relaxed atmosphere of a pub. Another Inn that manages to combine this very well is the Dartmoor Inn at Lydford run by Philip and Karen Burgess. These pubs have also been the source of some of the recipes for this book (see chapter 16).

But to return to the all important breweries, there is a fine one in the East Devon, O'Hanlons of Whimple, a village long associated with Whiteways cider. Liz and John O'Hanlon relocated from Clerkenwell in 2000 and the rest is history. They produce a fine port stout which is dark chestnut brown with ruby highlights and has the aroma of roasted malt and mocha coffee, and tastes almost like wine. They also make several other ales.

At Newton St Cyres, a village normally associated with Quickes cheddar cheese, (see chapter 5) there is an old Railway Hotel built in 1853, which is now a pub called The Beer Engine. Here they have brewed their own beer since the 1980s with beers called Rail Ale, Piston Bitter, Sleeper

The Hoops Inn, Horns Cross, Near Clovelly, Bideford, recently re-thatched after a major fire

Heavy and Silver Bullet. The Dartmouth Inn, East Street, Newton Abbot also brews its own beer. Micro breweries are popping up all over the place which is a very healthy sign. In North Devon even Hartland now has its own brewery, the Forge Brewery run by David Lang who makes such ales as Maid in Devon, Dreckly, Forged Porter and Hartland Blonde. Beer festivals are held regularly in Devon and CAMRA make every effort to supply the best ale they can lay their hands on. Occombe Farm near Paignton have a Beer Festival every year at the beginning of June sponsored by Bays Brewery who even have a new beer called Devon Dumpling. Another beer festival at the end of September is AbbFest held at Fermoys Garden Centre, Abbotskerswell. Here you can sample over 100 different Devon beers and the money goes to charity, the beer being donated by the brewers and sponsored by local businesses – a wonderful showcase of Devon's beer expertise.

There are about 30 breweries in Devon some of which operate from public houses, others from garages, old farm buildings and even back rooms. The quality is often excellent and there are some very good porters in there. These include The Country Life Brewery, The Big Sheep, Abbotsham Barton; Clearwater Brewery, Torrington; Fremington Brewery, Yelland, Barnstaple; Combe Martin Brewery; Bridgetown Brewery, Albert Inn, Totnes; Branscombe Vale Brewery, Branscombe; Gargoyles Brewery, Holcombe Village, Dawlish; Jolly Boat Brewery, Bideford; Barum Brewery, Barnstaple; Bays Brewery, Paignton; Exeter Brewery, Exminster; Hunter's Brewery, Ipplepen; Scattor Rock Brewery, Christow; Quercus Brewery, Churchstow, Kingsbridge; Red Rock Brewery, Bishopsteignton; Ringmoor Craft Brewery, Shaldon; Exe Valley Brewery, Silverton; The South Hams Brewery, Stokenham; Wizard Ales, Ilfracombe; Union Brewery Holbeton. Greg Towning now runs Topsham Brewery, Devon's smallest brewery set up in 2009. Topsham also has its own Community Brewery with 30 members and they will be soon by all accounts be brewing in the courtyard of the Globe Hotel, Topsham. Many of these bottled beers can be bought at Darts Farm near Topsham (see chapter 15) or at Tuckers Maltings. Brewing is now once again big business in Devon, no doubt to assuage the thirst of fishermen, farm workers and tourists alike.

Coming full circle and back to Plymouth, there is still a brewery there, Summerskills, which produces beers such as I.K.B. (named after Brunel), Menacing Dennis, Tamar, Devon Dew and Winter Warmer. Another outlet for beer in the city is a shop called Moor and More Beer run by Dave Moor at Frankfort Gate at the western end of Royal Parade. It would perhaps have staggered Scott of the Antarctic that this shop now stocks 110 beers from 27 different breweries. No need to go down South. Devon beer is definitely back on the map.

11/

GRAPE EXPECTATIONS
Devon Wine

A family affair – grape picking Pebblebed Vineyards, near Topsham

A FIDDLER IS WALKING UP AND DOWN rows of vines playing Irish jigs, and in the distance a recorder can be heard. It is a glorious autumn day, early morning mists have lifted and the sun is shining. From the top of a small hill near Ebford, not far from Topsham, there are glorious views looking out across the wide and glittering estuary of the River Exe. Perfect grape picking weather in a unique setting and all within five miles of Exeter Cathedral. This is grape picking with a difference, celebrating what Devon is increasingly gaining a reputation for – good food and drink.

Croissants and coffee in the Ebford vineyard supplied by the Pebblebed 2CV van

Geoff Bowen

There are around 80 or 90 volunteers ranging from A&E consultants to teachers, friends and their families, small children and dogs are racing excitedly around the vineyard. A queue of pickers are having a brief break, enjoying coffee and croissants from the stylish grey Pebblebed 2CV van before getting their secateurs out to finish this morning's grape harvest. Their reward comes later in the year, either in the form of wine or a celebratory harvest lunch in October.

Back in 1999 Geoff Bowen and a group of friends started a small community vineyard, each investing £100 and in a good year receiving a limited number of bottles of wine in return for their work. More than a decade later 20 families are still involved.

"A lot of community projects die out probably because of the demands on people, we try to keep the demands as little as possible. Certainly it's about making friends, and losing them," Geoff explains.

Like many of the producers in this book he is deeply aware of reminding people of the importance of the area that produces his food. He wants to put Devon wines on a par with other great wine producing areas.

Bacchus calling

Yearlstone Vineyards, Bickleigh, near Tiverton. Cricket pitch in middle distance

"A Frenchman in Burgundy or Bordeaux, he will only drink Burgundy or Bordeaux. We're never going to get that but I'm hoping to get Devon people being proud of their wines, and I'm seeing that more and more."

While the community vineyard has thrived, so too has Geoff's enthusiasm for growing grapes. He also has a cellar in the old wharf area of Topsham.

A former environmental geologist he recognised that the soils in this part of East Devon, where the pebble beds run right across the area, were well suited to growing vines. His is the only organic vineyard in Devon, but he freely he admits that commercial pressures may well mean that part of the 22 acres that he has planted will have to be treated more conventionally.

Today the pickers are working on Pinot Noir and Madeleine Angevine grapes; he also grows Seyval Blanc and Rondo, with a little Cabernet Sauvignon and Merlot on another site nearby. His wines are either rosé, white or sparkling rosé, with the occasional red in a good year. "We won't make a red every year because I will only make a red when I think I can produce reds I am happy with myself. And most English reds I think are still not that great. Some good ones are being produced, but if the wines are not that great they shouldn't be sold."

Another much older vineyard lies a dozen or so miles upstream from Exeter where a much younger river Exe is meandering languidly down the valley through water meadows where cattle are grazing. There are no fiddle

players here but below my hilly viewpoint, a village cricket match is in progress far below. It is a bright, warm early autumn afternoon, a quintessential picture of rural England with white figures quietly dashing from one end of the pitch to the other. The only difference about this slice of Devon is that the slopes of the hill are covered with vines, and there are pickers everywhere starting the harvest. Welcome to Yearlstone Vineyard, near Bickleigh, the oldest vineyard in Devon. Set up in the 1960s by brother and sister Tim and Gillian Pearkes, it was at the heart of the revival of English winemaking, which, half a century ago, was largely in the hands of a group of enthusiastic hobbyists. Some, like Gillian Pearkes, who was an authority on grape growing, and Raymond Barrington Brock, were very knowledgeable, but others were coming to this as a second or even third career, something to amuse themselves with in their retirement. The grape varieties tended to be sweeter, Germanic style making rather dull, sweetish white wines that were regarded as a bit of a joke, and an acquired taste. But these were the pioneers and very important they were too.

Out of all that, like a phoenix from the ashes, has come a new generation of young and professional viticulturists, growing different vines, often earlier ripening and more suited to northern climates, combined with using the latest technology to make their wines. English wine has been transformed and has come of age and is now taken very seriously indeed, many of these wines winning international prizes and awards. In 1975 there were 196 hectares under vines; in 2008 this had risen to 1,106

hectares in 416 vineyards, many of them planting vine varieties that would have been unthinkable a decade ago – Pinot Noir, Chardonnay, Pinot Meunier for example, the classic grapes for sparkling wine. More widely grown are Reichensteiner, Seyval Blanc, Madeleine Angevine, Phoenix and Bacchus. Some of the older vineyards are being replanted with these vines

Juliet and Roger White in the winery at Yearlstone Vineyard

Madeleine Angevine grapes at Yearlstone

suited to cool climate wine production – disease resistant, early ripening and able to crop in cooler years. However many viticulturalists also have one eye on global warming, which is predicted to bring more benefits, suggesting that within a few decades wines more in keeping with French, Italian and Spanish styles will be made while the winemaking areas of those countries will be too hot and dry to continue.

Over the last few years Yearlstone too has been transformed – the original 1976 vineyard has been added to and transformed with new plantings. By autumn 2009 all of the old vines, now over 30 years old, have all been pulled out. Mostly they have been replaced with Madeleine Angevine vines, with small numbers of Pinot Noir and Pinot Gris. The western half of the Old Vineyard was fully replanted with grafted Reichensteiner in 2008. The new section has been posted and re-trellised on the Double Guyot pruning and training system, widely used in Bordeaux.

The Experimental Vineyard has been replanted in spring 2008 with own-grown 1-year old cuttings of Seyval Blanc propagated by David & Simone Mills for Yearlstone at nearby Becklong Vineyard in Bickleigh. The total acreage planted is around 7.5 acres, and the number of vines around 6000.

In the winery Roger and Juliet White have invested heavily in new

*Picker's perks – lunch break
Yearlstone*

stainless steel tanks, a membrane press from Slovenia (with a capacity of 3 tons) as well as a new bottling line. Their storage capacity has trebled since 2004 and is now around 75,000 litres. i.e. 15,000 gallons.

The warm and sunny autumn of 2009 saved what had seemed like another precarious vintage for South West vineyards, and led to a low to moderate crop of beautifully ripe grapes – potentially one of the best vintages of the decade for wine quality. Yields for most were between 1 and 2 tons to the acre – with near-record sugar levels along with decent acidities promising much for the wines of 2009.

Roger and Juliet White have recently revisited the vineyard's teaching role, holding courses for aspiring English winemakers intent on learning all they can about cool climate wine production.

But what of vineyard history? While Yearlstone may be the oldest of Devon's vineyards, grapes have in fact been grown in England since Roman times. After the Romans there was a decline over several centuries until in the 9th century King Alfred helped re-establish Christianity which probably also encouraged a return to viticulture. Certainly by the time of the Doomsday Book (1085-6) there were 42 vineyards, many of them in the South West; 12 were attached to monasteries, the rest belonging to nobility, who cultivated them to provide wine for their own consumption. However once the links with Bordeaux were established through Henry II's (1154-89) marriage to Eleanor of Aquitaine, ease of importing French wines and the difficulty of making decent wines in England led to the gradual decline of what wine industry there was.

Over the next 400 years two other events contributed to the disappearance of these early vineyards, the Black Death and the Dissolution of the Monasteries. Following the Black Death in the middle of the 14th century there were fewer people to work the land, and the monks, recognising they no longer had the workforce they needed, leased much of their land. Their tenants needed crops that would provide an annual return, and planting vines did not fit their requirements. After the Dissolution of the Monasteries in 1536-40 domestic production was displaced by the thriving import trade from France. It is also thought that around this time the English climate went through a long cool period.

This left English viticulture in the hands of a few enthusiastic amateurs who relished the challenge of growing grapes in a damp, maritime climate. In the 17th century Robert Cecil, the first Lord Salisbury, planted 20,000 vines while Charles II's gardener wrote a treatise on cultivating vines, "The English Vineyard Vindicated". Then in 1875 the Marquess of Bute planted three acres of vines at Castle Coch in Wales which over the next 35 years was extended to 11 acres. The last vintage was made in 1911 and the vineyard was grubbed up during the Great War. For the next 30 years English wine was consigned to history.

The revival came in 1951 thanks to pioneers such as Major General Sir Guy Salisbury-Jones, who planted three acres of vines at Hambledon in Hampshire. Ray Barrington Brock, Edward Hyams and George Ordish had also seen the possibilities of a new English wine industry.

More vineyard plantings followed in the 1960s, including Gillian Pearkes at Yearlstone, who was to become an acknowledged expert on growing grapes. Germanic varieties such as Muller Thurgau and Huxelrebe dominated these new vineyards. The switch to the industry as we know it came in the 1980s and early 1990s, with new varietals reflecting the changing tastes for drier, more complex wines and the influence of the wave of New World wines that were becoming available. Plantings continue in both new vineyards and old, many of the longer-established extending their acreages.

One of Devon's newest vineyards is Eastcott Vineyard in Northlew near Okehampton, which has so far produced just two vintages. This is run by Robert and Hilary Waller, escapees from corporate life elsewhere. As an example Devon's vineyard owners and wine makers include a former BBC

VINEYARDS IN DEVON

ASHWELL VINEYARD
Bovey Tracey, TQ13 9EJ
Run by Bill and Diane Riddell

BLACKDOWN HILLS VINEYARD
Monkton, Honiton, EX14 9QH
Run by Roger and Marcelle Bootes

EASTCOTT VINEYARD
North Lew, Nr Okehampton,
EX20 3PT
Run by Richard and Hilary Waller

LILY FARM VINEYARD
Knowle, Budleigh Salterton,
EX9 3QA
Run by Alan and Faye Pratt

KENTON VINEYARD
Helwell Barton, Kenton, Nr Exeter
EX6 8NW
Run by Matthew and Jo Bernstein

MANSTREE VINEYARD
Shillingford St George, Nr Exeter,
EX2 9QR
Run by Tim and Simon Boyce

OAKFORD VINEYARD
Holme Place, Oakford, Tiverton,
EX16 9EW
Run by Peter and Susi Rostron

OLD WALLS VINEYARD
Bishopsteignton, Nr Teignmouth,
TQ14 9PQ
Run by Ken and Paul Dawe

PEBBLEBED WINES
46a Fore Street, Topsham, Exeter,
EX3 0HY
Run by Geoff Bowen

SHARPHAM VINEYARD
Ashprington, Nr Totnes, TQ9 7UAT
*Run by Mark Sharman and
Duncan Schwab*

WILLHAYNE VINEYARD
Willhayne Cottage, Colyton,
EX24 6DT
*Run by Dave and Kathryn
Baxendale*

YEARLSTONE VINEYARD
Bickleigh, EX16 8RL
Run by Roger and Juliet White

producer, an environmental geologist and a mining engineer. The Wallers have planted 12 acres with varieties including Rondo, Chardonnay, Pinot Noir and Pinot Meunier, planning to make a range of wine, white, red, rose and sparkling wine, which is probably the English wine industry's best, and best regarded, wine style. The state of the art winery has all the latest equipment they might need for the entire process from pressing the grapes, through fermentation, maturation and bottling. Like most of Devon's winemakers Richard took himself off to Plumpton College in Sussex, to learn about wine production. The first rosé, made from Rondo and Madeleine Angevine grapes, was fruity with overtones of mango and redcurrants, soft, easy to drink.

Half a century ago winemakers in England were almost without exception indulging themselves as a hobby, present Devon vineyards show that these have become thriving commercial businesses. However their owners are also realistic and realise that their produce will never replace the £3.99 supermarket bottle that is likely to be drunk within 24 hours of purchase. As Geoff Bowen says: "It's only going to be drunk as a weekend wine because people are going to continue, quite understandably, to buy their cheap wines for every day drinking …However people buy it as gifts, or dinner party wine, and they say look this comes from down the road."

Another vineyard I visited late in the autumn is not on the Exe but on the River Dart in South Devon. Vineyards seem to like river climates…

I'm on my way to meet Mark Sharman, Managing Director of Sharpham Vineyard in South Devon. It's been raining everyday for about six weeks and today is no exception. Then, quite suddenly, as I drive up the hill out of the little village of Ashprington near Totnes towards the Sharpham Estate, the sky clears, sunlight floods the landscape. Down the steep drive towards the vineyard on the bank of the river Dart, a panorama opens before me, a sweeping landscape of river, town and moorland stretch away to my left. Totnes, church spire pointing to the sky, sits huddled snugly at the top of the valley beneath the misty backdrop of Dartmoor. The river runs from moor to the sea beneath me.

Maurice and Ruth Ash bought the beautiful Palladian mansion, set in five hundred and fifty acres of Capability Brown landscape running along three miles of the Dart, in 1961. They came from Essex bringing with them their herd of Jersey cows and a vision way beyond the farming norm of the 1960s and 70s. Maurice Ash had an MA from the LSE and wanted to create rural employment at a time when farm workers were loosing their jobs at a tremendous rate due to rural mechanisation. He went against the flow.

During the 1960s and 70s cheese making also began at Sharpham "on the kitchen table". At the same time Maurice Ash was talking to Gillian Pearkes, famous viticulturist of Yearlstone Vineyard and the Southwest Vineyards Association. He had wine as well as cheese in his sights. She suggested vines that might be suitable for both the landscape and climate and in 1981 the first planting began. A two acre larch wood was cleared to make way for a trial sight on a warm south facing sheltered slope running down to the river. In 1985 the first grapes were harvested and the first Sharpham wine was produced.

More vines were planted. German rootstock was favoured which produced a dry hock style wine popular at the time: Reichensteiner, Huxelreb and Madelaine Angevine. Then 1988 proved to be a turning point. Mark Sharman, now Sharpham's Managing Director, arrived.

Duncan Schwab of Sharpham...involved with grape analysis

DEVON WINE WEEK

Devon Wine week usually happens in the last week of May and gives the public a real taste of the land at a wonderful time of the year. Here you can visit all the main vineyards and sample their wines and ask all the questions you want. It is a real education and shows how the Devon wine world has become an important part of Devon's landscape and terroir. Alastair Peebles of the Devon Wine School has even organised blind tastings between Devon sparkling wines and French champagnes.

Devon Wine Week was started by Roger White of Yearlstone Vineyard in 2004 and it has run every year since then. The events linked to Devon Wine Week have proved very popular indeed and include open days and guided tours, as well as river cruises and musical evenings with Devon wine, local food and tasting menus. Many restaurants and gastro pubs also get involved and feature Devon wine during that week. There are even artists in residence! For more information see www.devonwineweek.co.uk

But due to bad weather that same year most of the crop failed. Oddly enough, this proved invaluable because the only grape to produce a worthwhile harvest was Madeleine Angevine giving an average two tons per acre. Now this vine is the backbone of Sharphams white wines.

In 1990 Mark Sharman began extending the vineyard. With the help of two friends he doubled the size in one long, hot weekend. Suffering from sunburn, they planted five acres of vines in some four days. With a ten acre vineyard, wine production grew. Up until this time the grapes had been taken to the Three Choirs winery in Gloucestershire but as the harvest increased a decision was taken to "take control of our own destiny". A barn was converted and at last Sharpham had its own winery. The first vintage, a white wine, was produced that same year.

Staff were recruited and in 1992 Duncan Shwab arrived. Duncan is now Sharpham's Head Winemaker. Things began to develop fast. The winery barn, freezing in winter and unbearably hot in summer was gradually updated. As equipment was needed so it arrived, adding to the original two tanks, a crusher and a pump.

They were on a roll. In 1993 red grapes were planted for the first time. Dornfelder and Rondo did well in the Devon soil and were resilient enough to thrive in the local climate. Duncan's expertise came into its own, particularly his knowledge of pruning, training and canopy management, that is to say the skill required to control the plant leaf canopy to optimise the maximum amount of sunlight to promote productivity and ripening of the grapes. Even though the light on Kent's east coast is better, Devon's milder climate makes for a longer growing and ripening season.

Now two hundred acres of the estate make up the Sharpham Partnership. The ten acre vineyard produces some ten wonderful wines, red, white and rosé, all of which have won countless awards while the Jersey herd grazes the remaining land producing milk for Sharpham cheese. The combination of excellent cheese with excellent wine and one of the best views in all of Devon, if not southern England, is breathtaking.

The Sharpham wines include Madeleine Angevine, Dart Valley Reserve – Phoenix & Bacchus, Sharpham Barrel – Madeleine Angevine Oaked Sharpham Rosé – Dornfelder, Sharpham Red – Dornfelder & Rondo, Beenleigh Red – Cabinet Sauvignon & Merlot, Bacchus and a Sharpham Sparkling – Pinot Noir & Pinot Blanc. They have won many prizes.

The vineyard is open to the public for tours and hosts expert wine tastings. The Vineyard Café serves delicious food from May to October. Maurice and Ruth Ash's vision has indeed come to fruition.

But Devon has one other well kept secret apart from its vineyards, it has its own wine school run by Alastair Peebles and his wife Carol. Here at Redyeates Farm, Cheriton Fitzpaine near Crediton, deep in the folded hills of mid Devon they run a large number of fascinating courses to train your palate in any direction you could wish for. Essential training one might say before planting vines. Why go anywhere else? Alastair Peebles has been in the Wine Trade for more than 30 years, including 10 years as wine director at Berry Bros & Rudd, St James's. He has also made wine programmes for BBC and has worked with some of the world's top vineyards.

And then there is Devon Wine week which usually happens in the last week of May and gives the public a real taste of the land. Here you can visit all the main vineyards and sample their wines and ask all the questions you want. It is a real education and shows how the Devon wine world has changed emphasis. Not since the days of medieval monasteries has Devon produced so much good wine.

Tasting wines – Sharpham Vineyard

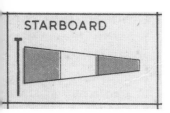
Plymouth Gin

Tucked in neatly behind the Hoe and below the imposing citadel, is Sutton Harbour and an area called the Barbican, the oldest part of Plymouth. Many of the houses are either medieval or Elizabethan. It was from here in 1620 that the Pilgrim Fathers, clutching their Bibles, set sail for that land of hope and freedom now known as the United States of America. As you walk from the harbour down Southside Street into the depths of the Barbican you pass several old pubs and shops that were once stores and ship's chandlers. There is Jacka's bakery, Plymouth's oldest bakery, countless fish and chip shops, tattoo parlours, ice cream shops and a chocolatier. There is even gypsy palm reading to be had. Eventually as the street curves round you reach an old white warehouse and a tall distinctive chimney with the words 'Plymouth Gin' emblazoned on it. You have arrived at the Black Friars Distillery, with its elegant copper still, still in place: a real gin palace.

Still in use – Plymouth's hidden treasure, Black Friar's Distillery

Local historians still argue about whether these old buildings were actually a Dominican monastery or not, however they include a fine Refectory, built in 1431, which is now a cocktail bar. The Plymouth Gin distillery was founded in 1793 by Mr Coates with two distillers, Mr Fox and Mr Williams. This was the same year that saw the start of the long Napoleonic wars with France. The large copper still stands at the back of the warehouse with a magnificent swan neck. By 1850 Coates were supplying over 1000 barrels of navy strength gin a year to the Royal Navy, which was drunk either as pink gin with water and angostura bitters or as a gimlet: gin and lime juice. Navy strength gin is 100 per cent proof, ie 57% ABV, and was so called because it was combustible which meant that if a barrel of gin leaked onto the gunpowder, the gunpowder would still ignite. An important consideration when on hostile operations.

In 1881 there was a ruling from Chancery that Plymouth gin had to be

The seven essential botanicals

distilled within the city walls of Plymouth and in 1882 there was a ruling to prevent the name of Plymouth Gin being used elsewhere, thus giving it a protected geographical status as opposed to London gin or even Dutch gin. By the start of the 20th century Plymouth had become so fashionable that is was the best-selling gin in the world, with 1000 cases a week going to New York alone. Gin cocktails were popular in the 1920s in Prohibition times in America.

The Dutch had invented gin, jenever, ie. grain spirit flavoured with juniper berries in the 15th century. A recipe is recorded in Leyden in 1492 but gin only became popular in England when Butch Billy, William of Orange, became William III in 1688. Today gin is still made from neutral grain spirit and re-distilled with botanicals to give it the distinctive flavour.

In the Black Friars Distillery the tall 155 year old copper still is heated with steam and as the gin vaporises it is mixed with the 7 magical herbs or botanicals. These are added to give it the full range of aromatics. In this case, juniper berries, sweet orange peel, lemon peel, coriander seed, cardamom, angelica and powdered orris root which binds them all together. The secret is in the proportions. The gin is then condensed with the flavour just right, a skilled art in the hands or should I say the nose and taste buds of Sean Harrison, the master distiller. Plymouth Gin also make some very fine Sloe Gin where the sloes are steeped in gin for at least four months.

The Navy of course still drinks gin and every new ship is equipped with a Plymouth Gin kit. The Navy even have a green and white flag now called the gin pennant which, when raised in port, invites other ship's officers over for a drink.

If you want to find out more about this ancient Devon art simply turn up at the Plymouth Gin Distillery in Southside Street and go on a conducted tour which is well worth it with tastings – but best to phone first to check the timings. The guides are always good fun. Plymouth Gin was favoured by such notable individuals as Winston Churchill, Franklin D Roosevelt, Ian Fleming, and Alfred Hitchcock.

Plymouth Gin has a Brasserie upstairs which is a very good place for lunch and is run by the Tanner brothers who also run an up market restaurant round the corner in Prysten House, Finewell Street. Most of the fish will come fresh from the Plymouth Fish market in Sutton Harbour.

LOAFING AROUND
Baking bread

daily loaf is
delicious + satisfying.
We use organic
flour from
Shipton Mill
available to buy here.

OVERLEAF
Occombe Farm Shop,
Paignton

*Otterton Mill – This waterwheel
was made in Exeter in 1827
and is driven by the River Otter.
Twelve revolutions a minute is
optimum for milling*

O UTSIDE the mill wheel is lazily turning fed by the mill leat that comes directly from the River Otter. Inside it is dark, and the dusty air is full of the quiet but regular thump, thump, a tune of giant wheels regularly turning and clattering as grain is fed down a shute, grinding organic wheat grown in Dorset into the purest, organic wholemeal flour. "Nothing taken out, nothing put back in," as head miller Brian Hart explains to a fascinated audience. Once the water has been released to turn the mill wheel and the granite stones start to grind at full speed the mill can produce half a hundredweight of flour in ten minutes.

Otterton Mill has been a working mill since Norman times, and during the Middle Ages was one of the biggest mills in the county, handling most of the wheat grown on local farms. It fell into disuse in the middle of the last century, and its revival was entirely due to Desna Greenhow's hard work. She set about restoring and revitalising the mill in 1977 and by 1979 was producing wholemeal flour for which Otterton is justly famed.

In the 21st century milling is restricted to a limited number of days each month – led by a team of enthusiastic amateur millers. The flour that comes down the shute into the paper sacks does not have far to travel. Most of it makes its way into the mill's bakery and kitchens, while the rest is packed and sold to visitors.

Before the advent of the supermarket, every town had at least one bakery and many villages as well. But – for the busy farmer's wife in the most rural areas without a bakery to hand – cakes, bread and other baked goods had to be good natured, not reliant on precise timing as often she would be elsewhere, such as in the dairy making butter or clotted cream or feeding the hens. As a result Devon has many bread-based recipes eg Devonshire Splits and Cut Rounds which rely on a yeasted dough, that could be left to prove for as long as necessary. Cakes such as fruit cake, Devonshire Yeast Cake and gingerbreads also fitted into the cook's timetable.

Splits, so called because of the way they should be split lengthways, from side to side, before filling with cream and jam were also known as Chudleighs, and in West Devon and East Cornwall as Tuffs. Cut Rounds were another vehicle for the cream tea, a handful of bakeries still bake these and splits to order, but they are becoming increasingly rare as the Scottish interloper, the scone, takes precedence. Cut Rounds seemed to be small, soft bread rolls closely baked together on a tray so that the baker had to separate them when cooked.

The craft baker that was once found on the high street of every town and village is becoming something of a rarity. But look a little closer in rural areas and there are still some to be found – Crediton, South Molton and

Brian Hart, the head miller

▸
Tony Suliauskas

Chulmleigh are examples. In Chulmleigh the tiny shop belies the work that goes on in the almost Tardis-like bakery behind the shop.

Anthony Suliauskas has been baking here for 32 years, first for the previous owners and then in his own right. Seventeen years ago he and his brother Andrew bought the bakery to ensure it survived. The Suliauskas are two of a rare breed – craft bakers. Every morning they are in the Chulmleigh Bakery by 3.30 am to start the day's work. The cast iron bread oven, more than 100 years old, has been heating up since late the previous night and is ready for the first batch of bread.

Today the brothers are baking Cut Rounds. The dough is rolled out into a cylinder then sliced on the angle, before being briefly baked. This is a slightly sweet, light yeasted dough and produces something that is the

Preparing Cut Rounds
▾

Chulmleigh Bakery

Fresh out of the oven

perfect vehicle for a cream tea (see chapter 13).

In the face of competition from the supermarkets they are somehow surviving, possibly helped by their very rural location in North Devon.

Inside their tiny shop there is a mouth-watering display of bread, rolls and fancy cakes. The display in the glass-fronted counter includes several varieties of rolls, meringues and chocolate éclairs. The tempting cakes and biscuits range from egg custard tarts to large chocolate cakes. Like all bakeries of its time – a rapidly disappearing breed in Devon's market towns and villages – it also relies on a lunchtime custom for pies, pasties and sandwiches. Without its wholesaling trade – supplying bread to pubs, restaurants, cafés and hotels within a 15-mile radius – the business probably wouldn't survive.

What sets them apart is that not only is this a real family affair – the other two bakers are Anthony's nephews, they are one of the few bakeries that still make the Devon speciality of Cut Rounds. These, like Devonshire Splits, were part of the traditional cream tea. Other items rarely found, but which they will bake to order, include Half Moons, made with yeasted dough and cooked by drying out in a cool oven to give a crunchy texture.

"We will make anything that people ask for," says Anthony.

Sadly his view is that this type of craft baking is a dying art, and to set themselves apart from the supermarkets the brothers know that they have to do something different.

Fortunately the revival of interest in real bread and the ability of these bakers to "do something different" has encouraged a new breed of artisan bakers who are reinventing breads made from ancient grains such as rye and spelt and older, natural ways of making the bread such as naturally forming sour doughs.

It is hard to believe now that rye was once one of the most commonly grown grains. There are extensive records from Tavistock Abbey showing that they grew rye from 1298-1538, but its use had died out by the end of the 18th century and isn't mentioned at all by Vancouver in 1808. Sourdoughs and modern, European-influenced breads such as focaccia are also part of the range of new breads.

In Devon, bakers such as Emma's Bread, Common Loaf and Bread of Devon are responding to consumers' interest in eating something quite different, and more satisfying to the appetite than the pappy, tasteless, pre-wrapped sliced loaves found at unnaturally low prices on supermarket shelves.

Emma's Bread is an artisan bakery, near Exeter owned and run by Emma Parkin – who gave up a safe job in marketing to follow her dream of becoming a craft baker. She uses organic flours from Shipton Mill in Gloucestershire – a working mill since the time of the Doomsday book. Amongst her appetite satisfying loaves are white sour doughs, a nutty, dense, stone-ground wholemeal and seeded varieties – all hand formed and tin baked. Also included in her range are 100% rye sourdough breads. "Sourdoughs are made without using conventional bakers yeast", explains Emma. "A natural leaven is produced by mixing a little flour and water and allowing it to ferment naturally by absorbing wild yeasts from the atmosphere." A time honoured method that produces a denser, chewy crumb and more easily digestible loaf with excellent keeping qualities.

Emma Parkin of Emma's Bread, Exeter

The 100 Years War helped to develop Plymouth as a port and many troops sailed for France from Sutton harbour. By the end of the 14th century it was Britain's fourth largest town with a population of 7,000. Not surprisingly Plymouth is thought to be home to Britain's oldest bakery still in business today. Jacka's Bakery in Southside Street, not far from the Plymouth Gin Distillery in the Barbican, was previously known as the Fone Warren Bakery, and has been trading since 1597. Reputedly they supplied adventurers such as Drake and Raleigh and no doubt the Pilgrims' boats as they set sail for the Americas.

Water to power the flour mills was essential and Drake's leat, completed in 1591, brings water down to Plymouth from the River Meavy near present day Burrator reservoir. The leat is seventeen miles long. Legend has it that Drake rode a white horse ahead of the water as it first raced its way into Plymouth. The leat not only provided fresh water for the city but enabled Drake to lease six important flour mills en route. Also this feat of building the leat was celebrated in the famous 'Fyshinge Feaste' – otherwise known as the "Mayor's Annual Survey of the Water Works", first held in June 1594. Here the assembled company, including the Mayor of Plymouth and the Aldermen, would each partake of a goblet of water from the leat to check its purity followed by a goblet of red wine to wash it down. Then they would all retire to a local Inn and whilst they were having an extended lunch the leat would be fished out for trout with nets and the

Emma's bread

trout then became the feast in the evening. The real purpose of the feast being of course to inspect the leat and make sure its banks and small weirs were in good order. The feast still continues to this day and is now over 400 years old. Devon's own version of loaves and fishes. The dignitaries now gather at Burrator Lodge. Anyone for more smoked salmon sandwiches?

For centuries bread formed the centre of the diet, at all social levels, it was bulky, filling, comfort food and also useful as part of the table etiquette and in some feasts and banquets actually provided the vessel from which the food was eaten. Hard to believe now that almost all bread was what we would think of as wholemeal, and that white bread became fashionable at high tables while the rest of the population had no choice.

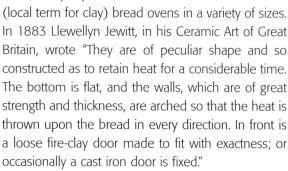
Not only was bread a staple part of the diet, its baking was easy to accomplish in every home. The grain would be stored and taken to the local miller as required. For homes with no bakehouse – the majority – the baking took place in the main living area. As these homes were without bread ovens, once the dough had been mixed and prepared it would be baked over the fire on flat stones, or inside a cooking pot on the range, which would often be covered by hot ashes. Instead of a bakestone sometimes the loaves would be set on a slightly raised metal trivet.

In some towns and villages local residents were obliged to use their lord's oven for all their baking, and pay for the service. Bakers ovens were often used on Sundays to cook people's roast dinners whilst they were in church listening to an improving sermon and the roast dinners in baking trays would then be carried swiftly back home before they got cold.

Devon is the 'home of cloam' says Allaleigh's food guru and one time judge of The Good Food Guide, Tom Jaine. And he should know, he has written two books on bread making and ovens.

Primitive ovens seem to have developed as a combination of the 'bakestone and covering pot method', combined into one bell-shaped device made of clay, and evolving to the more sophisticated brick design of Roman times.

From the 16th to the late 19th century, up on the North Devon coast potteries in and around Barnstaple produced their own renowned cloam

(local term for clay) bread ovens in a variety of sizes. In 1883 Llewellyn Jewitt, in his Ceramic Art of Great Britain, wrote "They are of peculiar shape and so constructed as to retain heat for a considerable time. The bottom is flat, and the walls, which are of great strength and thickness, are arched so that the heat is thrown upon the bread in every direction. In front is a loose fire-clay door made to fit with exactness; or occasionally a cast iron door is fixed."

They supplied not only local needs, but enjoyed a considerable export trade throughout Devon, Cornwall and Wales and in the 17th and 18th centuries as far afield as America. No doubt, at least in part, because – as Jewitt also states – ". . . the bread baked in them is said to have a sweeter and more wholesome flavour than when baked in ordinary ovens."

Brick linings are said to have been introduced in the 18th century. Brick lined bread ovens, still commonly found in old cottages and houses

throughout Devon, are built into a recess in large open fireplaces. The oven itself often projected beyond the outside wall of the house. Access is from an iron door in the side of the fireplace. On baking day, the housewife would step into the hearth to load the oven with faggots of wood. When it was hot enough to use she scraped out the burning ash into the fireplace and loaded her prepared pies, cakes, and bread into the oven. The oven retained heat for several hours and she might do several bakes, starting with goods that required the hottest temperature and finishing with perhaps a meat stew that benefited from a longer, slower cook.

Devonians, like the late Cecil Venner, remembered their grandmothers using their bread ovens. He claimed that "everything cooked in it tasted bootiful – nothing to touch it from any of today's modern cookers".

White bread was finer and higher in status than the coarser breads found on most rural and urban tables. Sourdough leavens were used for coarser and trencher breads. Food historian Peter Brears explains "Since its high gluten content enabled wheat to rise better and produce a lighter, spongier bread than other grains, it was the chosen bread corn for those who could afford it, rye and barley reckoned decidedly inferior. Wheat did not produce just one kind of bread, however, but a number of different types, their quality and status depending on their degree of refinement."

Up until the mid 18th century wheat, barley, oats, peas, even some rye were used in various combinations as flat bannocks, or similar loaves, which were easy to bake on hot iron griddles or bakestones.

It was really only the industrial revolution that changed British bread eating for ever. Fortunately, Devon has more than its share of traditional bakers who have clung on against the onslaught of mass-produced loaves, made to the Chorleywood system which uses bleached and improved flour, and a baking method that is almost diametrically opposed to the artisan methods that are returning in popularity. Devon has some superb examples of these too, so is no longer any excuse to eat poorly made, cheap bread, given what is available around us.

Early each morning customers of Occombe Farm Shop (see chapter 15) will find general manager Suz Ley, or her assistant, loading their bakery stand baskets with an inviting array of breads, buns and patisserie – much still warm from the ovens and wafting a truly mouth-watering aroma throughout.

Many farm shops buy in frozen bread to "bake off", but Occombe is still relatively unusual in having its own, in-house bakery – situated upstairs next to the café kitchen. Here Rob Hooley and his assistant make every batch from simple ingredients – slowly raised and baked, using no shortcuts and no artificial additives.

Organic flour comes from centuries old Shipton Mill, Gloucestershire, respected by artisan bakers for traditionally milled, stone-ground flour, whose natural goodness needs no improvers or additives used in large scale factory production. As a leavening (raising) agent Rob uses a "sponge" – a mix of yeast, salt, flour and water which he sets aside to ferment for at least 24 hours. Nothing is hurried, batches are allowed to prove slowly, to produce a loaf with a deeper flavour and texture, more satisfying to the appetite.

The bakery operates 7 days a week and the bakers' "day", starting at 3am, is organised to use their bank of ovens at the hottest setting first, following on with batches that need lower temperatures. Starting with white breads (still the most popular) and rolls, then malthouse granary and wholemeal. In addition to these staples, on a typical baking shift they will make cheese bread and rolls, red onion, rosemary and garlic, baguettes and cheese straws. Then come iced buns, Danish pastries, perhaps chocolate brownies, slices of old fashioned bread pudding – and of course scones, of both the plain and cheese varieties.

As well as selling from their shop, the bakery is kept at full stretch supplying Occombe's highly popular café – bread for breakfasts and to

Anyone for flapjack?

accompany their home-made soups, cakes, buns and pastries for tea and morning coffee and, of course, scones for the ever popular cream tea.

Owned by The Torbay Coast and Countryside Trust, Occombe aims to reconnect people with food, farming and the countryside. Education rangers teach real bread making, and its philosophy, to pupils from local schools and guest bakers run courses for adults.

Where Cornwall had its pasty, essential for working men who had to travel long distances to work, Devon's cuisine seemed to be more focused on pies. Effectively the same principle, going back to the early method of encasing food in pastry in order to preserve it and make it easily portable. But by the late 18th century, the Rev Richard Polwhele, author of The History of Devonshire, was writing: "The squab pie, the herb pye, the leek and pork pye, on which clouted cream was profusely poured – the goose and parsnip, and the fish and apple pye were frequent". There was no need for the portable pasty as part of the working man's diet as distances travelled to work were not on the same scale as in Cornish mining areas. The equivalent of something filling and cheap to make was probably the Devonshire dumpling which could safely be left to steam for several hours.

Annual fairs such as Widecombe Fair, which started as a hiring fair and annual stock sale, also evolved into great social occasions – an excuse for

Dough hooks and beaters – Chulmleigh bakery
▼

special foods such as Revel buns. A rich treat for village festivals, the sweet dough mix was enhanced with the addition of currants, eggs, fat and cream and flavoured with saffron and cinnamon. The buns were wrapped in sycamore leaves before baking or sometimes formed into loaves.

Otterton is not Devon's only working water mill still in production today. In 1995 John and Judith Stephens bought the derelict Sidbury Mill, near Sidmouth and gradually restored it to full working order. They now supply stoneground wholemeal flour to Trumps in Sidmouth and several farm shops throughout East Devon. Powered by a waterwheel using water from the River Sid, their flour is milled from wheat grown on land only a few hundred metres from the mill. Judith says ". . . our wheat is always our own, – sown, grown, harvested and milled all on the same land – we do not import wheat from other sources."

Although not open to the public on a regular basis, look out for their series of open days and workshops through the summer. Pre-booking essential.

Two recent additions to Devon's high quality baking profile are Town Mill Bakery now based in Topsham and Blue Mango in Tavistock. Town Mill Bakery was set up in Lyme Regis in 2005 with master baker Aidan Chapman at the helm. Aidan had previously worked at Leakers in Bridport. In autumn 2009 the bread baking moved to Darts Business Park and is now run by Mark Mullins and a team of three bakers. Aidan is now running the Phoenix Bakery in Weymouth. The Town Mill Bakery bread is still available in Lyme Regis where they run a fine café and still bake the cakes. Their bread can also be found in various outlets in Devon: Darts Farm Shop on Saturdays, Route 2 Café in Topsham, Ocean House Cafe and Deli in Budleigh Salterton, Kenniford Farm Shop in Clyst St Mary. The bread is available to all those who use the Riverford Vegetable Box Scheme – a new and savvy way of distributing good bread over long distances.

On the other side of Dartmoor in Tavistock, another excellent baker has taken up residence in Plymouth Road not far from the old Abbey. Linda Tonkin used to run Blue Mango in Redruth and then Truro. In 2004 she won the Bakery category of the Waitrose Small Producer of the Year Awards and 'Supreme overall Champion'. In the same year Blue Mango collected a 'Gold' for their Cheese Biscuits in the 'UK Great Taste Awards'.

Linda now runs Blue Mango in Tavistock as a restaurant in the evenings and runs bakery courses. She also sells her bread on Friday mornings for the cognoscenti of Tavistock. Get there early…

Real bread – and by that I mean bread made with good non-adulterated flour, slowly fermented and proved – is well worth searching out. It is both nourishing and a joy to eat. A sandwich becomes an appetite satisfying revelation of infinite variety.

13 /

HIGH DAYS AND HOLIDAYS

OVERLEAF
*Orange Elephant Ice Cream,
Kennford, near Exeter*

EARLY TRADERS AND VISITORS to Devon used to navigate their way around the county using packhorse tracks and drove roads. Modern motorists, on the other hand, are much more likely to use motorways jammed packed with cars, bumper to bumper in their eagerness to reach the sandy beaches or high heather moorlands. On their way down they meet distinctive landmarks like Stonehenge on the A303 in Wiltshire or the giant wicker man running beside the M5 near Bridgwater in Somerset. Sculptures that have become part of the motorway driving culture. Not to be outdone Devon now has its own roadside landmark, an orange elephant standing in a field just south of Exeter.

"Our ultimate goal is a herd of distinctive, orange-red cows on the side of the A38, our icon of rural Devon. That's where the ice cream and the cream teas come in," explains Rob Taverner of Taverner's Orange Elephant

The Orange Elephant on the A38

Ice Cream. The Elephants are in fact South Devon cows, so nicknamed because of their size, colour, long faces and large drooping ears. There is a natural link between the 'elephants' and Rob and Helen Taverner's business, which is based on the milk they produce. This creamy golden South Devon milk has a slightly higher butter fat content, making exceptionally rich ice cream and clotted cream.

Although the South Devon is generally thought of as a beef breed, they were milked on this farm until the late 1950s. It was only in the 1960s, when imported breeds like the Holstein Friesian was thought to be more efficient and productive, that many farmers, including Rob's parents, followed the trend that put aside traditional breeds and allowed these four-legged, black and white milking machines to dominate British dairy farming.

The Taverners started making ice cream in the 1980s – based on the milk from their then herd of Holstein Friesians – but realised that in a highly competitive market they needed to differentiate themselves from the other farmers also turning to ice cream to help balance the books. Four years ago the orange elephants were reintroduced on the farm and Rob is building up the herd so that, in his words, he doesn't have to spend the rest of his life "tied to a cow's tail".

"When you are producing top quality milk there's nothing better than seeing the whole process, from the field to the person walking out with a

Katie Taverner enjoying a chocolate cone

Rob and Helen Taverner with some of their South Devons

cornet in their hand smiling. It's the perfect combination."

The first thing you notice in the ice cream parlour is a display cabinet with an array of mouth watering, catchily named, ice cream concoctions – such as Elephant Bocker Glory or Brownie Temptation. If you manage to resist these, the counter holds around 18 different ice cream flavours – all made with organic South Devon milk, cream and eggs from the free range hens strutting around outside a few yards away. Many are made with fresh fruit, such as raspberries and strawberries from the farm's kitchen garden, which grows a range of fruit and vegetables for the farm shop. The end products include the unusually named Muddy Green Wellies – in reality chocolate mint chip – Banoffee, and the prize-winning Elderflower and Lime. What makes this ice cream stand out is the use of fresh lime zest, which gives it a sharp, citrus taste.

"If we use lime zest the flavour is wonderful. We are doing things the old-fashioned way, you get a far better product."

Rob Taverner is rare in that he is not chasing high milk yields and has recognised the struggle that many British dairy farmers face. "Modern dairy farming is going to get bigger and bigger, and we'll end up with fewer cows grazing outdoors, milking three times a day. That's not something I want to do. I want to have a herd of cows that is big enough to make a living and making a milk price that is sustainable."

His next project is to reintroduce what he calls a proper traditional cream tea, using his South Devon clotted cream, scones made to his grandmother's recipe, or perhaps Devonshire Splits, and a choice of home-made preserves from a local jam maker.

"It's an opportunity to get people to taste a real cream tea, the way it should be done. The cream teas you get in other places, often the scones are too big, they're not fresh, never warm. Granny Taverner's recipe is so light that you can taste the cream and jam. You need to put in all the right ingredients so that it's an experience you can enjoy. The tea should be served in bone china – little things you can't compromise on."

Traditional tea time baking in Devon revolved around the cream tea and dishes that could cope with long slow cooking while the farmer's wife carried out her other tasks on the farm. These would not only have been the basis of farmhouse cookery but also widely available to visitors to Devon. They would have included Devonshire apple or cider cake, Dartmouth Pie – made with mutton, apricots and prunes – Devonshire dumplings, Exeter stew with doughboys, followed by Devonshire junket or a Devonshire cider sorbet. However the traditional favourite remained the Devon cream tea.

A proper Devon Cream Tea with cut rounds

There is an on-going debate about by whom and where this was invented, with recent claims that it was the Benedictine monks in Tavistock who created this to feed the masons rebuilding the abbey in the 11th century, and later to hungry travellers. If so it would have been very different from what we might expect today. Andrew Boorde writing in the 1542 says this: 'Rawe crayme undecocted, eaten with strawberries or hurtes (whortleberries) is a rural mannes banket' Hurts grow in abundance on the moor if you know where to look for them and it was often the summer's job of women to go and pick them with baskets, the purple juice staining their hands and lips.

There would have been honey instead of jam – although the monks cultivated strawberries, it is unlikely they were preserved in the sense we know as sugar was not imported in any quantity until the 16th century. Bread would have been the basis, but again this would be unfamiliar, although the monks would have eaten white bread in preference to the darker brown bread that was available to most. Clotted cream was probably the one recognisable element, as clotting cream and making butter were the most reliable ways of preserving surplus milk.

Although the cream tea became a special treat for festivals and local revels, it also evolved as more visitors came to Devon. It was a highlight for painters and writers who visited the county in search of inspiration – both Daniel Defoe and Celia Fiennes commented on enjoying cream teas when in the county. By the late 18th century East Devon's coastal towns had found a new popularity thanks to the then Prince of Wales' penchant for sea bathing. By 1820 Sidmouth had become a very fashionable Regency resort. Travellers who had previously taken grand tours through Europe were prevented from doing so by the Napoleonic Wars, adding to the nascent tourism trade. Exmouth had the advantage of being the first sandy beach on the East Devon coast, attracting visitors from Exeter.

Boosted by Brunel's Great Western Railway, from 1848 tourism took hold in Devon, as travel by train suddenly made the area easily accessible. Torbay began its steady expansion at around the same time, earning a reputation as a watering place thanks to its mild winters and balmy summers.

As more road traffic arrived, making some of these seaside resorts less exclusive, small fishing villages such as Salcombe started catering for the upper and middle class tourists. A century later this has been followed by a rash of farmhouse bed and breakfasts, guest houses and self-catering accommodation.

Tourism has become a major industry for Devon. For most visitors the appeal lies in the beaches and landscape and, in the last decade, the quality of the food and drink. Even for the less foodie tourists, there are two not-to-be-missed treats to enjoy while in Devon, Devonshire ice cream and a cream tea.

Today most tea rooms and cafés serve scones, local clotted cream and jam, preferably home-made using local fruit or at the very least from one of the county's many small-scale preserve makers. But purists argue that the basis of a cream tea should really be Devon Splits (also known as Chudleighs) which are round buns made from a yeasted dough. Another variation, even rarer than the Devon Split, is the Cut Round (see chapter 12). There are also Devon Flats, a sweet biscuit made with clotted cream, and Devonshire biscuits, a rich mix using eggs and ground almonds, although neither would have been the vehicle for the cream tea.

Which comes first, the jam or the cream? This is where the distinction between a Devon cream tea and the Cornish version becomes clear. Given that the vehicle will most likely be a scone, in Devon the cream goes on first, as you would use butter, followed by the jam. However should you be lucky enough to find a Devonshire Split, the argument becomes academic

Wine

Bacchus, Bob and Sam Lindo, Camel Valley, Nanstallon, Bodmin

Pebblebed Rosé, Geoff Bowen, Pebblebed Cellar, Topsham

Sharpham Red, Mark Sharman, Sharpham Vineyard, Totnes

Beer, Apple Juice & Elderflower Cordial
Otter Brewery, Luppitt

Tamar Valley Apple Juice, Halton Quay, St Dominic.

Real Drink, Stoke Gabriel, Nr. Totnes

Heron Valley, Loddiswell

Elderflower Cordial, Lori Reich, Shute Farm,
Bishopsteignton

Jazz
Confederation New Orleans Jazz Quartet,
Somerset

Cranfields
Damson Preserve
Great Taste 2007 Gold Award

▶
*Leaf tea brewed for exactly
4 minutes*

The Singing Kettle, Dartmouth
▼

because of the way it is split down the middle and filled.

One of the scores of tea rooms offering something special is the Singing Kettle Tea Shoppe in Dartmouth. Here afternoon tea is served with just the right amount of deference. Loose leaf tea in a silver teapot, a timer to tell you the precise moment to remove the leaves, beautifully presented sandwiches, cakes, all home-made, or the cream tea. Sadly there is little evidence of any tea shop or café selling a traditional cream tea with chudleighs (splits) or cut rounds, although chudleighs can sometimes be found on the tea menu at Torquay's Grand Hotel (see chapter 16).

Another traditional favourite was Thunder and Lightening, splits filled with clotted cream and treacle drizzled over the top. Unfortunately for the Devon cream tea the scone is quick and easy to bake in regular batches rather than the yeast-based dough used for splits.

It would be invidious to pinpoint any one establishment as the height of excellence; there are many across the county that serve a good tea.

▶
Richard Hunt doing the Splits at the Grand Hotel, Torquay

Names that are regularly singled out for praise include the Georgian Tea Room in Topsham, the Captain's Cottage in Beer, The Quay Café at Fremington and the Corn Dolly in South Molton. Beware those offering a couple of dry, pre-plated scones, with pre-packed pots of jam and clotted cream.

So apart from the cream tea what other foodie treats would have drawn these eager tourists to the county for more than 200 years? Newer than the cream tea and even more universal is Devonshire ice cream, featuring in the top three on every holidaymaker's food hit list. Devon is blessed with many craft ice cream makers, who lovingly hand-make their products in small batches, using milk, cream, eggs, sugar and flavourings, usually containing no additives or anything unnatural of any description.

The early travellers to Torquay and Sidmouth would already have been familiar with ice creams, served in the great country houses from the middle of the 18th century. Many of Devon's wealthy estate owners had built ice houses to provide the freezing capacity needed to make ices for the high table. The first ices would have been cream flavoured with aniseed, almonds, flowers or fruit, poured into a tin which was kept cool in a bucket of ice. While we get excited about complex and often unusual ice cream flavours, some of the earliest were equally sophisticated, including pistachio, jasmine, elderflower, white coffee, burnt filbert cream ice and parmesan cream ice. Elaborate deserts, including the fashionable iced cream, joined growing exotic fruit and vegetables as two of the

benchmarks of competition between grand houses in the 19th century.

When the newly completed ice house at Killerton House in East Devon was filled in 1809 it took 30 men more than five days to store 40 tonnes of ice. They found that if the ice was packed hard enough it would last all winter and into summer. The ice was not good enough quality to be used in food but was principally used for chilling food and drinks.

By the mid nineteenth century the combination of easier access to ice and new machinery meant that ice cream could be manufactured on a commercial scale. The influx of Italians, with a long tradition of ice cream making, influenced its development and brought ice cream onto the streets of London and other major cities. Suddenly ice cream entered the mass market. Everyone could afford a hokey pokey – a two or three coloured Neapolitan ice cream, cut into small squares or slices – or penny licks, which were small portions of ice cream sold in a re-useable dish.

One business with a long history attached to it is The Good Intent in Dartmouth, now trading as the Dartmouth Ice Cream company but locally still known by its former name. The Good Intent is unusual in that this historic ice cream parlour has been making delicious ice creams for more than 80 years. For visitors arriving on the ferry from Kingswear it is the first thing they see. The present owners continue a long tradition of making ice cream fresh each day on the spot, alongside running an old-fashioned sweet shop, selling traditional sweets and fudge made here on the premises.

The ice creams come from a selection of 60 closely guarded recipes, some inherited from the previous owners. Flavours change each season, so in any year there may be 20 new ices that are either sold in the shop or made especially for local hotels and restaurants who commission one-offs such as a beetroot sorbet, which is served as part of a starter. Unusual flavours include Devon cream tea, complete with scones and jam, or liquorice. Watch out too for for their stop-me-and-buy-one ice cream tricycle.

After the Second World War ice creams made on this scale, or in the home, were rare indeed. The continued dominance of the Milk Marketing Board meant that ice cream, unavailable during the war years because of milk rationing, moved onto a massive industrial scale, given that virtually all the milk went straight from the farm gate to the manufacturers. These were the days when Lyons and Walls ruled the ice cream roost and ice cream had little sign of any connection with a cow, the ingredients of these mass-produced versions being mainly vegetable oils and air, stabilisers and emulsifiers.

But in 1984 the European Union, (EEC as it was then) decided to introduce milk quotas to try to drain the milk lake appearing across the

union, the result of post-war policies that had encouraged farmers to produce more at all costs. Suddenly dairy farmers were faced with the option of not being able to sell all their milk, or having to cut back production. Diversification was the name of the game and for several farms in Devon this meant ice cream. Rookbeare Farm and Devonshire Farmhouse Ice Cream were among the first. They recognised that a back to basics approach was needed, using high quality ingredients – their own milk, cream and eggs – to make something as close to home-made ice creams as possible, a craft product with a depth of flavour and a clear taste that is incomparable with the factory-made product.

The milk for Ian and Samantha Vincent's Devonshire Farmhouse Ice Cream is produced by Ian's brother Duncan's herd of Guernsey cows, and travels only a few yards from the milking parlour to the ice cream dairy. Made in relatively small batches, the fresh milk is mixed with clotted cream, eggs and sugar; the mixture is heated and then chilled in large vats for 24 hours. Finally it is poured into the ice cream machines and it is only then

▶ ▶
Cream Tea – Vincent's cream and
Lori Reich's Jam, with Chulmleigh
Bakery cut rounds

that flavouring is added, the ice cream is churned and frozen. As much of the fruit and other flavourings as possible are sourced locally, so for instance strawberries come from Shute Fruit and Produce at Bishopsteignton.

Many of the early on-farm ice cream makers initially made a limited range of flavours, probably the standard vanilla, strawberry and chocolate. But responding to the challenges of international companies such as Ben and Jerry's and Haagen Daz, they started to develop flavours encompassing everything from the weird to the wacky. Many of these artisan ice cream makers refresh and update their lists each year – some of the most interesting I have seen recently include Pimms and summer fruit, chocolate with chilli and lemon zest, and cherry and amaretto biscuit. We want flavour and innovation, and bags of it.

Like their competitors, the Vincents' range has extended to dozens of flavours and they expect to introduce a couple of new ones each year, but still find that vanilla is their best seller by a ratio of three to one.

Devon's artisan ice cream makers are proud of their authentic, creamy ices, bursting with natural flavour. These are not the so-called "dairy ice cream" imposters full of air, additives and artificial colourings that have come to dominate supermarket and convenience store frozen food cabinets. These craft ice cream makers excel at making sophisticated, top of the range, gourmet ice creams, something for both grown ups and youngsters to enjoy.

They are part of an unstoppable ice cream renaissance, with Devon chefs now falling over themselves to invent their own flavours and put genuine ice cream at the heart of their menus rather than served as an afterthought (see chapter 16). All this has changed our perception of eating ice cream from more than just a holiday highlight to a truly hedonistic experience, to be enjoyed whenever there is a need for a brief moment of self-indulgence.

WELL
PRESERVED

◄

*Wild Honey comb on display
Devon County Show*

*Peter Hunt, Black Aller Apiary,
North Bovey*

▼

BUSY AS A BEE, hiving off production, the sweet smell of success, the land of milk and honey, the Queen Bee, worker bees and drones – just a few of the words and phrases that have crept into our language through the ancient art of keeping bees. Without these small, loyal, colourful, highly intelligent and organised insects, little of the food we eat would appear on our plates. We take their work of pollination for granted but without bees our planet would be infinitely poorer with little in the way of fresh fruit, flowers or even cider. The common honey bees, apis mellifera, collect nectar to feed themselves and store it in the hive for the winter and on the way they pollinate the plants as they go from flower to flower with the yellow pollen sticking to their furry legs. It is a win-win situation. The bees collect the nectar, the plant or tree gets fertilised and we get the excess honey they produce.

Devon beekeepers are a mixed bunch, some seeing a better future for their bees than others. Some only have a few hives. Gilbert Warne, the last surviving tin miner on Dartmoor, who in his youth once worked in the Golden Dagger mine, was a beekeeper in Princetown. In later years when pottering around his garden he said that he was 'as contented as a bumblebee.' His bees liked the heather which abounds around the Warren House Inn, a great purple swath of undulating flowers that merges with the dips and hollows down to Soussons, not far from where the mine was worked as late as the 1930s. One summer Gilbert got very concerned because his bees got mixed up with Brother Adam's bees which were foreign… More about Brother Adam later.

Another bee keeper not far from the open moorland is Peter Hunt of North Bovey. There is a quiet buzz around Peter Hunt as he tends his bees – smoking them out to inspect the hives and remove the honey frame by frame.

As Peter explains, "I have kept bees on and off since I was 12. I had a friend whose father was a jeweller and he kept two or three hives in Truro. I once asked him if I could go down the garden to look at what was inside the hives. I was hooked. It is a fairly addictive thing to do. That's how I started."

Peter has kept bees on and off ever since then. He has kept bees at Chagford with a man called Wilf Fitzpatrick, who ran a garage, an Irishman whose father came over to help build Fernworthy Reservoir.

After a fourteen years working in the Middle East, Peter came back and ran the Blackaller Hotel in North Bovey. Aller means alder and the River Bovey is lined with alder here.

As Peter says "I wanted to paint this picture of rural bliss so I kept bees and kept Jacob sheep".

The hotel had ten bedrooms and Peter used to put the honey on the breakfast table and his guests really liked it. So much so, that he has now given up the hotel in favour of full time beekeeping. For a few years he also worked with the bees at Buckfast Abbey and got to know Brother Adam, the famous bee keeper. Peter now has nearly 100 hives and they are located not just in North Bovey, but in Manaton, Postbridge, Crediton and Exeter.

Most of the honey is sold at farmers' markets: "One of the beauties of farmers' markets is that you can actually tell people about bees and the flowers that the bees have been working on. They start to fly as soon as the snowdrops are out, then celandines and buttercups, some of the tree flowers, catkins, alder sycamore, (a really good honey producing tree), then dandelions, clover, with blackberry and bramble in June and July. Ready for the heather in August."

If you want to talk to Peter and buy his honey you can usually catch him at Tavistock, Crediton, Exeter or Okehampton Farmers' Markets.

Beekeeping is now very popular but he says that people have to understand that it is hard work and you have to be very attentive. "The most important part of my job is trying to keep my bees healthy and putting them in good locations. In winter or summer. Constantly when I am driving around, I am thinking – where is a good location south facing? What forage is available? You have to think like a bee."

In some ways Peter is still in the hospitality trade. Only he has over 60,000 customers…per hive. And often there will be ten hives in each location. And he has to keep them all happy. In a good year he might be able to take 30 pounds of honey off each hive. He reckons his Dartmoor honey is special because of where he lives. "I am privileged to live here as the farming around here is not intensive, not a lot of fertiliser goes on. That is why it is so special. We have an abundance of wild flowers. I don't have too many disease problems. I don't overstock. North Bovey is a very friendly community and we have a good pub, a really good pub."

Peter has a great respect for bees and thinks that their creation of wild honey comb is a work of art. "So beautiful we don't seem to respect the amount of time bees take and the ingenuity to make it totally amazing. They are so versatile, they can do everything."

At the other end of the county in North Devon is Quince Honey Farm in South Molton, UK's largest honey producer which is run by the Wallaces. It was started in 1949 by George Wallace, who, after surviving the war as a glider pilot and a parachutist, needed a change. He was inspired by reading a novel about beekeeping and wanted to become England's

▸ ▸
Peter Hunt inspecting a frame.
Dartmoor Honey in kit form…

biggest commercial beekeeper. So in 1947 he was one of only six people to enlist in a demob beekeeping course. He then settled in North Devon where his father had built a war time bungalow at Rose Ash called 'Little Quince'. Six hives soon became 600 hives. George married Kate, a local teacher, and in 1959 they bought a premises in East Street in South Molton. Their son Paddy soon joined the business. "Back in 1972 one ton of honey sold to the packers paid one man's wage for a year. It now takes 6 tons to pay one annual wage"

They had by now 1500 hives and bought the Old Workhouse in South Molton where they also set up an innovative exhibition to educate the visitors about the delights of Devon honey and the extraordinary and quirky nature of bees. One colony had even taken residence in an old red post box.

Their hives are spread across North Devon over 400 square miles with colonies of about 20 hives at about 2 mile intervals. The stages of honey production are governed by the time of year. A colony of bees in a single hive requires about 100lb honey or sugar syrup to live for 1 year. In an average year they feed 20 tons of sugar syrup and harvest about 30 tons of honey. In 2008 they fed 44 tons of syrup and production was only 9 tons. Wet weather doesn't help at all.

As they the colonies grow, boxes (supers with lids) are placed on top of the hives for the bees to deposit their honey. From mid-June onwards they produce more than they need to live because they store honey to live through the winter. Only honey bees do this. Like many other beekeepers Paddy has a great respect for these industrious insects:

"I am very fortunate to have spent all my life with honey bees. They

Starter comb

are truly fascinating and there is nothing better than a fine day in July when out with the bees while they are working the flowers."

By the end July they have produced a significant surplus and the supers are brought home, the wax cappings are removed by hand with a knife or a flail. A centrifuge machine then forces out the honey. This drains into a baffle tank and the honey is then separated from the wax and filtered. Clear honey is gently warmed to 120°F and stirred regularly as overheating will destroy the flavour. Set honey is warmed to 80°F. The honey is then poured into jars and labelled by hand. Honey 'Keeps Forever' but the law requires a 'best before date' so many give it a 6 year shelf life.

In August after removing the main crop, all the hives go to Exmoor. Some of the honey is from Bell Heather, but mostly from Ling with a bit of Gorse. The reddish heather honey is an acquired taste but as Paddy says it is "Beautiful strong flavoured honey that tastes like the heather blossom smells on a hot day."

Honey was of course for thousands of years the universal sweetener. Many historical documents record monks tending their bees for their honey and wax for candles, a long tradition that survived into the 20th century at Buckfast Abbey, where the late Brother Adam became a world authority on bees and bred the disease-resistant Buckfast Bee. The Abbey's hives still produce honey and queen bees are bred and sold. They have a breeding station on Dartmoor near Hexworthy. After a long career of bee keeping Brother Adam died in 1996 aged 99. The bees are now looked after by Dr. Dhafer Behnam who is from Iraq.

Long before sugar was available monks and the kitchens in the big houses used copious amounts of honey in their cooking. It was probably the original sweet element in what was to become the cream tea. (see chapter 13) . Up until the Stuarts honey was widely used to sweeten food but, although sugar had been expensively available since Elizabethan times, it was from this time onwards that it replaced honey. Preserving, sweetmeats, candies and fruit pastes, became a widespread activity across the great houses in Britain before jellies and jams as we know them.

Since the Tudor era, jellies would have been made from soft fruit such as strawberries and raspberries as well as apples. Jam, however, was a later addition to the kitchens of the big country houses, first appearing in a printed cookery book in 1718. Much of this was related to the availability and high price of sugar, but as it became more widely available so the kitchens extended their repertoire of preserves and jellies to absorb the seasonal gluts of fruit and vegetables.

It was the industrial revolution, and the large population shift to urban areas that brought to an end the soothing annual cycle of pickling and conserving that had featured in every rural home. By the end of the 19th

century there were big jam factories in many cities that would take any surplus fruit. The end of season fruit from the Tamar Valley would be sent to the local jam factory at Weir Quay or factories in Plymouth and Bristol.

It was the Womens' Institute that was the beacon of jam making during the 1914-18 war. Jam came before Jerusalem (first sung at the national AGM in 1924), as one of the reasons the organisation was set up in 1915, so that its rural members could help the war effort by getting involved with farming and food production. This included making jam from surplus fruit, an enduring image that has, perhaps unfairly, stuck to the WI ever since, given the range of its other activities. Its members were called upon to take on the same role during the Second World War. Although sugar was strictly rationed between 1939 and 1954, the Government allocated the WI extra sugar expressly for jam making.

Up until the Second World War jam making and preserving fruits and vegetables was also a given seasonal activity in almost every village and market town. For those living in rural areas the war years strengthened the urge to conserve, and during the summer and autumn families gave up sugar in tea and would save their sugar rations to use for jam. Sometimes honey would be substituted if it was available.

In 1952 the Government was persuaded to free up sugar supplies so that a bumper plum crop did not go to waste, although there was a long debate about whether to take the sugar from the sweet ration.

Anyone who grew up during the war years, and under the continuing rationing through the 1950s, emerged from that time with a horror of food waste, remaining the generation that would preserve or pickle any surplus garden produce. But for the Baby Boomers of the 1960s and 1970s the supermarkets simply made it too easy for the next generation to bother. The changing culture of how our food has been manufactured and sold in the post-war years, and a greater choice of imported foods, meant that the imperative to conserve and stock up for the dark winter months was replaced by an "anything at any time" attitude. This left a dwindling band of domestic jam and jelly makers spending hours over steaming preserving pans, hoping that the finished product would be good enough to win prizes at the annual village produce show. Recently however there has been a renewed interest in 'growing your own' and this has spawned a new generation of home-made pickle and preserve enthusiasts who often have their own allotments.

Thursday Cottage began life in the 1960s in Somerset making preserves on a small scale in open pans. Its founders, Kurt and Jill Kunzli, concentrated on marmalade, and it was only when Hugh and Pam Corbin took it on in 1989, and moved it over the border into Devon at Uplyme, that the marmalade was supplemented with jams. These too were made in small

Lori Reich stirring it

Bottling it up in jars

batches, with the highest attention paid to quality and taste, effectively traditional preserves made the old-fashioned way. They also made even smaller batches of unusual seasonal preserves, such as pink rhubarb, using the earliest rhubarb from Yorkshire's famous rhubarb triangle. They were definitely pioneers, and at their first visit to the International Food Exhibition were virtually the only preserve makers exhibiting in the speciality food section. Sadly the Corbins decided to retire in 2002, although the brand and its values live on in the careful ownership of Tiptree.

Where Thursday Cottage went, others followed, and now Devon has dozens of small-scale preserve makers, many of whom see this as a way of starting a genuinely cottage business in their own homes. They can be seen at county markets, farmers' markets and food fairs. Some go on to make a proper living from this, some linking it in with existing businesses such as farm shops or smallholdings, where this is the natural end use for any fresh produce that goes unsold.

We have already come across Lori Reich and David Lamboll in a previous chapter, (see chapter 13) but Lori also takes credit as one of the county's most original preserve makers. One of her strengths is her ability to maximise the crops that the couple grow by turning the surplus into preserves, pickles or fruit vinegars. Using some traditional, family recipes, but also keen to experiment with more contemporary ideas, everything is carefully made in small batches, so her award winning, legendary strawberry preserve will have masses of whole fruit and no additives of any kind, courgettes become Bread and Butter Pickle, French beans go into Bean Piccalilli, blackberries become Spiced Blackberry Vinegar.

Lori admits that in some cases she creates many of her recipes by instinct. One vegetable that surprised her was the pumpkin, which she transforms into Cinderella Truffles – a humble vegetable bringing the rich truffle taste.

Perhaps she is best known for her luscious elderflower cordial, made each year when the elderflower bushes along the banks of the River Teign are looking their loveliest. She freezes the flowers to keep up a year round supply of this refreshing drink – one taste and few people can resist. Her sublime Strawberry Jam, often named for the specific variety of strawberry used, has become for some customers the essential ingredient of their "at home" cream tea. Her raison d'etre, she says, is that she "wants to be a farmer and preserve maker, not a farm shop".

At almost the diametrically opposite end of the county near Barnstaple is another preserve and conserve maker with a range of products that reflects the county and her garden around her. Victoria Cranfield gave up a lucrative career in the legal profession thinking she would set up a hamper business aimed at the London market. "Now I'm in other people's hampers instead of my own," she jokes. The reason she is in other people's hampers began with abiding interest in cooking with flowers. This started the idea of making flower vinegars and fruit vinegars, using

Exeter Food Festival

Victoria Cranfield

ingredients such as lavender and rose petals. Her passion for preserves led to jellies, followed by pickles, preserves and marmalades. Many of these are made using locally grown or her own produce – fruit, vegetables and herbs – grown in her extensive garden – everything from Morello cherries to apples, damsons and quinces. She also sources soft fruit from South Devon and takes surplus produce from friends and private gardens.

Visit her stand at any food fair or festival and the eye is delighted by the range of jewel bright jars including ginger, lavender and elderflower jellies. Her versatile lime pickle is a sensation, designed for those who don't enjoy the chilli burn, brilliant with blue cheese but just as good with curry. Her benchmarks are flavour, taste, avoiding using too much sugar, or any artificial preservatives. Her low sugar and high fruit content means that her preserves fall outside the accepted definition of jam, and this intense fruit concentration means you should be in no doubt about what you are tasting. "You ought to be able to tell what jam you are eating with your eyes shut," she says.

As most jam makers would agree, backed up by the evidence of the Devon cream tea, strawberry outsells every other flavour, yet for Victoria damson jam comes out tops. "Damson on a cream tea knocks spots off strawberry."

Chilli peppers from the South Devon Chili Farm, near Loddiswell

Another innovation is the South Devon Chilli Farm near Loddiswell in the South Hams. Started in 2003 by Jason Nickels and Steve Waters they now have 10,000 chilli plants a year and employ eight people. Business is hot and they have many products which include chillies; chilli jam, chilli chutney, hot apple chilli jelly, pepper relish and a wide range of sauces as well. They even put chillies in chocolate. Mind you I can't see them getting away with putting chilli in honey. Gilbert Warne and Brother Adam might just draw the line at that.

Pick Your Own – Shute farm Bishopsteignton

15/

TO MARKET
TO MARKET

THE MID DEVON TOWN of Cullompton entered modern history books in 1998 as the location of Britain's second farmers' market, following hard on the heels of the inaugural farmers' market held in Bath. For those who have grown up with the supermarket shopping culture it is very easy to overlook the fact that farmers' markets are merely a reincarnation of what was once the only commercial form of food marketing across Devon. But they were more democratic and down to earth.

Having to feed cities such as Plymouth and Exeter, as well as having good access to rail and sea routes to London and Bristol, always gave Devon a trading advantage. But local markets were an indigenous part of Devon's culture and farmers wives regularly travelled to the nearest market towns to sell their surplus produce weekly or monthly.

In medieval times markets were held under charter, usually issued by the king or local landowner. In 1105 the Benedictine monks at Tavistock Abbey were wealthy enough to pay the king for the right to hold a weekly market on Fridays, still trading more than 900 years later. Moretonhampstead and Okehampton were already established market towns and Tavistock's monks benefited by charging a levy on sales of produce and livestock. In 1765 there was even a potato market at Two Bridges and many of the farmers from the west of the moor came over to buy the potatoes and stored them in potato caves, no doubt also clamped in straw to protect them from the frosts. Some caves can be still seen around Burrator.

In towns across Devon traders would line the side of the main street with their baskets or panniers. In places such as Tavistock these grew and grew into considerable commercial activities so that by 1859 the moorland town had livestock, corn, meat, poultry, eggs, fish, fruit, vegetables, hay and many other markets all competing for space. The solution, through the Tavistock Markets Act, was to build a fine granite pillared corn market, a new livestock market and a pannier market – named after the most common mode of transporting the goods to the market.

Barnstaple's pannier market, like Tavistock, still offers a changing selection of stalls for six days a week. It was completed in 1855, while others were built from Tiverton in the east to Plymouth in the far south west of the county. In South Molton the public market and assembly rooms were commissioned by the mayor in 1863. The covered pannier market still operates every Thursday and Saturday, many stalls offering local produce including: meat and sausages, West Country cheeses, bakery goods, preserves and locally landed fish. Even seasonal local fruit and vegetables slip in when available. Market days are a real social occasion as friends meet for a coffee and a gossip, then go shopping.

Okehampton, Tiverton, Holsworthy, Torrington, Newton Abbot and Ilfracombe are among those that have survived. Some remain relatively unchanged, others have been "restored" or enclosed, but most still fulfil their original retail function in some way or another.

Game Pies – The Moorland Larder – Barnstaple

Some of these pannier markets are housed in magnificent Victorian buildings – the one in South Molton was much photographed by James Ravilious – while in Barnstaple the market runs parallel with Butchers Row, once, as the name suggests, home to 33 butchers. Today there are still a couple of butchers, two fishmongers, a bakery, a delicatessen and so on. Devon still has many other bustling market towns like Totnes in the south or Honiton and Topsham in the east.

Although some farmers' markets are criticised for their irregularity, i.e. functioning only once a month rather than once a week, the idea of farmers' markets has caught the imagination of local people and foodies alike. In Devon, at the last count, there were more than 30 farmers' markets including produce or village markets held in a motley collection of parish halls, car parks and town centres. Although a few are held every week, some are fortnightly, some once a month, and others less frequent. Some are seasonal. They have emerged in response to consumers' desire to meet the producers face to face and make the connection between food and the countryside. They enable buyers not only to discover some new gems or unusual foods but also give the opportunity to find out more about their provenance, by asking the producers face to face. The producers on the other hand use the markets as a testing ground for their new ideas. It is very much a two way process and many friendships are made upon which good trade relies.

Purple sprouting

The award-winning Crediton farmers' market, which is blessed with a picturesque setting in the town's market square, is the epitome of how a farmers market should be – lively, good atmosphere, well-informed stallholders passionate about their produce, a good range of genuinely local food and drink, and food that tastes good when you get it home. This is where shoppers learn about what is in season, what is eating well, what not. The relaxed approach – for the shoppers rather than stallholders – becomes a highly social occasion. Hot drinks are available and friends take time out to share gossip and catch up on recent news. Then it's time to

Francis Hancock with Charles Ross and Nouveau Poitou local grown pears

Hartland Farmers Market

The Deli counter at Darts Farm Shop Topsham

browse around the more than 24 stalls offering honey, fresh fish, local organic vegetables, cheese and dairy produce, eggs, bacon, sausages, local lamb and beef, fresh rainbow trout and other trout products, apple juice, venison and wild boar, bread and cakes. It is an event, something that makes you feast your eyes and encourages you to feast more when you get home.

While farmers' markets may have captured the public's imagination they have their limitations, one of the most difficult being the infrequency of some, making it hard for all but the most dedicated to keep up. This is where the growing number of farm shops found across Devon has a role to play. From a simple stall at the side of the road in the Tamar Valley to the retail experience of Darts Farm near Topsham, there is something for everyone. Many prefer the simplicity of an old barn adapted for a new use; others prefer the slightly less characterful but familiar feel of purpose-built new shopping environments.

Darts Farm started in the 1970s as a pick your own operation with a small roadside hut on the outskirts of Topsham. Like Topsy this has grown and grown, and Michael, James and Paul Dart, the third generation of the Dart family, decided in 2002 to take this to a completely different level, with a brand new farm shop and other retail and office developments. According to James "we wanted it to be a showpiece in the south west of

the local food and drink available, and to support and champion many local producers and farmers". Although the purists might sneer at the AGAs and fancy furniture areas, there is a lot here to go for.

The underlying philosophy is that the majority of products should be baked, caught or processed in the region. The impressive farm shop, following the model of food halls in large department stores, showcases an extensive range of local food and drink, wherever possible from Devon or the South West. So this is one place you can find many different local foods not found elsewhere, everything from milk and cream from small businesses such as West Down Farm, to fresh pies and tarts from the shop's bakery. A local butcher is franchised to run an in-house butchery and tucked away in one corner Chris Coles, of Green Valley Cyder, can be found, creating four different styles of Devon cider each year for connoisseurs to take away. These include still or sparkling Stillwood Vintage Cyder and dry, bottled and carbonated Dragon's Tears. These award-winning Devon ciders are sold alongside an extensive range of Devon wines, apple juices, and Devon beers as well as other Devon ciders and perries from further afield.

A relatively new addition is the Fish Shed run by a local fishing family, combining a wet fish counter, selling fresh day boat fish direct from Lyme Bay, with a fish and chip shop. If you are feeling peckish simply select your fish and enjoy it cooked there and then, on the spot.

Just as at any multiple retailer, when it comes to food and drink you could easily do your weekly shop here, but the experience could not be more different. The original ethos remains – the farm still grows acres of different crops specifically for the shop, everything from sunflowers, lettuce and runner beans, to endive and cauliflower. The Dart Brothers are also very committed to encouraging their customers to make the connection between the food on their plate and the fields around the farm from where much of it has been freshly delivered that morning. There are farm walks to get customers into the fields to see the crops being grown and regular food club events which might cover seasonal cookery demonstrations or masterclasses featuring Devon wines.

"We believe farming is at the heart of our community, our economy, our cultural heritage. Farmers and local food producers can link people with the landscape and the environment," says James Dart.

Further east is another farm shop institution – Millers at Kilmington. As

Malcolm Miller of Millers Farm shop at Kilmington

▼

you drive along one of the Blackdown Hills' many ridges above Honiton, nothing prepares you for the cornucopia offered at Millers Farm Shop.

A shed by the side of a busy road may sound like an unlikely setting but after 25 years trading the Miller family knows otherwise. They believe in selling quality produce but without any frills or furbelows. They recognise, as all supermarkets have, that we are lazy consumers and want as much convenience factored in as possible – easy parking being paramount, but also in this case access to plants, cut flowers, fertiliser, compost, kindling for fires, logs and – a recent innovation – fresh seafood supplied by local fishmonger Simon Bennett.

One of the earliest farm shops in Devon, it started in a small way on the Millers' farm, and moved to its present site in 1988. At the same time Malcolm Miller and his wife Angela spotted the early signs of a new interest in local produce and good quality food, and that people liked the experience of shopping in a place where the staff know and care about what they sell.

"I was fed up with running my own lorries and staff to get my produce to market and not getting much back so I thought why not sell direct?" explains Malcolm. This has become a real family concern with their son, daughter and their partners all involved. In addition to stocking their own

The fish counter at Churston Farm Shop, near Brixham

Churston Farm Shop, near Brixham

vegetables, herbs and salad leaves, the shop is supplied by eight other local growers. There are also local meats, cheeses, dairy produce, jams and preserves, ciders, fruit wines from Lyme Bay Winery, beer, ice cream, patés and dressings from nearby Branscombe. This is no elitist farm shop, although top quality products are there, many of the customers are either

families with young children, retired pensioners and everyone with incomes and lifestyles in-between.

If Malcolm Miller thinks that farm shops should not be elitist so do Richard and Caroline Haddock. One of the newest kids on this growing block is Churston Traditional Farm Shop, located between Paignton and Brixham. As livestock producers themselves the Haddocks are keen to support local farmers and vegetable growers – all carefully named on blackboards and shown on stunning photographs on the walls – they also know that their average customer in their part of Torbay has a limited budget and keen pricing reflects this.

The kitchens turn out patés, cakes, pies, tarts and individual ready meals, there is a wet fish counter where the fish comes direct from Brixham each morning. The butchery not only processes the carcases but also makes sausages, often more than 20 varieties, burgers, kebabs and cures its own bacon. Richard takes great pride in talking to customers and

Riverford Farm Shop, Staverton, near Totnes
▼

persuading them that buying good quality local meat is not only helping to support Devon's farmers, but is also usually cheaper than buying from supermarkets as they can buy a single chop or a small quantity of mince rather than a pre-pack which often ends up being wasted.

At the time of writing the couple were also planning a café, garden centre and green visitor centre to add another dimension. This will also have an educational element, with raised beds growing vegetables and a wind turbine showing how wind power is converted into electricity.

The name Riverford pops up in this chapter too. Ben Watson was another pioneer and in 1984 started his first farm shop in the garage on his parents' farm, before his brother Guy's organic vegetable business had planted its first seeds. Originally set up to sell the farm's pork and charcuterie it has expanded to sell a wide range of either organic or ethically produced food and drink much, but not all of it, local. Devon cheeses, dry goods, organic fruit and vegetables from a range of nearby growers, including his Riverford Organics, are complemented by an in-house bakery making a mouth-watering array of bread, pasties, cakes, savouries and tarts. All starting from the principle of using the best, freshest, predominantly organic ingredients, with no artificial colourings or flavourings.

Riverford Organic Veg Box

The butchery makes sausages, chorizo and cures its own hams and bacon. This side of the Riverford business has expanded from the original shop at Staverton into Totnes – Riverford Goes to Town – and Kitley, where there are also a café and pick your own operation. Meat and other food from the shop can be ordered in the Riverford Organic vegetable boxes.

While on the subject of box schemes, if the prospect of more vegetables than you can shake a stick at bores you, a box of top quality, prime Devon meat, delivered to your door, may be the carnivore's dream.

The appropriately named Well Hung Meat recognised that plenty of customers are happy to pay a premium for organic meat with a genuine provenance and to have it delivered to their door. A large part of the meat either comes straight from owner Geoff Sayer's farm on the south Devon coast, or is supplied by a network of trusted local organic farms. The original box scheme is supported by a small butchery on the A38 at Dean Prior — worth a visit if you are passing.

In the early 1980s, whilst not exactly a box scheme, Anne Petch set up a mail order service to sell rare breed pork. One lucky piece of publicity in a national newspaper and Heal Farm was transformed into one of Britain's first nationwide mail order butchers selling top quality red ruby beef, reared locally, and traditional breeds of lamb and pork, setting a template that many others have followed. A huge range of other produce has been added from Devon butter to ready meals made on the premises with top quality local ingredients.

Two early pioneers were Tim and Jo Budden at the award-winning Higher Hacknell Farm, who started selling their own organic meat boxes in the 1980s, later adding a range of mouth-watering ready meals; Others who have extended this idea include Pipers Farm with its local delivery service to parts of Exeter, complementing its mail order business and Exeter shop.

South Molton Pannier Market

Of course the explosion of availability of great products is not a recent phenomenon. In the middle of the 19th century stores such as Trumps in Sidmouth and Crebers in Tavistock were already setting out their stalls as traditional grocers and purveyors of fine foods. Today they are strong supporters of Devon's produce at the same time as recognising that to remain distinctive in a crowded grocery marketplace they must stock a wide range of cheeses, olives, salads made in the shop's kitchens, great wines and everything from fine teas and coffees to saffron and carnaroli risotto rice. Many of the new generation of Devon's delicatessens have cafés to showcase local produce, while others such as Effings in Totnes (see chapter 16), have followed the French traiteur route, making tempting dishes to take away, everything from pesto sauces to cooked meats, pâtés and patisserie. There are too many to mention and the spread across the county means that we are spoilt for choice.

Visit Occombe Farm Shop for a fascinating farm experience linked to top class food and drink. Here an education centre combines with a farm shop and café showcasing the most local of foods. Some of the best of Devon's foods including dairy, vegetables, preserves and eggs sit proudly next to freshly baked bread from the bakery, (see chapter 12) along with blackboards and whiteboards explaining food miles and provenance. The in-house butchery draws on Occombe itself and other local farms for red ruby beef, lamb, pork and poultry. Occombe is dedicated to preserving its surroundings, using organic farming methods, and raising public awareness of environmental issues through nature trails and 'educational rangers', who run workshops and other family events. It also has a vital role to play ensuring that future generations grow up understanding why we should value the land, farmers and food producers and understand how local food gets from the farm onto our plates whether it be at home, in the kitchen, or in the restaurant or gastro pub.

Ruby Red Cows
We are Ruby Red cows from North Devon. We live in the barns in Winter (eating hay + silage) and in the fields in the Summer. There are about 100 of us in the herd and our bull is named Headland Hero.
Our cow pats are used as a natural fertiliser! Ruby Reds are beef cattle and prized for the quality of their meat.

16/

CHEFS AND
RECIPES

NICK COILEY
AGARIC IN ASHBURTON

Herby Pancakes with English Asparagus and Sorrel Hollandaise

Serves 4

Nick Coiley at Agaric in Ashburton is passionate about cooking according to the seasons. Spring is a great relief, he says, as so much new produce is bursting into life. Inspired by his time working with Joyce Molyneux at the original Carved Angel in Dartmouth, where he was head chef and a director, the Agaric menu is underpinned by a network of local growers, fishermen, butchers and foragers, all from within a short distance of the restaurant. "Our ethos is to work with local suppliers who grow, rear and harvest the exceptional produce from this part of Devon," he says. Nick found the fresh ingredients for this recipe while weeding his herb garden; sorrel, chives, thyme, marjoram and mint. On his smallholding he produces salad leaves and more herbs. He suggests that this dish makes a great lunch but would also make a tasty starter.

50g mixed fresh chopped herbs: sorrel, chives, thyme, marjoram, wild garlic and mint

1 egg yolk

1 whole egg

300ml milk

125g plain flour

25g melted butter

Butter for frying

Freshly ground salt and pepper

2 bunches of asparagus, washed and trimmed

Chive or rosemary flowers to garnish

To make the pancakes mix the milk, egg and the melted butter together and beat in the flour and a little salt and pepper. Chop the herbs by hand so they don't bruise too much. Add them to the batter and mix in. Leave the batter to stand for a while in the fridge.

Heat a heavy based pan and add a little butter. When the pan starts to smoke (but not burn), add a small ladle full of the mixture, enough to cover the pan but to make a thin pancake. Flip or turn with a palette knife and as they are ready stack the pancakes with a piece of parchment between each. This should make eight thin pancakes according to the size of the pan.

For the asparagus, lightly season the trimmed asparagus and steam for 3 – 4 minutes depending on the thickness of the stems. Keep warm, ready to roll up in the herb pancakes.

Sorrel hollandaise:

1 whole egg

200g unsalted butter

Juice of half a lemon

Salt and pepper

50g fresh chopped sorrel (or any fresh leafy herb, e.g. basil – if sorrel unavailable)

Make the hollandaise by putting the herbs, lemon juice, egg and seasoning in a blender. Melt the butter. Start blending and gradually pour in the hot butter. Blend until you have a beautifully green emulsion. Serve immediately or keep warm until needed. The hollandaise can be poured over the asparagus tips.

To serve, roll 3 or 4 asparagus spears in each pancake and warm in the oven for 3 minutes, serve on warm plates with the sorrel hollandaise and a few chive or rosemary flowers sprinkled on as a garnish.

Chef's Note

A hand stick blender is invaluable for this recipe.

ELSPETH BURRAGE
CADELEIGH ARMS
CADELEIGH,
NEAR TIVERTON

Devon Blue
Twice-Baked
Soufflé

Serves 4

This recipe comes from the Cadeleigh Arms in Mid Devon. When Elspeth Burrage and her manager Jane Dreyer took over this pub it had been neglected and was very run down. They have revitalised it, making it an inviting space for families, children and dogs and put it back at the heart of this very rural community. Their ethos is firmly based in its Mid Devon locality, working with many local suppliers, creating a menu of pub food "served with an innovative twist, all at a reasonable cost". This could be anything from a sandwich, to one of the daily specials or something more sophisticated for dinner. Local ingredients finding their way into the kitchen, most travelling no more than a few miles from farm to fork, include local eggs, meat, game, fruit and vegetables from the local farm shop, Devon cheeses, preserves and ice creams. The pub also serves wines from Yearlstone Vineyard, one of Devon's oldest vineyards, which is almost on its doorstep, along with local beer and cider.

Jane Dreyer

225ml whole milk
½ onion cut in two
25g butter
25g plain flour
2 eggs separated
Freshly ground black pepper
75g Devon Blue cheese

Pre-heat oven to 180°C, 350°F, Gas 4.

Grease 4 ramekins with butter – we use 9 cm diameter ramekins but you can use the size that best suits your needs.

Put the onion in the milk and bring gently to the boil, then remove from the heat and put aside for 20 minutes, then remove the onion.

Make the béchamel sauce by melting the butter in a saucepan. When it is bubbling add the flour and stir over a moderate heat to make a roux. When it is smooth gradually add the milk, stirring all the time to ensure a smooth sauce. When all the milk has been incorporated, add the egg yolks and grated cheese and then remove from the heat. Season with black pepper.

Whisk the egg whites to stiff peaks, and fold into the cheese sauce.

Pour the mixture into the prepared ramekins and bake in the oven for 15 - 20 minutes.

At this stage you can hold the soufflés and then re-heat at 180°C, 350°F, Gas 4 for about 8 -10 minutes, until they start to puff up.

Otherwise serve immediately with mixed salad leaves, and a sliced pear and walnut salad with a walnut oil dressing.

Chef's Notes

This works particularly well with Devon Blue cheese but other blue cheeses could be substituted.

The soufflés can be held overnight in a fridge and re-heated the next day.

KARL RASMUSSEN
EFFINGS IN TOTNES

Devon Rabbit Terrine

*serves 5 - 6 as a light lunch
or 10 - 12 as a starter*

This recipe comes from Karl Rasmussen at Effings in Totnes. Effings for fine foods is the ethos behind this top class delicatessen that Michael Kann and Jacqueline Williams have run for some years. The small, intimate café at the back of the shop offers coffee, lunches and teas, and the daily changing menu focuses on the freshest, seasonal produce, anything from herb-crusted spring lamb with hispi cabbage and a tomato and olive sauce to pan-fried lemon sole with Effings' own tartare sauce and local vegetables. Alternatively you can buy a range of traiteur-type produce to take away, from patés and fresh pesto, to salads or sweet and savoury tarts and some very superior ready meals, all made on the premises.

2 whole rabbits

2 chicken legs

6 rashers rindless, smoked streaky bacon, diced very small (lardons)

250g belly pork

170g pork fat

2 tbsp white wine

2 bay leaves

2 tsp brandy

3 or 4 sorrel leaves - or basil if sorrel is unavailable

2 cloves garlic

1 tsp green peppercorns

1 large or 2 small shallots

Unsmoked Streaky bacon (thinly sliced) rashers to line the terrine (see Chef's Note)

Remove meat from rabbits and chicken legs, removing the silver skin, and cut into bite-sized pieces and put into a non-metallic bowl.

Combine the white wine, bay leaves, garlic, green peppercorns, brandy and shallot and pour over meat to marinate for several hours.

Pre-heat oven to 180°C, 350°F, Gas Mark 4.

Line the terrine with the thin slices of bacon.

Remove the meat from marinade and strain off the shallots and other marinade ingredients.

Mix the pork belly, pork fat and the strained shallots etc and mince.

Mix into the rabbit and chicken meat, with the lardons, season and add the chopped sorrel or basil and marinade liquor.

Push into the lined terrine and cover with more bacon.

Cover with cling film and foil and place in a tray of simmering water. Bake for 2 hours.

Cool in a tray of iced water and press overnight.

Serve cold with some salad leaves, a few gherkins, pickled cucumber or chutney.

Chef's Note

When cooking pâtés it is the depth of the terrine that determines the cooking time. Ours is rectangular - external measurements are approximately 30cm x 10cm, the depth to the rim – just under 9 cm.

DEBORAH SMALLBONE
THE GROVE INN
IN KINGS NYMPTON

Laver Soup with Poached Scallops

Serves 4

The Grove Inn in Kings Nympton is a quintessential Devon pub, thatch and whitewashed cob outside, inside a proper community pub that combines its role at the heart of village life with being a good place to eat. The menu shows a strong sense of the pub's location in North Devon, featuring local wild venison chops or individual beef wellingtons made with beef from Lakehead Farm only a few miles away. Deborah and Robert Smallbone also offer good pub standards such as sandwiches, steaks or ham and eggs, complemented with a range of guest ales from Devon breweries including O'Hanlons and Otter Brewery, Sam's Dry Devon cider, and 30 single malt whiskies.

Sometimes described as the marine equivalent of Popeye's spinach, laverbread is an edible seaweed, porphyra umbilicalis, with high nutritional values, and was traditionally served with bacon for breakfast on the North Devon coast or in Wales, or served with vinegar, salt and pepper. Most people buy pre-cooked laver, which freezes well. Fresh spinach can be used as a substitute.

25g butter

1 large onion, finely chopped

25g plain flour

900ml vegetable stock

Juice of half a lemon

250g cooked laver

150ml milk

50ml single cream

9 scallops, with their corals

Finely shredded green cabbage, for optional garnish

salt – see Chef's Notes

Melt the butter and cook the onion gently for 10 minutes, making sure not to colour. Stir in the flour and cook gently for a further two minutes. Gradually add the stock, lemon juice and cooked laver.

Cover, bring to the boil and simmer for about five minutes. Cool a little then purée in a liquidiser.

Return the soup to a clean saucepan and stir in the milk and the single cream.

At this point place a single scallop with its coral in the soup, reheat and simmer gently for about 10 minutes. This will add sweetness.

Remove and discard the single scallop. Place the remaining eight raw scallops in the soup and poach for two minutes.

Serve in shallow bowls with a glass of dry Devon cider or chilled dry sherry.

Chef's Notes

Replace the 250g laver with 750g fresh, washed spinach. Only take it off the stalks if the leaves are large. Add the spinach when you add the stock.

Finely shredded green cabbage, briefly deep fried, makes a lovely crispy garnish.

For vegetarians the scallops can be omitted altogether. Robert Smallbone says that adding the single scallop to the soup adds sweetness, but the soup is just as good without any scallops.

Salt – the Laver is already salted, so not needed unless you are substituting the laver with spinach.

MARTIN REYNOLDS
VENUS CAFE
BLACKPOOL SANDS, NEAR
DARTMOUTH

Venus Café Bigbury Bay Oysters Mornay

*Serves 4 as a starter,
or 2 as a main course*

This dish was created in collaboration between the Venus Company and Jacques Marchal, who for many years ran Plymouth's first Michelin-starred restaurant, Chez Nous. Michael Smith, who set up the Venus Company, is also the chairman and one of the driving forces behind Food and Drink Devon. The Venus Company has a range of relaxed and informal beach cafés, all in stunning beachside locations in

Devon and Cornwall, all run on the principles of sourcing locally, organically and ethically, even down to the crockery which is disposable and recyclable. The biggest plus is that the cafes serve top class food – either to eat al fresco while admiring the view or to take away – which tastes good and has no sense of hair-shirtedness. This recipe features Bigbury Bay oysters which travel literally a few miles up or down the River Avon to their Venus destination.

---

1 doz Bigbury Bay Oysters

250ml organic, semi-skimmed milk

25g plain flour

25g salted butter

'tiny pinch' of salt (or omit altogether – oysters and cheese are both salty)

small 'pinch' white pepper

125g grated organic mature Cheddar

100g leeks, trimmed, cut lengthways and washed thoroughly

25g salted butter to soften leeks

Gather together all the ingredients. Keep the oysters unshucked and refrigerated until needed.

Sieve the flour, melt 25g butter in a non-stick saucepan. Add flour and start to mix vigorously until the mix starts to turn slightly white and thin. Place in fridge to cool to arrest cooking.

Put the milk onto the heat, add salt and pepper and bring to the boil.

Take sauce mix out of the fridge, add the hot milk and 80g of the cheese – whisking constantly – until mix rolls off the spoon.

Finely chop the leeks, melt 25g butter in a pan and gently soften leeks for 2 minutes.

Shuck the oysters and remove from the shell. Place the shell liquor in another pan. Wash the shells thoroughly.

Bring the oyster liquor to the boil, gently place oysters in liquid for 3 seconds, then drain in a colander.

Place the leeks in the bottom of each shell (dividing the leeks up equally between the 12 shells). Add $1/2$ tsp of sauce on top of the leeks. Place an oyster on the sauce and add 1 tbsp sauce to cover the oyster.

If desired sprinkle the remaining grated Cheddar on top. Place under a hot grill for 2 - 3 minutes until sauce browns.

Serve immediately with some organic leaves drizzled with extra virgin olive oil, a wedge of lemon and perhaps some cherry tomatoes.

Chef's Note

At the Venus cafés these are also served in a box with French fries as a take away meal.

Taw Mussels in Cider and Leek Cream Sauce

*Serves 6 as a starter
or 3 as a main course*

Sue Harty has won several awards for her café/tea room on the quay at Fremington, set in a glorious location on the banks of the River Torridge, with views stretching across the estuary to the Bristol Channel. Her cream teas are renowned for the freshly baked scones – on the table within an hour of coming out of the oven – served of course with clotted cream and home made jam. But the café is about more than cream teas. Passionate about the wealth of local produce around her in North Devon, she makes many traditional Devon dishes, such as rabbit pie or gammon, leek and potato pie in a cider cream sauce. "In Devon they want good, hearty food, poor man's food, all the things people don't generally eat but that's delicious."

Sue is another pioneer who followed the 'source local and cook seasonal' principle long before it became a fashionable foodie concept. Training as a chef in France showed her that using what was local and available was the best way to create food with taste and flavour.

Not only is this her favourite mussel recipe, this is probably the café's best selling dish, using local Devon cider, fresh local garden-grown leeks and the best local organic clotted cream. These all complement the hand-picked mussels uniquely grown and harvested in the estuary close to her café.

2 litres (or 2 kg) Taw mussels, cleaned and debearded

50g butter

2 leeks, finely chopped

500ml Devon cider

3 tbsps clotted cream

Salt and freshly milled black pepper to taste

1 tbsp chopped fresh parsley

A few small sprigs of thyme

In a large wide bottomed pan melt the butter, gently soften the leeks then pour in the cider. When it comes to the boil, tip in the mussels. Cover and leave on a high heat for four minutes.

As they open, lift out the mussels and place on a warm dish in a very low oven while you make the sauce.

Strain the cooking liquid, discarding the leek, and return to the pan. Simmer to reduce by about a quarter and add the clotted cream. Season well and pour over the mussels resting in their shells.

Sprinkle with the parsley and a few thyme leaves.

Serve with freshly baked crusty bread and some chilled organic Devon cider.

Chef's Notes about mussels

Commercially grown and harvested mussels are depurated for 42 hours using ultra violet light to ensure that they are safe to eat.

Any mussels that are open when cleaning, and refuse to close when tapped sharply on the side of the sink, should be discarded. When the mussels are cooked they should all be open. Discard any that remain closed.

PHILIP BURGESS
DARTMOOR INN
LYDFORD

Brixham Scallops with Ginger, Lemon Grass and Chilli Relish

Serves 4 as a starter or a light lunch with salad

Philip and Karen Burgess have been running the award-winning Dartmoor Inn at Lydford for more than 10 years. Long before it became fashionable they were great champions of local produce and had no hesitation in naming suppliers in the menus – from butchers, to fishmongers and vegetable growers. So while beef comes from the uplands around the pub and from graziers on Bodmin Moor, the freshest of fish comes straight from day boats in Looe, or as here from Brixham. Fruit and vegetables are even more local, travelling only a few miles from nearby growers. Philip and Karen have created something unique; a gastropub perhaps but certainly somewhere where the food is equally good in the bar or restaurant. Their award-winning breakfast is one of the inn's best kept secrets, available not just to overnight guests but hungry walkers who know to book in advance. The difference between the Dartmoor Inn and Devon's other great eating places is the art, featuring pictures, crafts and ceramics from local artists, creating what Karen describes as a "challenge to people's perceptions of what a pub could be, and as part of the community to offer events and exhibitions to make a nice way for people to see art in a relaxed environment".

12 shelled and washed scallops - with roe left on

I piece of root ginger, about 3cm long

I shallot

I stick lemon grass

I red chilli

Soya sauce

1 small bunch chives, chopped

1 lemon

Salt and pepper

Olive oil

Small salad leaves for garnish

Make the relish. Finely chop the ginger, chilli, shallot, lemon grass and chives.

Place in a bowl and add a squeeze of lemon juice, two tablespoons of olive oil and one dessertspoon of soya sauce. Mix well.

Pat the scallops dry with kitchen paper.

Heat a little olive oil in a heavy-bottomed pan to almost smoking.

Season the scallops with salt and pepper and pan fry for two minutes each side until cooked. Remove and place on serving plate.

Cover with the relish and garnish with small leaves.

Serve immediately.

Chef's Notes

Make sure that your pan is really hot, with the smallest amount of oil in the bottom – too much will deep fry them and the scallops with be soggy not crisp as they should be – the scallops should really sizzle as you sear them on each side.

Finish them off with a squeeze of lemon just as you pull them off the heat, this will add piquancy and enhance the flavour.

DAN GARNETT
CLOVELLY

Roast Clovelly Herring with Bread and Butter and Tea

Serves 1

For fishmonger Dan Garnett the late autumn is always a time of year to look forward to, when the herring arrive in Bideford Bay. "The taste is rich, the fish full of creamy roes or 'peas', the hard female roe", he says. Later in the year, while they are waiting to spawn at Christmas, they do not eat, so their gut is empty. After spawning, the spent herrings swim away to return the following year. Dan and the few remaining Clovelly herring fishermen catch

them in small wooden boats, drifting on the tide and using traditional cotton nets. This is the ultimate slow food, with a low impact on the fragile coastal and marine environment. Herrings are often known as the 'silver darlings', because for hundreds of years they were a valuable source of income for fishing communities right around the British coast. Locally the Clovelly Herring is known as the King of Fish, as catching herring was once the mainstay of this fishing village's economy.

Dan is a great champion for local fish, and his mission in life is to get more of his customers to enjoy the harvest of the sea. He suggests that the best way to enjoy herrings is to roast them and to eat them accompanied by malted brown wheat bread and butter and a mug of strong tea.

2 Clovelly herrings (scaled and cleaned)
1 lemon
50g salted butter
Chopped parsley
Salt and pepper
A slice of buttered malted brown bread
Lemon wedges
Tea

Pre-heat oven to 200°C, 400°F, Gas 6.

Pre-warm an ovenproof dish.

Prepare the herrings, remove the head and gut, leaving the roes in, or you can ask the fishmonger to do this, making sure the roes are left in.

Brush the hot dish with a little melted butter. Place the herrings in the dish and brush with the remainder of the melted butter. Season with salt and pepper and roast uncovered in the oven for about 7 minutes.

Meanwhile pre-heat the grill. Remove the herrings from oven and check the flesh at the backbone, it should not be bloody.

Sprinkle the herrings with chopped parsley and grill until sizzling and golden brown.

Serve immediately with lemon wedges, bread and butter and tea of your choice.

Chef's Notes

These are good as a breakfast, lunch or supper dish. If children (or adults) are challenged by the fine bones, tell them they are 'sea whiskers'!

If you can't get Clovelly herrings, which have a very limited season, use locally caught herrings.

The Clovelly Herring Festival celebrates this special fish each November, for details see www.clovelly.co.uk

MATT MASON
JACK IN THE GREEN
ROCKBEARE,
NEAR EXETER

Fillet of Sea Bass with a Carrot and Vanilla Purée

Serves 4

Matt Mason has been head chef at the Jack in the Green for more than 12 years. He and owner Paul Parnell have been pioneers in not only sourcing the best local, seasonal produce, usually from within a 25-mile radius of this pub, but in telling their customers what they are doing. Vegetables come from a smallholding only a few miles away, fish from Brixham, meat is locally reared and butchered, beer and cider also fly the flag for Devon. Paul Parnell eschews the term gastropub, describing his establishment as both restaurant and pub.

This recipe would be served in the restaurant while the bar offers classic pub food with a Jack in the Green twist.

"I could not think of a better fish to represent our region," Matt says. "Sea bass has class and is always a real favourite with our customers, and features on our menus regularly."

Whenever possible he uses line-caught bass from local fishermen. "Its firm creamy white flesh and wonderful distinctive flavour benefits from being just simply cooked and at the same time is robust enough to compete with the heady flavours of the orient when required."

50g carrots peeled and finely chopped

30g unsalted butter

125ml freshly squeezed orange juice

1 vanilla pod split and de-seeded

Salt and pepper

4 x 150g sea bass fillets

Oil and butter for cooking

Salt

Ground white pepper

Lemon juice

Place the carrots in a saucepan with the vanilla and butter. Cover with the orange juice and a sheet of greaseproof paper. Bring to a gentle simmer and cook for 25 to 30 minutes.

Remove the paper and reduce the liquid by two thirds. Remove the vanilla pod.

Transfer to a liquidiser and blend until smooth. Season to taste.

Trim the fish if necessary and lightly score the skin at close intervals using a sharp knife. Season the fish well on both sides with salt and freshly ground white pepper.

Warm a non-stick pan over a medium heat. When the pan is hot add a little oil, gently place the sea bass in the pan, skin side down, gradually increase the heat.

When the skin is nice and coloured add a little butter and turn.

Baste with the butter and continue to cook for about a minute longer, depending on the thickness of the fillet, ensure that the butter does not get too hot and burn. Finish with a little lemon juice.

To finish the dish, warm through the carrot and vanilla purée, place a good spoonful on each serving plate and sit the fish on top.

Serve with some buttered new potatoes and good seasonal local vegetables.

Chef's Notes

Choose line or net caught bass in preference to trawled.

Most fishmongers will be happy to gut, scale and portion your fish.

MITCH TONKS
THE SEAHORSE
DARTMOUTH

Spider Crab as you would find in Venice

Serves 2

Mitch Tonks is a passionate advocate for Devon's fish and shellfish. As the founder of Fishworks, The Seahorse in Dartmouth, and also the Rockfish Grill and Seafood Market, he knows a thing or two about fish and shellfish. He is also involved with the regeneration of Brixham harbour, where he hopes to run a restaurant, fish shop and cookery school.

Spider crabs are highly underrated and although many are landed along the south Devon coast, most are exported to France, Spain and Italy. "We don't appear to have as much of a taste for them in the UK," he says. "We should really champion them because they are local and plentiful and therefore priced well." Despite their appearance they are easy to prepare. The tools he uses are a pick and a small hammer for cracking the legs. "It is wonderfully sweet with a very fresh taste and more like the flavour of lobster or prawn than traditional crab." Mitch suggests using four crabs to serve two people as they don't yield a lot of crabmeat.

4 cooked spider crabs

1 round lettuce

A grind or two of white pepper

3 tbsps of your best olive oil

1 lemon

Remove the back of the crab by turning it on its shell with its back facing you, then with your thumbs prise it open (the brown stuff you will see is also meat).

Remove the "dead man's fingers" that will be attached to the body, then take off the claws and legs.

Chop the body into four and pick out the meat; then crack the claws and legs and do the same.

Rinse out the top shell and line it with a lettuce leaf.

Rub the crabmeat in your hands to make sure there is no shell in it and mix it with the olive oil and a squeeze of lemon and season with white pepper.

Serve by placing the meat back in the shell on the lettuce with nothing more than a slice of lemon. Simple and classic.

Chef's Notes

You should be able to order a cooked spider crab from any reputable fishmonger.

If you want to buy a live one dispatch it in the same way as any other crab. Turn it on its back with its legs upward. Underneath towards the back of the shell you will see a small pointed flap, lift this flap and you will find a small hole in the shell. Using a small screwdriver pierce down through this hole, with a sharp tap on the top of the screwdriver, until you feel it hit the other side of the shell. Move the screwdriver handle sharply towards the back of the shell then withdraw it. Cook in boiling water, salted with a good handful of salt, for 8 -12 minutes.

TIM BOUGET
ODE

Poached Teign Salmon Peel with Rhubarb and Devon Cider

Serves 4

From March through to the end of July Tim Bouget, of Ode in Shaldon, is fortunate to have occasional supplies of wild salmon, peel (sea trout) and during June and July, wild salmon caught just a few yards away on the Teign estuary. Both species are caught using the traditional method of seining. (see chapter 7).

This dish has many dimensions and was inspired by Tim's days working with

Gaulteiro Marchesi in London. Tim, who is chef-proprietor of one of the county's few organic restaurants, has adapted the recipe to champion the finest Devon produce. The apparently unusual combination of the underrated rhubarb chard, local cider and salmon peel is wonderfully complex yet simple to prepare, he says. The sharpness and texture of the rhubarb replaces lemon and combines with the sweetness of the cider to balance the richness of the salmon and cream.

---

4 x 120g pieces of wild salmon peel - skin removed (see chef's notes)

300g rhubarb cut into fine batons (4cm x 5mm)

150ml organic double cream - we use Riverford Farm Dairy

1 tsp Cornish sea salt

1 tsp black pepper

1 sprig of thyme and 1 bay leaf

400ml dry Devon cider

50g rhubarb chard, also known as ruby chard (optional) or 100g sea lettuce, lightly steamed

---

Bring the cider to the boil and add the thyme and bay leaf.

Add the batons of rhubarb and chard leaves if using, simmer for 1 minute, remove and set aside in a warm place.

Add the seasoned wild salmon fillets to the cider, presentation side up (skin side down) and cover with greaseproof paper.

Poach the fish in the simmering cider for about 2 - 3 minutes until cooked, ensuring the centre of the fish is soft to touch and slightly pink. Be careful not to overcook the fish, this is a very quick process.

Remove the fish and place on a bed of chard (or sea lettuce) in the centre of your chosen plate, place the rhubarb batons on top of the salmon peel and set aside.

Sieve half the poaching liquid into another pan and reduce by half, add the double cream and reduce again until the sauce coats the back of a spoon.

Pour the warm cream cider sauce over the fish.

Serve with a small mixed salad, vegetables or new potatoes

Chef's Notes

Rhubarb is great in salads, raw, sliced thinly, sprinkled with sugar and salt, and served with sweet vegetables such as cooked beetroots. High in fibre it originated in Asia.

Rhubarb chard is also known as ruby chard, it has bright red stalks.

For this recipe we use our home-grown rhubarb chard leaves to accompany the dish but watercress or Swiss chard are great alternatives.

Wild salmon could be used in place of the salmon peel, or at a pinch organic farmed salmon. At ODE we only purchase wild caught or sustainably caught fish.

Monkfish Loin wrapped in Prosciutto, Potato Purée, Orange and Balsamic Vinegar

Serves 4

2 medium sized monkfish, giving 4 fillets of approx 160g each

8 slices of prosciutto ham

8 sage leaves, briefly blanched in boiling water

150ml orange juice

20g sugar

1 dsp balsamic vinegar

150ml double cream

olive oil

A few lightly blanched French beans, briefly tossed in butter

Potato purée, made by sieving cooked potato, and re-heating with butter and cream

Spinach, gently wilted

I orange, cut into segments

Mushrooms, sliced if necessary, and fried in a little olive oil

This recipe comes from Mark Dodson at the award winning Mason's Arms in Knowstone. Now in his fifth year in Devon, Mark runs this pub with a restaurant with a sharp focus on Devon ingredients, when they are the right quality, consistency and available in sufficient volume. When he first moved to Devon after 12 years as head chef at Michel Roux's Waterside Inn in Bray, he was pleasantly surprised by the quality of the ingredients available in the county. He uses exclusively Devon beef and game, preferably from nearby Exmoor, fish comes from Brixham.

"I knew about the dairy produce but I found a lot of products I wasn't expecting," he says.

He tries to combine the values of being a village pub with the Michelin-starred restaurant. Describing it as "a restaurant in a pub". Simplicity is the key, he adds. "If you've got good ingredients my philosophy is not to mess about with them, let the ingredients speak for themselves."

Wrap each monkfish fillet with two pieces of ham and two blanched sage leaves. Then tightly wrap each fillet with cling film, giving a sausage shape.

Boil together the orange juice, balsamic vinegar and sugar. When it is syrupy add the cream. Cook until the sauce is slightly thickening then pass through a sieve and reserve.

Poach the monkfish fillets in boiling water for approximately 8 -10 minutes.

Prepare the garnish of orange, beans, spinach and reheat the potato purée.

Once the monkfish is cooked, remove the cling film, pat dry then pan fry lightly in some olive oil.

Carefully put the potato in the centre of the plate and make a small well in the centre to hold the spinach, then place the garnish around the plate.

Slice the monkfish into three at an angle which will give the dish height. Place the pieces around the potato and finally pour the sauce around.

Chef's Note

Girolles or chanterelles if available make a lovely garnish.

BEN BOISDEVES
SAUNTON SANDS HOTEL
BRAUNTON

Lundy Lobster, Tomato Caponata and Devon Asparagus

Serves 2 as a generous starter or main course

This late spring and early summer dish comes from Ben Boisdeves, second sous chef at the Brend family's Saunton Sands Hotel perched high on the dramatic North Devon coast overlooking miles of sandy beach and across the World Heritage Site of Braunton Burrows.

This Frenchman, who grew up in South West France, thinks of this as his signature dish, and is particularly keen to use Braunton asparagus, local salad and lobster from Lundy when they are at their best. Their lobsters are supplied by Walrus Fisheries of Ilfracombe who pride themselves on responsible, sustainable fishing - catching lobster and crab by traditional potting.

1 x 800g lobster, either cooked or live

15 plum tomatoes

10 spears Devon asparagus - this would work well using sprue, the thinnest and often earliest asparagus

2 tsp baby capers, washed and drained

2 tsp finely chopped basil

1 bouquet garni

1 orange cut into quarters

Frisée lettuce

Olive oil

Cornish sea salt

Sarawak black pepper

To cook a live lobster (see Chef's Note) put the bouquet garni, orange, some salt and 6 Sarawak peppercorns into a pot with two litres of water. Bring to the boil and simmer for 10 minutes.

Put the live lobster in the boiling bouillon and cook for ten minutes. Remove and put into iced water to cool.

When the lobster is cool split it open and remove the body meat, cutting into very small dice. Try to remove the tail and claw meat in one piece, if possible. Keep the tail and claw meat to one side.

Peel, de-seed and finely chop the tomatoes.

Put some olive oil in a pan and when it is hot cook the tomatoes over a low heat until all the moisture has evaporated and the consistency is like tomato paste. Sweeten to taste if it is too acid.

When it is cool add the capers and basil, season with salt and pepper and chill for at least six hours.

Trim the asparagus to 5cm lengths, discarding the lower half of the spears.

Briefly cook them in salted boiling water for 2 minutes, then cool in iced water.

When they are cold, dry and slice in half lengthways.

Oil two cutters or rings with olive oil. Build a fence inside each ring with half the asparagus.

Fill with alternate layers of the tomato caponata and the diced lobster until it is about three-quarters full. Top with some frisée lettuce, with a little olive oil drizzled over. Place the remaining lobster meat on the plate.

For a simpler presentation layer up the caponata and chopped lobster meat in a ring, but serve the asparagus alongside, with the remaining lobster meat.

Chef's Notes

The lobster can be either pre-cooked or live.

Ben chooses Sarawak pepper because of its slightly spicy taste. However white peppercorns can be substituted.

The tomato caponata can be made the day before.

JANE BAXTER
RIVERFORD FIELD KITCHEN
WASH BARN,
BUCKFASTLEIGH

Braised Artichokes with Broad Beans and Mint

Serves 4

4 globe artichokes

juice of 1 lemon

3 tbsp olive oil

1 garlic clove, crushed (wet garlic can also be used)

a handful of shelled broad beans

1 tbsp chopped mint

sea salt and freshly ground black pepper

This recipe comes from the popular Riverford Farm Cook Book which combines information from Guy Watson about the vegetables grown at Riverford Organics near Buckfastleigh with mouthwatering recipes from Jane Baxter who runs the Riverford Field Kitchen. Both the book and the restaurant are a showcase for the fresh organic vegetables, salad leaves, herbs and fruit grown here.

Jane has long been passionate about promoting the virtues of eating local and seasonal foods, having worked with Joyce Molyneux, the founder of the Carved Angel in Dartmouth, and later at London's River Café, another restaurant based on the best seasonal produce.

The Field Kitchen is not a restaurant where anyone can turn up on spec. Diners must book ahead and take a farm tour. Afterwards they sit at long wooden refectory tables to share the no choice menu that offers five or six vegetable dishes, and one meat or vegetarian dish.

What's special about the Field Kitchen, Guy says, is the fact that it is on a farm and the whole experience should reinforce the experience for farm visitors of remaking the links between food production and the land. This is nothing new to the Watson family. More than 30 years ago John Watson, Guy's father, was one of the first to open the farm to the public, trying to bridge the gap between consumers and agriculture.

Prepare the artichokes by pulling off the dark outer leaves, working round the artichoke until you are down to the pale green leaves. Then cut off the tops of the remaining leaves and trim the artichokes so no dark green bits are evident. Lightly trim the stems if the artichokes are young. Remove the hairy choke with a teaspoon. Cut each one into sixths or eighths. Place in a bowl of cold water with the lemon juice added to prevent them going black.

Heat the oil in a frying pan over a high heat, add the artichoke wedges and stir constantly until they start to brown. Lower the heat, add the garlic and a few tablespoons of water and season with salt and pepper. Stir well, then reduce the heat, cover and cook for about 10 minutes, until the artichokes are tender.

Blanch the broad beans in a pan of boiling salted water for 4 - 5 minutes, then drain and add to the artichokes. Stir in the mint and adjust the seasoning.

Chef's Notes

You can add chopped parsley and chopped dried chilli when you add the mint.

DEZ TURLAND
BREND HOTELS

Exmoor Partridge

Pumpkin 3 ways
Chestnuts Girolles
Elderberry Jus

Serves 2

Dez Turland is Group Development Chef for Brend Hotels, overseeing the overall food policy for the family-owned hotel group. This recipe typifies the approach taken by Brend Hotels who were sourcing locally, long before it became a fashionable foodie concept. According to Peter Brend senior "it simply seemed the natural thing to do". Dez and his team of chefs work closely with a handful of local farmers and producers.

Dez says "This is a fantastic autumn dish using fresh grey partridge from Exmoor that's in season between 1st September and 1st February, we purchase ours through Smythacott Farm at Frithelstock Stone, Great Torrington. Patrick and Tristan Cockerill have been running the farm for the last 6 years and shoot twice a week during the season, ensuring the freshness of the partridge is maintained on a regular basis.

The sharpness of the elderberries complements the sweetness of the pumpkin and the roasted chestnuts and wild mushrooms give the dish a lot of depth".

Partridge & Jus

1 Partridge - cleaned and ready for roasting legs and breasts removed

100ml Game Stock - made from the carcase

100ml Red Wine

50ml Red Wine Vinegar

25g Elderberries

25g Redcurrant Jelly

50g Shallots / Carrot / Celery - finely diced

50ml Brandy

Bay Leaf / Thyme /Clove Garlic / Juniper Berry

100g Duck Fat

Olive Oil / Butter

salt - see Chef's Note

Place Partridge legs in a small, ovenproof saucepan, cover them with duck fat and half the spices and herbs, place a tight fitting lid on the pan and cook in a preheated oven at 125°C, 250°F, Gas ½ for 4 hours, or until tender. Keep warm.

For the Jus - sweat off any partridge trimmings, the diced vegetables and the rest of the herbs and spices, caramelise, deglaze with brandy, add vinegar and reduce until almost dry. Add the red wine and reduce again, then the game stock, reduce until you have the correct consistency, (like single cream) pass through a fine sieve, add elderberries and redcurrant jelly.

Panfry breasts in a little oil until brown on skin side, turn over and continue to cook for 5 minutes, add a knob of butter and cook for a further 2 minutes - keep slightly pink. Remove from heat, cover and allow to relax for 5 minutes.

Pumpkin

175g Pumpkin
25g Unsalted Butter
100ml Chicken Stock
25g Dried Pumpkin Seeds

Cut pumpkin into even sized dice, cook 125g with chicken stock until soft and blitz with 20g of butter until smooth.

Panfry 50g of pumpkin in rest of butter until browned.

Panfry the dried pumpkin seeds until they start to brown and release an aroma.

TO FINISH THE DISH

50g Whole Chestnuts - roasted and shelled

25g Girolles mushrooms - cleaned washed and sautéed in a little butter

a little olive oil if liked

Chef's Note

Season with salt to your own taste as you go along. Season the Jus only after all the reductions.

PETER GORTON
HORN OF PLENTY
GULWORTHY, NEAR
TAVISTOCK

Roasted Loin of Venison with a tangle of Greens and Red Wine Sauce

Serves 6

6 x 140g trimmed venison loin

Salt and freshly ground black pepper
Clarified butter or vegetable oil

Chef's Notes

You could replace the venison with almost any meat. I particularly love venison both for its taste and healthy qualities. I have it on the menu at every opportunity I can.

The tangle of greens is also delicious without the smoked bacon and works very well with grilled goats cheese for a vegetarian alternative.

The Horn of Plenty Hotel, is set in lovely gardens with sweeping views across the Tamar Valley to Dartmoor. This charming country house hotel, owned and run by Paul and Andy Roston and Master Chef Peter Gorton, is warm and welcoming, with friendly and well trained staff for whom nothing seems too much trouble. The hotel has its own fruit and vegetable garden and is also supplied with a wealth of local ingredients, all contributing to the delicious and elegant food.

Peter told me "My philosophy is simple, I use the freshest, local, seasonal produce available and cook it in the most simple flavoursome way I can. We have world class produce on our doorstep which makes cooking a great pleasure.

I have many great suppliers but Dave Williams the pig farmer is an inspiration, the quality of the meat and sausages are wonderful. The pigs are called 'Large Blacks' which is a rare breed. The sausages contain 95% pork and are fantastic.

Finally I love to teach people how to cook in a friendly relaxed way and have been running cookery courses at The Horn of Plenty for 16 years. I also demonstrate in schools, work places and in people's homes".

Tangle of Tart Greens

1 head of Savoy cabbage
2 rashers of smoked bacon
1 red onion, thinly sliced
1 bunch watercress, coarse stems removed
1 tbsp sugar
3 tbsp balsamic vinegar
Salt & freshly ground pepper to taste

Core & coarsely shred the cabbage with a sharp knife. In a 10-inch saucepan sauté the bacon over a medium heat. Add the onion & cabbage & sauté until the cabbage begins to wilt. Add the sugar & vinegar & cook until the cabbage is tender but still a little crisp. Remove the saucepan from the heat, toss in the watercress & season to taste. Serve warm.

Apple Aïoli

2 eggs yolks
1 clove of garlic
1 tbsp Dijon mustard
1 tbsp cider vinegar
100ml vegetable oil
200g apple purée
Salt & pepper

Put eggs yolks, garlic, mustard and vinegar into a food processor and with the motor running slowly add the oil. Finally add the apple purée, season with salt and pepper and keep in the refrigerator until needed.

Red Wine Sauce

40 ml vegetable oil
6 shallots, finely sliced
1 carrot roughly diced
1 stick of celery, diced
2 cloves garlic
2 bay leaves
10 crushed black peppercorns
2 sprigs thyme
1 sprig Rosemary
400ml red wine
200ml crème de cassis
300ml chicken stock, beef stock or
    vegetable stock
200ml water

Heat the oil in a large saucepan until hot, add shallots, garlic, celery and diced carrots, cook until caramelised. Add bay leaves, peppercorns, thyme, and Rosemary. Deglaze with cassis, red wine and reduce by two thirds.

Add stock and water and bring to the boil then lower the heat and simmer for one hour skimming off any scum that rises. Pass through a fine sieve then return to a clean pan and reduce over a high heat until the sauce has thickened. Allow to cool.

TO COOK THE VENISON

Pre-heat oven to 230°C, 450°F, Gas 8

Lightly season the venison with salt and pepper. Heat the clarified butter or oil in a frying pan and when hot add the venison and seal on all sides, lift the venison from the pan and put onto a clean tray, cook in the oven for six minutes then remove the venison from the pan and allow to rest in a warm place for five minutes.

TO SERVE

Place two spoonfuls of the greens on a pre-heated dinner plate. Cut the venison loin steak in 2 and place on the greens. Spoon a line of apple aïoli on the plate and spoon the red wine sauce around. Serve with vegetables of your choice.

ROSS TREGIDGO
THE HARRIS ARMS
PORTGATE, LEWDOWN

Slow Cooked Local Pork Belly with Cider Sauce and a Black Pudding Potato Croquette

Serves 4

Six years ago Andy and Rowena Whiteman escaped from corporate life and bought The Harris Arms, with the idea of creating a welcome and relaxing atmosphere for "our customers to enjoy honest food with substance and style, using the best of local ingredients". They certainly have succeeded. The pork and black pudding in this recipe is supplied by Phillip Warren & Son, Launceston family butchers for 130 years, who still farm their own livestock as well as buying direct from other local farmers.

Head Chef Ross Tregidgo, a local young Cornish chef, who cut his teeth at the renowned Horn of Plenty, was inspired to create this dish through his desire to use local produce and less expensive cuts of meat. His twist combining the mashed potato and black pudding into a unique croquette adds his own magic touch of creativity. Additionally he uses Sam's Poundhouse Cider - made about 25 miles from the Harris Arms - in the sauce, and spinach supplied by a local grower.

3½ kg belly pork - deboned and skinned by your butcher (wgt with skin/bone on)

1 litre stock - you can buy Bouillon

3 carrots

2 sticks celery

1 onion

10 sprigs of thyme

1 bulb of garlic

olive oil to fry

salt and pepper (see Chef's Tip)

Chef's Note

If you are using bought in Bouillon, check for seasoning and add salt and pepper if necessary. Some makes have plenty and others not enough.

Cut the carrots, celery and onion roughly into 2cm. Cut the garlic bulb in half.

Heat olive oil in a casserole dish on a high heat, then add carrots, celery, onion and garlic and colour till golden brown.

Add warm stock (see chef's tip) and the thyme to the vegetables and bring to the boil. Turn the heat down.

Add the belly pork and cook on low heat for 2½ hours until the pork is tender.

Take pork out of the stock and put it in a tray. Let it cool. Place another tray on top with a heavy weight and put the pork in the fridge for 1½ hours. Once pressed, take pork off the tray and portion into 12 equally sized pieces.

Heat a heavy-duty frying pan on high heat, add a little oil, when hot add the pork - flat side down and colour till golden brown.

Once golden brown, place the pork in a hot oven (200°C, 400°F, Gas 6) for 12 -14 minutes to warm the pork through. Make sure it is hot in the middle - if not place in oven for a further 5 minutes. When ready, serve with black pudding croquette, cider gravy and vegetables.

Black pudding croquette

500g potatoes - peeled

200g black pudding (chopped up into small dice)

2 tsp dried oregano

50g Flour

4 eggs

100g fresh white breadcrumbs

salt & pepper to taste

Fill a medium size saucepan with water, place on a high heat and bring to the boil. Cut peeled potatoes into 5cm pieces and boil them until soft. Once cooked, strain potatoes and leave to stand for 5 minutes. Then place them in a mixing bowl and mash until most lumps are gone.

Add chopped black pudding, 2 beaten eggs and oregano and season and mix all together. Place in fridge to firm up for about 20 minutes. Once firm, mould the mixture into 4 sausage shapes about 6 cm in length and place on a floured baking tray.

Coat sausage shapes in flour, shake off excess, then coat with beaten egg, then breadcrumbs. Repeat one more time then place the tray in a pre-heated oven 190°C, 375°F, Gas 5 for 25 minutes until golden brown and hot in the middle. Cut in half and arrange as shown in the photo.

Cider sauce

500ml cider

800ml Bouillon

10 black peppercorns - crushed

4 leaves fresh sage, chopped

1tsp cornflour

salt

Place cider and peppercorns in a saucepan, reduce by half, add stock (bouillon), reduce by half again. Add sage, simmer for 20 minutes then strain. Return to heat and bring to the boil. Thicken with cornflour, season and pour over the pork.

Pan-fried Sirloin Steak with roasted shallots, celeriac puree wild mushrooms and a Madeira Cream Sauce

Serves 4

4 x 200/250g sirloin steaks
120g mixed wild mushrooms
½ small, peeled shallot, chopped finely
200g young spinach
20 shallots, peeled and blanched
Sherry vinegar
Unsalted butter
Vegetable oil
Salt and pepper

Celeriac Puree

300g celeriac, peeled and chopped
25g celery, chopped
25g onions, chopped
250ml chicken stock
250ml milk
25g unsalted butter
¼ tsp salt
Pinch of ground white pepper

Michael Caines is Executive Chef of Gidleigh Park, the prestigious 2-star Michelin country house hotel on the edge of Dartmoor and, in partnership with hotelier Andrew Brownsword, is in the process of creating a group of individual ABode hotels throughout the United Kingdom. The first to open was the Royal Clarence, in Exeter's Cathedral Yard.

Born in Exeter and adopted into a large and loving family, Michael gained his passion for food from his mother. Says Michael, "I grew up in a large family, and my love of food and cooking came from the big family meals we always shared together, prepared by my mother, who was a wonderful cook. My father loved to grow vegetables and fruit in our garden, and so I grew up appreciating the flavours of the freshest foods, picked that day and simply prepared."

After Exeter catering college, followed by three years under his mentor Raymond Blanc, and a spell in France, he returned to take up the post of Head Chef at Gidleigh Park.

Michael is passionate about using local produce and firmly believes that the food culture in the south west is much stronger than anywhere else - that the relationship between the growers , local producers and artisan cheesemakers and those they supply, is much closer here than elsewhere. "In Devon in particular there's a lot of producers here on our doorstep".

For this dish Michael always uses Richard Vines' beef (see chapter 1), sirloin or fillet - "I prefer sirloin for the flavour. Richard hangs it for us for 4 weeks and it's not unusual for us to add a week on top of that"

Firstly make the celeriac puree. Place the onions, celery and salt into a saucepan with the butter and sweat. Then add the milk, chicken stock, then the celeriac and pepper. Bring to the boil, then reduce to a simmer and cook for 30 minutes and then allow to cool. Pass the mixture through a colander and place into a mixer and mix until fine. Remove from the mixer and place into a blender and blend to a very fine puree. Place back into the pan and add a little butter and correct the seasoning. Keep warm

Madeira Cream Sauce

40g shallots, peeled and sliced
50g button mushrooms, sliced
100ml Madeira
150ml chicken stock
150ml double cream
50g butter
2 sprigs thyme
Salt and pepper

Chef's Notes

Add a little fresh butter when cooking the steak. This helps to colour the steak and produces a lovely caramelised effect to the meat to add to the intense flavour.

The roasted shallots can be part boiled in water, with salt, thyme and a bay leaf, to aid cooking.

When making the celeriac purée it is best to use a blender rather than a food processor. Always ensure that your celeriac is nice and softly cooked through before blending to acquire the correct consistency.

Then make the Madeira cream sauce. Sweat the shallots in 25gr of the butter, add the salt and cook until transparent. Add the mushrooms and continue cooking until they are slippery in texture, then add the thyme. Add the Madeira and cook until reduced by half. Follow by adding the chicken stock and reduce by half again, then add the cream and reduce this by half. To finish, add the remaining butter and pass through a fine sieve and season with salt and pepper.

Then, using a thick bottomed pan take some butter and slowly roast the blanched shallots with a little salt and pepper, turning from time to time. When soft, deglaze with the sherry vinegar and leave to rest.

Season the steaks with salt and pepper and seal them in a hot pan with a little vegetable oil and butter then cook them in the resulting foaming butter, turning as you go until you reach the required degree (rare, medium etc). Remove the steak from the pan and leave to rest on a tray for a few minutes.

Remove the excess fat from the pan the steaks were cooked in and add a little water before adding some Madeira sauce. Bring to the boil and reduce to a sauce consistency. Then in a separate frying pan heat some butter and sweat the finely chopped shallots, then add the wild mushrooms and sauté until cooked. Now add these to the Madeira sauce. In the same pan as the shallots and mushrooms were cooked, wilt the spinach and season with salt and pepper.

To serve, place the spinach onto the right side of the plate, slice the steaks and fan on top of the spinach. Using a large spoon, place a tear drop of celeriac purée onto the plate. Dress 5 roasted shallots around each plate and then spoon the mushrooms and sauce over the meat.

Serve and enjoy

HADLEIGH BARRETT
COMBE HOUSE
GITTISHAM

Roast Rump of Spring Lamb with Braised Neck, Crushed Jersey Royal new potatoes, Aubergine Purée and Fried Capers

Serves 4

Head chef Hadleigh Barrett has been cooking top notch local ingredients at Combe House for several years. He is particularly keen to serve spring lamb, properly hung, at the appropriate time, and sources his from Blacklake Farm, just two miles away. He describes this brief six-week season as the highlight of the seasonal produce that passes through the kitchens. Ken and Ruth Hunt, owners of this award-winning country house hotel, have been passionate about the provenance of the produce that makes its way into the kitchen from the day that they arrived. More than a decade on they have a dedicated team of local suppliers and the hotel's walled garden produces 40 per cent of the fresh vegetables, soft fruit and herbs used in the kitchen, from chervil and basil to broad beans, redcurrants and gooseberries.

2 spring lamb rumps

2 spring lamb necks

2 aubergines

1 onion, chopped

1 carrot, chopped

2 cloves of garlic

1 sprig of rosemary

400ml of lamb or brown chicken stock

500g Jersey Royal new potatoes, cleaned

100g capers

Sea salt

Olive oil

Chopped parsley

Salt and pepper

Cut the aubergines in half lengthways. Score with a knife and sprinkle with sea salt, leave for one hour. Dry with kitchen towel, drizzle with olive oil and cook in a pre-heated oven at 150°C, 300°F, Gas 2 for 2 hours. When cooked, scoop out the middle and blend in a food processor until smooth, season with salt and pepper.

Season the necks with salt and pepper and fry in a heavy based frying pan with olive oil, until browned all over. Transfer to a casserole dish and add the onion, carrot, garlic, rosemary and stock, bring to a simmer. Cover and transfer to a pre-heated oven at 140°C, 275°F, Gas 1 and cook for 2 hours. When cooked, remove the necks, pass the stock through a fine sieve into another pan, skim off any fat, return to the heat and reduce to sauce consistency. Keep the necks warm until needed.

Turn the oven up to 200°C, 400°F, Gas Mark 6. Season the rumps with salt and pepper. In a heavy based pan, fry them in olive oil until browned all over. Put the rumps on an oven tray and cook for 14 minutes, turning them half way through cooking. Once cooked, take the rumps out of the oven and rest for 10 minutes before carving.

Chef's Note

Jersey Royals, or possibly Cornish Earlies, are the only new potatoes available when the spring lamb comes on stream, but local or Westcountry new potatoes could be substituted when available.

Put the potatoes in a pan and cover with salted water, bring to the boil and cook for about 15 - 20 minutes, drain and peel. Roughly crush the potatoes with the back of a fork, drizzle with olive oil and season with salt, pepper and parsley.

In a heavy based pan, heat some olive oil, add the capers and fry for about 30 seconds. They should start to puff out and crisp up a little.

Arrange the potatoes on the plate, cut the lamb necks in half and place on top. Slice the rump, spoon on the aubergine purée, sprinkle the capers around and pour on the reduced stock/jus. Serve with spring greens, young leeks and broad beans.

Summer Salad of Braised Ham Hocks, Broad Beans and Garden Herbs with Caramelised Apples and Sherry Vinegar Dressing.

Serves 4 to 6

Angus McCaig and his brother Joe run the Holt in Honiton which is fast gaining a reputation for good pub food, based around local ingredients.

It is difficult to describe the Holt's atmosphere because it is more chic and elegant than a pub, not a super smart restaurant and not quite a bistro. In fact, it is entirely individual to the McCaigs' vision of "stylish yet accessible, and definitely warm, welcoming and comfortable".

Head chef Angus radiates energy and enthusiasm - inspired by the idea of marrying local produce with unusual combinations of aromatic spices that complement, but do not overpower the main ingredient of the dish. All carried through with meticulous attention to every detail on the plate, including own recipe breads, flavoured and smoked butters, home made vegetable pickles and dressings. Yet somehow his highly individual dishes are strangely simple, and clean and fresh on the palate.

The Holt has its own small smokehouse, producing a diverse and fascinating range of smoked ingredients used in the kitchen and on sale to take home.

Over the five years since the McCaigs took over The Holt, Angus has built relationships with an increasing number of local suppliers, including fruit and vegetable growers Paul and Caroline Bellinger of Ottery St. Mary who supplied the salad and vegetables for this recipe and free-range farmers and butchers "Devon Rose" who provided the ham hock.

500g ice mixed with 300ml cold water

2 local ham hocks

1 leek, washed and roughly chopped

1 carrot, roughly chopped

1 onion, roughly chopped

3 bay leaves

3 juniper berries crushed

5 whole black peppercorns

2 star anise

200g podded broad beans

100g mixed fresh basil, flat leaf parsley, mint

30g rocket

20g watercress

2 local Cox's apples

3tbs sugar in a small bowl

50ml sherry vinegar

20g palm sugar, or caster sugar if you can't find palm

1tbsp whole grain mustard

100ml extra virgin olive oil

1x pinch salt and pepper

Put a large ovenproof pan of water onto the heat. Place the hocks in the pan, making sure they are covered, and bring to the boil. Discard the water and re-fill the pan with a fresh batch of cold water.

Add the leek, carrot, onion, bay leaves, juniper berries, peppercorns and star anise. Bring to a simmer, then cover with a lid or tin foil and braise in the oven at 150°C, 300°F, Gas Mark 2, for 4 to 4½ hours.

When the hocks are cooked, they should be almost falling apart. Let them cool in the liquor, until they are about 50°C (1 - 2 hours), discard the jelly-like skin. Flake the meat into a bowl and discard the bones.

Bring another pan of water to the boil and add the broad beans for 45 seconds, lift out with a slotted spoon and place in the iced water and leave for 3 - 4 minutes. When cool, skin the beans by squeezing them between thumb and fore finger. Discard the skins.

Put the sherry vinegar, olive oil, mustard, palm sugar, salt and pepper in a jam jar and shake vigorously to emulsify. Taste, and add more sugar to sweeten or more sherry vinegar to sharpen to your taste.

Pick the herb leaves from any tough stalks and set aside.

Use a melon baller to cut five little apple balls per person. Place 2 - 3 at a time in the caster sugar and swirl the bowl to coat them with sugar. Place these on a flameproof surface then use the blowtorch to caramelise the sugar. Set the caramelised balls aside.

Warm the flaked meat gently in a little of the cooking liquor on a low heat for 20 seconds.

Mix the salad leaves and herbs with some of the dressing and the broad beans.

Place a stack of the salad in the centre of each plate, lay a few pieces of the ham hocks on top, put 5 of the caramelised apples around the outside edge, scatter a few extra broad beans around, and add a little extra dressing to finish.

Chef's Notes

The first stage of the recipe should be done in the morning or the evening before. Doing the recipe in two stages makes it a very easy dish to finish.

You can save the stock in which the hocks are cooked for a lovely pea and ham soup.

STEPHEN PIDGEON
THE ARUNDELL ARMS
LIFTON

The Arundell Arms Beef Sandwich

serves 1

Owned since 1961 by the legendary Anne Voss-Bark, MBE - this 15th century hotel is justly proud of its reputation for good food in relaxed surroundings. The kitchen is run by Head Chef Steven Pidgeon, one of only 80 Master Chefs of Great Britain, who prides himself on beautifully presented food, meticulously prepared, using only the finest quality produce sourced from local suppliers.

Their Devon beef (Red Ruby or South Devon breeds) is from nearby Phillip Warren, who buys 'direct from the farm'. Predominately grass fed, and naturally reared on the grasslands surrounding Bodmin Moor, the beef is hung for three weeks. The result is well marbled, succulent, tender meat, bursting with flavour.

Steven says that "the cut used for this stunning sandwich is always ribeye, chosen for its full flavour".

This shows that even something as quick and simple as a sandwich can still be a gourmet treat, providing you use the very best ingredients. *At home, this is a great way to use the remainder of a family roast.*

4kg Ribeye of Devon Beef - (this cut is from the forerib - ask your butcher to bone out the ribeye and tie for roasting)
2 slices granary bread
horseradish cream
unsalted butter
olive oil

Preheat the oven to 200°C, 400°F, Gas 6. Rub the joint with olive oil and roast for 1½ hours, turning it every 20 minutes. Once cooked, allow the beef to cool and "relax". It will be a perfect medium rare.

Horseradish Cream

1 horseradish root
300ml double cream
3 tsp French Mustard
1 tsp sugar
1 lemon

Wash, peel and finely grate the horseradish and mix with the lemon juice, mustard and sugar. Whip the double cream until it forms a peak and fold into the mixture.

ASSEMBLE

Butter some granary bread and spread the horseradish cream on both slices. Thinly slice the beef, place on one of the slices of bread and roll the beef across the bread to form a roll in the middle of the bread. Then place the other piece of bread on top and push down either side of the beef to form a humpy shape. Remove the crusts and cut into three. Serve with a salad garnish.

Chef's Tip

When cooking meat, always allow it to cool and "relax" before serving - to retain all the juices and maintain full flavour and tenderness.

SCOTT PATON
JACK IN THE GREEN
ROCKBEARE, NEAR EXETER

Summer Pudding with Blackcurrant Posset

Makes 10 individual puddings

Described by his boss as "pastry chef extraordinaire" Scott Paton has been cooking at the Jack in the Green since leaving school. Passionate about desserts, in 2008 he won the international Pastry Chef of the Year competition at his second attempt. He is responsible for all the bread, desserts, petits fours and ice cream served in both the pub and restaurant. He devised this take on summer pudding by turning the fruit inside the bread case into a mousse. "Personally the idea of a summer pudding is so lovely and I often look forward to tucking in, but in the first mouthful I am greeted with an unpleasant bitter berry that is unwelcome on my palate. This recipe eliminates that problem and is very satisfying," he explains.

Summer Pudding

150ml summer berry coulis

2 eggs, separated

120ml double cream

120g caster sugar

2 leaves bronze gelatine

10 - 15 slices white bread soaked in 500ml berry coulis

Make the summer berry coulis by blending 1kg of whatever seasonal berries are available with 50ml elderflower cordial (will make about 800ml coulis).

Start by lining the base and walls of 10 moulds (70mm in diameter) with cling film, then with the bread that has been soaked in the coulis. Cut strips for the walls and circles for top and bottom. Keep the tops aside until later.

Soften the gelatine in cold water for 5 minutes until pliable.

Whisk the egg yolks and 50g of sugar until pale and bring the coulis to the boil. As soon as it starts to boil remove from the heat. Add the gelatine and stir until dissolved.

Slowly pour the coulis over the egg yolks mixture as you whisk them and keep whisking until the mix is cool.

Make a meringue with the egg whites and remaining sugar.

Whip the cream until it forms ribbons in the bowl.

Fold together the cream, meringue and egg yolk mixture and pour into the lined moulds filling right to the top of the bread. Finally cap the moulds with the final circle of bread soaked in coulis and weigh them down evenly overnight.

Blackcurrant Posset

425ml double cream

125g caster sugar

90ml strained blackcurrant juice (made with 200g blackcurrants in the same way as the berry coulis)

25ml lemon juice

Bring the sugar and cream to the boil and simmer for 6 minutes.

Stir in the lemon and blackcurrant juice and return to the boil. Count to ten and remove from the heat. Pass the mixture through a sieve and leave to set in a bowl overnight.

To serve turn out the pudding and add some of the posset, some local summer berries (as many or as little as you like) and a blob of clotted cream

Chef's Notes

If you are short on time try just making the blackcurrant posset. It is extremely easy and delicious.

For the fruit coulis I use a mix of tayberries, cherries, blackcurrants, white currants, redcurrants, raspberries, golden raspberries, strawberries and blackberries, depending on what is season. You can use frozen berries. They are much cheaper. Any coulis left over can be frozen for a month or will keep in the fridge for 3 days. Try it on cereal for a kick start to the day.

ED CHESTER
OTTERTON MILL
OTTERTON

Rhubarb and Ginger Bavarois with a Beetroot and Scrumpy Coulis

Serves 4

This recipe comes from Ed Chester, head chef at Otterton Mill. This lively centre mixes food, art and local crafts in a unique location where water-powered milling has taken place for more than 1,000 years. The restaurant menu is led by whatever is fresh, seasonal and available locally, and the daily changing specials board might include classics such as hunter's pie, stuffed butternut squash, smoked fish platter, Mill salads and

contemporary dishes such as mezze. The restaurant is complemented by the mill's bakery and shop specialising in Devon food and drink. The owners Simon and Caroline Spiller describe the eclectic mix found here as offering a place to relax, to unwind, to explore, to escape to and enjoy.

200ml milk

200ml double cream

100g caster sugar

6 large egg yolks

3 sheets of leaf gelatine

250g rhubarb

50g peeled fresh root ginger

500ml dry Devon cider or scrumpy

125g peeled raw beetroot

10ml balsamic vinegar

75g icing sugar

Juice of a quarter of a lemon

Heat the oven to 200°C, 400°F, Gas 6.

Cut the rhubarb into 3 cm pieces, finely grate the ginger and mix well together. Put them into a baking tray, cover with parchment paper and bake for 20 minutes. Set aside to cool.

Put the milk and cream into a pan and bring to scalding point. While the milk mix is heating, whisk the egg yolks and sugar together until they are pale and thick.

Slowly add 150ml of the scalded milk/cream to the egg mix while whisking constantly. Pour the egg and milk/cream mix back into the milk pan and lightly whisk until fully incorporated.

Cook this crème anglaise on a very low heat stirring frequently until beginning to thicken noticeably. Remove from the heat.

Purée the rhubarb and ginger, and stir through the crème anglaise.

Soak the gelatine leaves in cold water for 5 minutes. Take out and squeeze gently. Lower sheets into the crème anglaise and whisk until dissolved. Pass the mix through a sieve and pour into lightly oiled ramekins or a 1lb loaf tin lined with clingfilm. Leave to cool in a refrigerator until required.

For the coulis, coarsely grate the beetroot into the cider and set on medium high heat in a saucepan. When the beetroot is soft and the cider reduced by about three-quarters, blend to a purée. Pass the purée through a sieve and set back on the heat.

Sift in the icing sugar and add the lemon juice and balsamic vinegar, stirring until thickened. Leave to cool.

To serve turn out each bavarois onto a plate and pour around some coulis.

Chef's Note

If turning out a ramekin is proving tricky, dip it in hot water for ten seconds then gently upend onto the plate.

KATE McCAIG
THE HOLT
HONITON

Rhubarb and Custard Ice Cream

Serves 6 - 8

Kate McCaig is the dessert and pastry chef at The Holt, the Honiton pub owned by husband Angus and his brother Jo. This recipe came about because Kate had a pudding on the menu served with a rhubarb compote. "It used the pinkest juiciest bits of rhubarb and therefore had all of the green stringy bits left," explains Kate, who also makes all the ice creams served there. "This is a really simple custard and a compote mixed together and frozen, it eats well with my brown bread biscotti which also came about using left over bread," she says.

300ml milk

300ml double cream

1 vanilla pod (split in half lengthwise)

8 egg yolks

100g caster sugar

1 tbsp skimmed milk powder

1 heaped tsp cornflour

300g rhubarb, washed and chopped into small pieces

200g caster sugar

Zest of ½ a lemon

To make the custard: put the cream and milk into a pan, scrape out the seeds from ½ a vanilla pod, and add both to the pan. Bring to the boil over a medium heat.

Whisk the yolks, 100g of sugar, milk powder and cornflour together until smooth, pour over the hot milk, off the heat, and mix well.

Return to a medium heat stirring all the time until the custard starts to thicken and just starts to bubble. Take off heat and put through a fine sieve. Leave to cool and place in the fridge until well chilled.

Place the rhubarb in a baking tray with the rest of the sugar, the remaining ½ vanilla pod (seeds and pod added separately) and the lemon zest. Bake in the oven at 200°C, 400°F, Gas 6 for 15 - 20 minutes until soft and tender (give it a stir 2 or 3 times whilst cooking to prevent crystals forming). Leave to cool and place in fridge until well chilled.

To make ice cream mix custard and rhubarb together and place in an ice cream maker and churn until thick, put into a tub and freeze overnight.

Serve with brown bread biscotti.

Brown Bread Biscotti

115g granary breadcrumbs

50g porridge oats

50g plain flour

100g light soft brown sugar

1 tsp vanilla essence

75g melted butter

2 medium egg yolks

Place all ingredients in a food processor and mix until a dough forms. Make the dough into a sausage the size of a roll of cling film (approximately 35cm long), and chill for at least 20 minutes.

Pre-heat the oven to 180°C, 350°F, Gas 4, and cook the sausage for 25 - 30 minutes until pale golden brown. Remove from the oven and leave to cool for 20 minutes.

Cut the biscuit sausage with a bread knife on a 45 degree angle, into slices 1cm thick. Place on a baking sheet lined with silicone paper and put back in the oven for 20 - 30 minutes or until golden brown. Remove and leave to cool and crisp up.

Chef's Notes

If you don't have an ice cream maker put the mix in a tub and freeze for half an hour and then mix with a fork until smooth. Return to the freezer for another half an hour and repeat until frozen and smooth and ice crystal free.

The biscotti also go well with rhubarb or other crumble fruits

RICHARD HUNT
GRAND HOTEL
TORQUAY

Devon Splits
or Chudleighs

Makes 14 approx

This recipe comes from Richard Hunt Executive Chef at Torquay's Grand Hotel, where he oversees the food for several restaurants and the hotel's bakery, the only commercial one west of London, which supplies many other hotels and restaurants in the area with bread and baked goods. The kitchens also make all the hotel's fudge, jams and marmalade. Since returning to Devon after many years working in London, he has made it his mission to change the perception of dining in a large seafront hotel from a stuffy, often disappointing, experience to a fine dining occasion, and as a showcase for local produce such as Devon beef and pork and River Exe mussels.

Richard was intrigued by the idea of Devonshire Splits and was happy to research this recipe for The Devon Food Book. Lighter than a scone, the split, also known as Chudleighs, was the traditional ingredient of Devon cream teas. As the dough is similar to a brioche it retains a soft crust after baking. Devonshire Splits feature regularly at the Grand Hotel, but elsewhere 21st century tourists will find that the scone is what virtually all tea rooms serve as the vehicle for the cream and jam. Scones are, of course, quicker to prepare as there is no yeast or rising process involved, and purists seek the split almost in vain. Whether they originated in the town of Chudleigh is open to debate. In West Devon and South East Cornwall they are also sometimes known as tuffs.

450g strong bread flour

30g fresh yeast or 2 tsp dried yeast

50g caster sugar

300ml water

80g unsalted butter

50ml single cream

50ml milk

To serve: strawberry jam, clotted cream
and icing sugar

Warm the butter, milk, cream and water together with the sugar in a saucepan. This mixture should be warmed to approx 30°C. If it is too hot it will kill the yeast.

Add the yeast to this mixture and dissolve well (see Chef's Note below).

Pour the mixture into a well in the dry ingredients and mix to form a soft dough. Knead well by hand for 10 - 12 minutes or for 5 minutes on a medium speed in a mixer.

Leave to prove in a warm place, covered with a slightly damp tea towel, until doubled in size.

Knock back the dough and divide into 14 equal pieces. Shape into rolls, cover with a tea towel and leave to prove again, about 30 minutes.

Bake in pre-heated at 200°C, 400°F, Gas 6 for 10 -12 minutes until slightly golden.

Leave to cool slightly then split and fill with lashings of clotted cream and jam, dust lightly with the icing sugar.

Chef's Note

Yeast – chef recommends fresh if you can find it. Dried Yeast – see instructions on container – if you can only find the "Fast Action" type then incorporate with the dry ingredients before adding the liquid.

Editor's Notes

Whilst reading the very many tributes to Carol Trewin that were sent in after her death in October 2009, it became very obvious that Carol had touched many people's lives, not just as a journalist or radio producer but as a friend and colleague. For many years she produced Radio 4's Sunday breakfast programme 'On Your Farm' and travelling around the country gave her an instinctive feel for people and high quality local food. Later on she ran the BBC Farming Today team and helped save it from annihilation after BSE. In the years spent working for the BBC and as Farming Editor for the Western Morning News, Carol had acquired a deep understanding of West Country food and farming and often gave very valuable advice and encouragement to small producers. If you turn the clock back to the dark days of 2001, when Foot and Mouth was rampant in Devon, it is nothing short of a miracle that the local food economy has been turned round in less than ten years. Even then Carol could see the light at the end of the tunnel and how the future could be shaped by farmers diversifying by selling their own products in farmers' markets and farm shops, as opposed to kow-towing to the factory methods so often demanded by the economics of supermarket chains.

I first met Carol in North Devon at Parracombe Village Hall in 1992. Later on I worked with her for eight and a half years on many food stories with trips around Devon, Cornwall, Somerset and Dorset. And what a great pleasure that was. Her time at the Western Morning News was much appreciated by the rural community. She had real commitment and would often be phoned up late at night by farmer's wives asking for advice. Nothing was too much trouble for her. So it was a very sad day, in May 2006, when she was diagnosed with acute leukaemia. She was given three months to live but managed, with intensive treatment, to keep working as a journalist for another three and half years. Sometimes she was too ill to work but more often than not she was also beavering away on a story behind the scenes. In whatever spare time she had, she not only produced a book on Cornish Fishing and Seafood, but managed to write and research most of *The Devon Food Book*. She was determined to finish it come what may, but knew that time was running out.

Carol was very grateful to all her friends who helped to drive her round the countryside when she could no longer drive herself. I worked alongside her for the last three months of her life and I can honestly say she was working right up to the very end. I would often take my laptop into Derriford Hospital in Plymouth and read out various bits of the book and get her approval for any alterations. And just as soon as I had got it all 'sorted', the chapter openings agreed and the introduction written, she died. It was 12.30 pm on the 14th October 2009, the same day as the annual Goosey Fair auction in Tavistock.

Since then it has been a major task for myself and Ann Wilson of North Devon to double check, research, re-organise and edit various sections. The book has grown in size dramatically and has become something of an icon for Devon Food and Drink. The good will of the sponsors and the support of the many food and drink producers featured has been truly amazing. Anyone who came to her funeral at the Crossways Woodland burial site in Cheriton Bishop or the beef sandwich and Dry Sack lunch at the Dartmoor Inn, Lydford or the Cream Tea Revel at the Horn of Plenty will know what an extraordinary event that was.

This book is therefore a tribute to Devon, to its farmers, the food and drink producers, and the chefs as much as it is to Carol Trewin herself. Hopefully this book will, alongside her Cornish books, become her legacy, and in that way her strong belief in local food and drink will live on for many years to come. She was a very good friend and companion.

Nothing gave her greater pleasure than to see the growing awareness and success of local Devon Food and Drink particularly at Food Festivals and the way in which families and children enjoyed experimenting with new tastes and flavours.

She was a firm believer that quality, honesty and innovation linked to terroir and local farming traditions were the way forward. Enjoy the book and the wonderful photographs of Adam Woolfitt. The book is a guide for both local people and visitors alike. What better way to explore to Devon's Food and Drink culture.

James Crowden February 2010

GAZETTEER

Some of these producers and retail outlets are featured in *The Devon Food Book.*

Devon has a wealth of businesses dedicated to producing and selling wonderful local food and drink - regrettably lack of space made it impossible to include them all.

Bakery

Craft bakers – those who make bread with good non-adulterated flour, slowly fermented and proved – are a rare breed and worth searching out. Often, even within this group, some of their staple varieties sound the same (e.g. white, wholemeal, sourdough rye) and yet the taste, flavour and appearance is individual to each bakery.

Blue Mango
19 Plymouth Road, Tavistock
01822 617581
www.bluemangobread.com
www.bluemango.org.uk
Fridays 10am to 2pm Best to phone first.

Chulmleigh Bakery
East Street, Chulmleigh
01769 580228

East & West Bakery
Butchers Row, Barnstaple
01271 377577
www.eastandwestbakery1.webs.com

Emma's Bread
Exeter Farmers Market, Fore Street/South Street
every Thursday 9am to 2pm
and see www.emmasbread.co.uk for stockists

Occombe Farm see Farm Shops & Delicatessens

Otterton Mill see Farm Shops & Delicatessens

Saveurs Bakery bread and patisserie
3 Victoria Road, Dartmouth
01803 835852

Town Mill Bakery
Darts Business Park, Topsham
01392 875150 phone for stockists

Dairy Produce

Glorious Devon - the county of butter, cream, real ice cream and artisan cheeses.

Country Cheeses
Market Road, Tavistock
01822 615035
Branches at Totnes and Topsham
www.countrycheeses.co.uk

Dunns Dairies
milk, clotted cream, home delivery, farm shop, cream by post
Beacon View, Drewsteignton, nr Exeter,
01647 231452

Elsa's Eggs
Higher Fingle Farm, Crockernwell, nr Exeter
01647 281281
www.higherfingle.co.uk

Holy Cow Organic
soft cheese, cottage cheese
01752 337723 phone for stockists
www.holycoworganic.co.uk

Langage Farm
clotted and other creams, yoghurt, soft cheese,
frozen yoghurts, ice cream
01752 337723 phone for stockists
www.langagefarm.com

Market Cheeses
4 Market Arcade, Holsworthy
07974 796715

Moorland Dairy
42b The Square, Chagford
01647 432479

Quickes Farm
cheese, butter, ice cream
Newton St.Cyres, nr Exeter
01392 851222
www.quickes.co.uk

Salcombe Dairy
Shadycombe Road, Salcombe
01548 843328,
www.salcombedairyco.uk

Taverner's Farm
ice cream parlour, farm shop and café
Kennford, nr Exeter
01392 833776
www.tavernersfarm.co.uk

West Down Dairies
organic milk, cream, yoghurt, cream cheese
West Hill Farm, West Down, Ilfracombe
01271 815477
www.westdowndairies.co.uk

Ice Cream

Clovelly Ice Cream
01237 431305 for stockists and farmers markets
www.clovellyicecream.co.uk

Devonshire Farmhouse Ice Cream
Moorland Dairy, 42bThe Square, Chagford
01647 432479
www.icecreamonline.co.uk

Dunstaple Farm
01409 261106 phone for stockists
www.dunstaple.co.uk

The Good Intent historic ice cream parlour
30 Lowry Street, Dartmouth
01803 832157
www.dartmouthicecream.com

Henaford Manor
01288 331193 phone for stockists

Langage Farm
01752 337723 phone fo stockists and own ice cream
parlours
www.langagefarm.com

Orange Elephant see **Taverner's Farm**
under Farm Shops and Delicatessens

Rookbeare Farm
01363 866424 phone for stockists
www.rookbearefarm.co.uk

Salcombe Dairy
shop and café open Easter to October every day
Shadycombe Road, Salcombe
01548 843228
www.salcombedairy.co.uk

Yarde Farm
01752 340888 phone for stockists
www.yardefarmeicecream.co.uk

Farm Shops, and Delicatessens

Some farm shops also have a café, some offer a range of activities, nature walks or farm tours, demonstrations and seasonal events. Delicatessens listed here also offer a good range of Devon produce.

Blacks Deli
28 The Square, Chagford
01647 433545
www.blacks-deli.co.uk

Bon Gout Deli
45 Magdalen Road, Exeter
01392 435521
www.bongoutdeli.co.uk

Churston Farm Shop
Brokenbury Quarry, Dartmouth Road, Churston, nr Brixham
01548 845837
www.churstontraditionalfarmshop.org.uk

Crebers Deli
48 Brook Street, Tavistock
01822 612266
www.crebers.co.uk

Darts Farm Shop
Topsham, nr Exeter
01392 878200
www.dartsfarm.co.uk

Effings Deli
50 Fore Street, Totnes
01803 863345
www.effings.co.uk

Exe Valley Farm Shop
Rudway Barton, Thorverton, nr Exeter
01392 861239

Millers Farm Shop
Gammon's Hill, Kilmington, nr Axminster
01297 35290
www.millersfarmshop.co.uk

Occombe Farm Shop
Preston Down Road, Paignton
01803 520022
www.occombe.org.uk

Otterton Mill
Otterton, nr Budleigh Salterton
01395 568521
www.ottertonmill.com

Quickes Farm Shop
Newton St.Cyres, nr Exeter
01392 851222
www.quickes.co.uk

River Cottage Local Produce Store & Canteen
Trinity Square, Axminster
01297 631862
www.rivercottage.net

Riverford Farm Shop
Staverton, Totnes and Kitley
01803 762523
www.riverfordfarmshop.co.uk

Royal Oak Farm Shop
opening times and days vary with the seasons
Cotleigh, nr Honiton
01404 831223
www.royaloakfarm.co.uk

Smith Street Deli
The Old Shambles, Smith Street, Dartmouth
01803 835900

Stokeley Farm Shop
Stokenham, nr Kingsbridge
01548 581010
www.stokeley.co.uk

Taverner's Farm Shop
Lower Brenton, Kennford, Exeter
01392 833776
www.tavernersfarm.co.uk

Treloar's Deli
38 High Street, Crediton
01363 772332

Wallace's Farm Shop
Hill Farm, Hemyock
01823 680307
www.welcometowallaces.co.uk

Fish and Shellfish

Beer Fisheries
41 Park Road, Beer
01297 20297
www.beerfish.co.uk

Britannia of Beesands
Beesands, Kingsbridge
0845 055 0711
www.britanniashellfish.co.uk

C & L FISH
9 Butchers Row, Barnstaple
01271-343097

Clovelly Fish
Starfish Cottage, Higher Clovelly
(Dan the Fishman) 07970 932566
www.clovellyfish.com

Exmouth Mussels
mussels, cockles, clams and oysters available at
Greendale Farm Shop
Sidmouth Road, Farringdon, nr Exeter
01395 232836
www.greendalefarmshop.co.uk

The Fish Deli
7 East Street, Ashburton
01364 654833
www.thefishdeli.co.uk

Gibson's Plaice
38 Magdalen Road, Exeter
01392 495344

Mark Lobb fish and game merchant
Old Telephone Exchange, Mill Lane, Stoke Fleming
01803 770743

Lloyd Down
The Fish Stalls, The Market, Plymouth
01752 228612

Passmores
16 Butchers Row, Barnstaple,
01271 343 677

Walrus Fisheries
12a Fore Street, Ilfracombe
01271 867206
www.walrusfisheries.co.uk

Meat, Game and Poultry

Devon boasts many butchers who specialise in superb quality, traditionally reared or organic local meat. These are but a few – apologies that lack of space prevents us from including more.

Chicken Shack
Roosters of Babylon, Silverton
01392 860430
www.arkchicken.co.uk

Beckland Game
Bay Cottage, Beckland Farm, Hartland
01237 441945

Gribbles
15/16 High Street, Ivybridge
01752 893030
www.gribblesbutchers.co.uk
and various Devon towns

Heal Farm
Kings Nympton, nr Umberleigh,
01769 574341
www.healfarm.co.uk

Higher Hacknell Farm
Burrington, nr Umberleigh
01769 560909
www.higherhacknell.co.uk

Higher Fingle Farm
Crockernwell, nr Exeter
01647 281281
www.higherfingle.co.uk

Little Comfort Farm
Braunton, North Devon
01271 812414
www.littlecomfortfarm.co.uk

Lloyd Maunder
Westcountry family butchers, various locations across Devon.
01392 432782
www.lloydmaunder.co.uk

Pipers Farm
57 Magdalen Road, Exeter
01392 274540
www.pipersfarm.com

Shapland & Searle
123 East Street, South Molton
01769 573411

Wallace's
see Farm Shops and Delicatessens

Well Hung Meat
Tordean Farm, Dean Prior, Buckfastleigh
0845 230 3131
www.wellhungmeat.com

Wilkinsons
6 Church Street, Modbury, nr Ivybridge
01548 830240

Vegetable Box Schemes and PYOs

Most vegetable box schemes operate year round, PYOs tend to be seasonal so best to check first.

Ashford Inn Fruit Farm
Braunton Road, Ashford, nr Barnstaple
01271 311147

Boyces of Manstree
New Barn Farm, Manstree Road,
Shillingford St George, nr Exeter
01392 832218
www.boyces-manstree.co.uk

Lifton Strawberry Fields
Lifton
01566 684785
www.liftonstrawberryfields.co.uk

Linscombe Farm New Buildings
Crediton
01363 84291
www.linscombe.co.uk

Luke's Fruit Farm
Great Trehills, Tamerton Foliot, nr Plymouth
01752 785022

Riverford Organic Vegetables
Wash Farm, Buckfastleigh
0845 600 2311
www.riverford.co.uk

Rod and Ben's
Bickham Farm, Kenn, nr Exeter
01329 833833
www.rodandbens.com

Shillingford Organics
The Barns, Barton Lane, Shillingford Abbot,
nr Exeter
01392 832729
www.shillingfordorganics.co.uk

Shute Fruit and Produce
Shute Farm, Bishopsteignton, Teignmouth
01626 777570
www.shutefruit.co.uk

Tea Rooms

Opening times of some tearooms vary with
the seasons and term times – so best to
check first. Some offer light meals as well as
delicious cream teas. Many Farm Shop
Cafés and Hotels included in this gazetteer
also offer excellent cream teas.

Brimpts Farm
Dartmeet, Dartmoor, nr Ashburton
01364 631450
www.brimptsfarm.co.uk

The Corn Dolly
115a East Street, South Molton
01769 574249

The Captains Cabin
Fore Street, Beer

Docton Mill Gardens
open March to October
Hartland, North Devon
01237 441369
www.doctonmill.co.uk

The Georgian Tea Room
35 High Street, Topsham
01392 873465

The Quay Café
Fremington Quay, Fremington
01271 378 783
www.fremingtonquaycafe.co.uk

Royal Oak Farm
see Farm Shops and Delicatessens

The Singing Kettle
6 Smith Street, Dartmouth
01803 832624

Apple Juice and Cider

All the producers included in this list sell direct to the public. As well as cider and apple juice, some make a whole range of fruit juices, cordials, pressés and vinegars.
* indicates please phone

Ashridge Cider*
Barkingdon Farm, Staverton
01364 654749
www.ashridgecider.co.uk

Brimblecombe's
Farrant's Farm, Dunsford
01647 252783

Countryman Cider
Felldownhead, Milton Abbot, Tavistock
01822 870226

Green Valley Cider
Darts Farm, Clyst St George, Exeter
01392 876658 & 878200
www.dartsfarm.co.uk

Four Elms Fruit Farm*
Harpford, Sidmouth
01395 568286

Hancocks Devon Cider*
Lower Blackpool, Clapworthy Mill, South Molton
01769 572513
www.hancockscider.co.uk

Grays Devon Cider*
Halstow Farm, Tedburn St Mary,
01647 61236

Heron Valley*
Crannacombe Farm, Hazelwood, Lodiswell, Kingsbridge
01548 820111
www.heronvalley.co.uk

WGF Hunt & Sons*
Yalberton, Paignton
01803 782309
www.huntsfarmcider.co.uk

Luscombe Cider
01364 643036
www.luscombe.co.uk
cider available from
Dean Court Farm Shop
Lower Dean, Buckfastleigh
01364 642199

Lyme Bay Cider
Lyme Bay Winery, Shute, nr Axminster,
01297 551355
www.lymebaywinery.co.uk

Mill Top
The Food Hall, Newton Abbot Market
01626 202180
www.milltop.co.uk

Ostlers Cider Mill*
Eastacott Lane, Northleigh Hill, Goodleigh,
nr Barnstaple
01271 321 241
www.ostlerscidermill.co.uk

Palmershayes Cider*
Palmershayes Farm, Calverleigh, nr Tiverton
01884 254579 or 252900

Real Drink*
Elmcroft, Broad Path, Stoke Gabriel
01803 782217
www.realdrink.org

Sandford Orchards*
Lower Parks Farm, Fordton, Crediton
01363 777822
www.sandfordorchards.co.uk

West Lake Farm*
Chilla, Beaworthy
01409 221991
www.west-lake.co.uk
group visits and courses

Winkleigh Cider
Western Barn, Hatherleigh Rd, Winkleigh
01837 83560
www.winkleighcider.com

Wiscombe Cider*
Wiscombe Park, Southleigh, Colyton,
07976 585465

Useful apple/cider/orchard related sites for Devon:
www.thornhayes-nursery.co.uk
for old varieties of Devon fruit trees
www.talatonplants.co.uk
for apple trees
www.orchardlive.org.uk
for North Devon apple matters
www.devon-apples.co.uk
for Devon apples
www.orchardlink.org.uk
for South Devon apple matters
www.commonground.org.uk
for Apple Day events

Beer

There are more and more Devon micro breweries starting up and many of the Devon pubs that "brew their own" can be found in Chapter 10. The breweries listed here make real ale that they sell to pubs, farm shops and off licences, but also sell to the public from their premises. For a full list of Devon real ale breweries see www.southdevoncamra.com

O'Hanlons
weekdays sell at the farm gate
Great Barton Farm, Whimple
01404 822412
www.ohanlonsbeer.com

Teignworthy Brewery
Maltings, Teign Road, Newton Abbot
01626 332066
www.teignworthybrewery.com

Tuckers Maltings
beer shop and guided tour of the maltings.
Tours seasonal, so phone ahead.
Teign Road, Newton Abbot
01626 334734
www.edwintucker.com

Vineyards + Gin

Viticulture is an increasing part of the Devon scene. These Devon vineyards welcome visitors, some have guided tours, a few a café. However opening days and times change with the seasons so you will need to phone ahead. Many farm shops, delicatessens and off licences sell Devon wines. For Devon wine week see:
www.devonwineweek.co.uk

Blackdown Hills Vineyard & Winery
Oaklands Farm, Monkton, Honiton
01404 47442
www.blackdownhills-vineyard.co.uk

Boyces at Manstree
New Barn Farm, Manstree,
Shillingford St George, nr Exeter
01392 832218
www.boyces-manstree.co.uk

Kenton Vineyard
Hellwell Barton, Kenton, nr Exeter
01626 891091
www.kentonvineyard.co.uk

Old Walls Vineyard
Old Walls Road, Bishopsteignton
01626 770877
www.oldwallsvineyard.co.uk

Pebblebed Wines
Ebford, nr Topsham
07814 788348
www.pebblebedwines.co.uk

Sharpham Vineyard
Sharpham Estate, Ashprington
01803 732203
www.sharpham.com

Yearlstone Vineyard
Bickleigh, nr Tiverton
01884 855700
www.yearlstone.co.uk

Plymouth Gin
Black Friar's Distillery,
60 Southside St, Plymouth
01752 665292 for distillery tours
www.plymouthgin.com

And to get your taste buds tuned up see:

The Devon Wine School
Redyeates Farm, Cheriton Fitzpaine, Crediton,
01363 866742
www.devonwineschool.co.uk

Farmers Markets and Country Markets

Markets are held in these locations at the time of printing. However they do change, so it is wise to ask locally.

Country Markets

Barnstaple Pannier Market, Town Centre
every Tuesday and Friday, 9am to 1.30pm

Hatherleigh The Old Cattle Market
every Tuesday, 9am to 1pm

Holsworthy Market Square
every Wednesday, 9am to 4pm

Honiton High Street
every Tuesday and Saturday, 8am to 4pm

South Molton The Pannier Market, town centre
every Thursday and Saturday, 7am to 1pm

Tiverton The Pannier Market
town centre every Tuesday and Friday, 8.30am to 4pm,
every Saturday, 8.30am to 3pm

Totnes Civic Square
every Tuesday and Friday, 9am to 1pm

Farmers' Markets

Ashburton Tuckers Yard
every Thursday, Friday and Saturday, 9.30am to 3pm,

Bideford The Quay
Easter to October, 2nd and 4th Saturday of the month,
9.30am to 12noon

Bovey Tracey Town Square, Union Street
alternate Saturdays, 8.30am to 1.30pm

Bratton Fleming Village Hall
4th Saturday of every month, 9.30am to 12noon

Braunton The Parish Hall
4th Saturday of every month, 9.30am to 12noon

Buckfastleigh The Town Hall
every Thursday, 9am to 1pm

Combe Martin Village Hall
3rd Saturday of every month, 9.30am to 12noon

Crediton Market Square
1st Saturday of every month, 10am to 1pm

Croyde Village Hall
April to November, 3rd Saturday of every month,
9.30am to 12noon

Cullompton Station Road Car Park
2nd Saturday of every month, 9.30am to 12.30pm

Dartmouth The Old Market
2nd Saturday of every month, 9am to 1pm

Exeter Fore Street/South Street
every Thursday 9am to 2pm

Exmouth the Strand Gardens
2nd Wednesday of every month, 9am to1.30pm

Hartland the Parish Hall, The Square
1st Sunday of the month from April to October
(not August), 10am to 1pm.

Ilfracombe The Lantern Centre, High Street
1st and 3rd Sunday of every month,10am to 12.30pm

Kingsbridge Town Square
1st and 3rd Saturday of every month, 9am to 1pm

Lynton The Town Hall
1st Saturday of every month, 10am to 12.30pm

Newton Abbot The Market, Courtenay Street
every Tuesday, 9am to 4pm

Okehampton
St James Chapel Square, town centre
3rd Saturday of every month, 9am to 1pm

Ottery St Mary Hind Street car park
1st Friday of every month, 8.30am to 1.30pm

Plymouth Sundial, Armada Way, city centre
2nd and 4th Saturday of every month, 9am to 4pm

Seaton Town Hall
3rd Friday of every month, 9am to 1pm

Tavistock Bedford Square
2nd and 4th Saturday of every month, 9am to 1pm

Teignmouth The Triangle
3rd Saturday of every month, 9am to 1pm

Widecombe The Church House,
last Saturday of every month, 10am to 4pm

Wrafton Heanton Church Hall
2nd Saturday of every month, 9.30am to 12noon

Chefs

All these chefs have contributed recipes to The Devon Food Book and are passionately committed to using local and regional food.

Agaric
Nick Coiley
Ashburton
01364 654478
www.agaricrestaurant.co.uk

The Arundell Arms
Steven Pidgeon
Lifton
01566 784666
www.arundellarms.com

Brend Hotels
Dez Turland
Saunton (& others)
01271 890212
www.brend-hotels.co.uk

Cadeleigh Arms
Elspeth Burrage & Jane Dreyer
Cadeleigh
01884 855238
www.thecadeleigharms.co.uk

Clovelly Fish
Dan Garnett
Higher Clovelly
07970 932566

Combe House
Hadleigh Barrett
Gittisham
01404 540400
www.combehousedevon.com

Dartmoor Inn, The
Philip Burgess
Lydford
01822 820221
www.dartmoorinn.com

Effings
Karl Rassmussen
Totnes
01803 863435
www.effings.co.uk

Gidleigh Park
Michael Caines
Chagford
01647 432367
www.gidleigh.com

Grand Hotel, The
Richard Hunt
Torquay
01803 296677
www.grandtorquay.co.uk

Grove Inn, The
Deborah Smallbone
Kings Nympton
01769 580406
www.thegroveinn.co.uk

Harris Arms
Ross Tregidgo
Portgate, Lewdown
01566 783331
www.theharrisarms.co.uk

Holt, The
Angus McCaig & Kate McCaig
Honiton
01404 47707
www.theholt-honiton.com

Horn of Plenty
Peter Gorton
Gulworthy Cross, Tavistock
01822 832528
www.thehornofplenty.co.uk

Jack in the Green
Matt Mason & Scott Paton
Rockbeare, nr Exeter
01404 822240
www.jackinthegreen.uk.com

Mason's Arms, The
Mark Dodson
Knowstone
01398 341231
www.masonsarmsdevon.co.uk

Ode
Tim Bouget
Shaldon
01626 873977
www.odetruefood.co.uk

Otterton Mill
Ed Chester
Otterton, Budleigh Salterton
01395 567041
www.ottertonmill.com

Quay, The
Sue Harty
Fremington
01271 378783
www.fremingtonquaycafe.co.uk

Riverford Field Kitchen
Jane Baxter
Buckfastleigh
01803 762074
www.riverford.co.uk

Saunton Sands Hotel, The
Ben Boisdeves
Saunton
01271 890212
www.brend-hotels.co.uk

Seahorse, The
Mitch Tonks
Dartmouth
01803 835147
www.seahorserestaurant.co.uk

Venus Café
Jacques Marchal & Venus
Bigbury Bay (& others)
01803 833338
www.venuscompany.co.uk

Food Festivals

Devon has a number of exceptional food festivals each year, including

Abbotskerswell Beer and Food Festival
www.abfest.org.uk

Clovelly Crab and Lobster Feast
www.clovelly.co.uk

Clovelly Herring Festival
www.clovelly.co.uk

Combe Martin Strawberry Fayre
www.exmoor.com

Dartmouth Food Festival
www.dartmouthfoodfestival.co.uk

Devon Celebration of Food county-wide
www.devoncelebrationoffood.co.uk

Exeter Festival of South West Food and Drink
www.exeterfoodanddrinkfestival.co.uk

Exmoor Food Festival
www.exmoorfoodfestival.co.uk

Flavour Fest Plymouth
www.plymouth.gov.uk/flavourfest

Fishstock Brixham
www.fishstockbrixham.co.uk

Maltings Beer Festival Newton Abbot
www.edwintucker.com

Marldon Apple Pie Fair Marldon, nr Paignton
www.englishriviera.co.uk

North Devon Foodfest Barnstaple
www.northdevonplus.com

Occombe Farm Beer Festival Paignton
www.occombe.org.uk

The Real Cheese Fair Tavistock
www.countrycheeses.co.uk

Tavistock Food Festival
www.tavistockfoodfestival.co.uk

Websites

Try these websites for more information about Devon farmers, producers, shops, markets and events.

www.visitdevon.co.uk
www.tasteofthewest.co.uk
www.lovetheflavour.co.uk
www.northdevonplus.co.uk
www.slowfooddevon.co.uk
www.visitsouthdevon.co.uk

Bibliography

A Guide to Good Food in the West Country 2000, ed Tom Jaine, Halsgrove 1999

A History of Devonshire, Rev Richard Polwhele, Kohler and Coombs, 1977

A Tour Through England and Wales, Daniel Defoe, J M Dent and Sons

Burcombes, Queenies and Colloggetts, Virginia Spiers, West Brendon, 1996

Cooking and Dining in Medieval England, Peter Blears, Prospect Books, 2008

Dartmoor Farm, Stephen Woods, Halsgrove, 2003

Dartmoor Worker, William Crossing, David and Charles, 1966

Dartmoor, Ian Mercer, Collins 2009

Dartmouth, Percy Russell, BT Batsford Ltd, 1950

Devon Household Accounts, 1627-59 part 1, Todd Gray, Devon and Cornwall Record Society and Todd Gray 1995

Down the River Dart, Gordon Hill, Bossiney Books, 2004

Exmoor Oral History Archive

England's Sea Fisheries – The Commercial Sea Fisheries of England and Wales since 1300, eds David J Starkey, Chris Reid & Neil Ashcroft, Chatham Publishing, 2000

Food and Drink in Britain, C Anne Wilson, Penguin 1984

Food in England, Dorothy Hartley, Little Brown, 1999

General View of the Agriculture of the County of Devon, Charles Vancouver, David and Charles reprints, 1969

Good Old-Fashioned Jams, Preserves and Chutneys, Sara Paston-Williams, National Trust Books, 2008

Historic Inns of Devon, Monica Wyatt, Bossiney Books, 1986

Icehouses, Tim Buxbaum, Shire Publications Ltd, 1992 (2002)

Industrial Archaeology of the Tamar Valley, Frank Booker, David and Charles 1974

Lost Devon, Felicity Goodall, Birlinn, 2007

Mazzards, Michael Gee, The Mint Press, 2004

Nine centuries of Tavistock Markets, Graham Kirkpatrick, Tavistock Market Charter Group, 2005

Preserves, Pam Corbin, Bloomsbury, 2008

Red Rubies, A History of the Devon Breed of Cattle, Clive Thornton, Gabriel Communications

Sovereigns, Madams and Double Whites, Joanna Lewis, Tamar Valley AONB, 2004

Tavistock Abbey, HPR Finberg 1952

Home Scenes or Tavistock and its Vicinity, Rachel Evans, Tavistock 1846

The Apple Source Book, Sue Clifford and Angela King, Hodder and Stoughton, 2007

The Art of Dining, A History of Cooking and Eating, Sara Paston-Williams, National Trust Enterprises, 1993

The Book of Meavy, Pauline Hemery, Halsgrove, 1999

The Devon Landscape, W. Harding Thompson and Geoffrey Clark, A and C Black Ltd, 1942

The Journeys of Celia Fiennes, edited Christopher Morris in 1947,

The History of Lloyd Maunder, 1898-1998, Henry Clarke and Hilary Binding, Halsgrove

The National Trust's Country House Cookery from the West, Elizabeth Lothian, David and Charles, 1978

The Outline of Dartmoor's Story, Sylvia Sayer, Devon Books, 1987

The Penguin Companion to Food, Alan Davidson, Penguin Books 2002

Illustration and photo credits:

Oxen manuscript illustration from the Luttrell Psalter originally published in East Anglia c 1325-1335 Courtesy of the British Library.

Cider press woodcut Courtesy of the Estate of Clare Leighton, from *The Farmer's Year*, 1933.

Windlass cider press and frontispiece from *Treatise of Cider* by Hugh Stafford 1753.

All photographs © Adam Woolfitt unless otherwise stated.

Clovelly Fishermen and Salmon Nets on the Dart by Rev F Partridge taken from *A Book of Devon* by Sabine Baring Gould 1899.

James Hannaford, Headland Warren, Three Rabbits, Tavistock Church and Arthur and Harold Stephens, Bere Ferrers © Chris Chapman.

Stag roof boss – Coldridge church © Sue Andrew.

Photo of Mrs Ware at Ditsworthy Warren, photographer unknown, but sourced originally by Brian Le Mesurier via Mrs Vanstone for Crossing's *Dartmoor Worker*.

Sponsors

Generous support from our sponsors has enabled us to research, photograph, print and publish *The Devon Food Book*.

Without the businesses and organisations listed below, the book would not have come into being. We are grateful to Michael Caines and Guy Crowden for supporting the project right from the start.

Michael Caines

THE **JACK** IN THE **GREEN INN**

Brend Hotels take pride in offering our guests the very best of the West. The family-run business, which has nine hotels and two restaurants in Devon, has a long history of supporting local food and drink and has won a number of awards for its food and use of local producers produce. **www.brend-hotels.co.uk**

Churston Traditional Farm Shop stocks local fresh meat and poultry, Brixham fish, fruit and vegetables, cheese and dairy produce and food prepared daily in our in-house butchery and kitchens. **www.churstontraditionalfarmshop.com**

Situated just outside the historic town of Topsham, **Darts Farm** offers a special shopping experience. While still a working farm, the farm shop focuses on food that is locally grown, reared, baked, caught or produced. The on-site master butcher, fishmonger, baker, delicatessen, cider and wine cellar all reflect the superb produce available in the South West. **www.dartsfarm.co.uk**

Devon Farms Accommodation is a group of farming families, offering Bed and Breakfast and self-catering accomodation in some of the most beautiful countryside to be found anywhere in England. Its members take great pride in giving their guests delicious local home-cooked fare, often produced on the farm itself. **www.devonfarms.co.uk**

Food & Drink Devon – 'Love the Flavour' represents a membership of like-minded businesses, dedicated to providing quality local food and drink. The association is committed 'to make Love the Flavour a nationally recognised brand for outstanding sustainable food and drink.' Our hotels, restaurants, cafes and shops are dedicated to serving and selling this delightful produce. **www.lovetheflavour.co.uk**

The food and drink industry is a major contributor to Northern Devon's economy. **North Devon+** has recognised the importance of the sector's economic impact to the region by providing tailored business support to encourage business growth and improve the overall visitors experience in the region. **www.northdevonplus.com**

Both restaurant and pub, the **Jack in the Green** oozes honesty, panache and that rare four letter word – CARE. With a crystal clear philosophy to serve only the best of Devon's artisan produce, seasonality comes through in every dish. Expect good local brews, a very warm welcome and superb service. Exceptional value for money and a dining option to suit any occasion. **www.jackinthegreen.uk.com**

Jackie Milsom at **Little Comfort Farm** provided us with a luxurious self-catering farm cottage near Braunton for a week of our early shooting and research. We were surrounded by blossom, lambs and piglets www.littlecomfortfarm.co.uk

Lloyd Maunder Ltd. has been a pioneering force in the South West food industry since it was founded in 1898 by Mr Lloyd Maunder, when he took over the management of his father's butchers shop. www.lloydmaunder.co.uk

Mole Valley Farmers is one of the region's most successful farmer-owned and run co-operatives. Set up in 1960 by a group of North Devon farmers, this supports and supplies many of the county's food producers through its 9 branches. www.molevalleyfarmers.com

Occombe Farm reconnects people with food, farming and the countryside. It is a unique opportunity to get close to local wildlife, experience the day-to-day workings of an organic open farm and sample authentic Devon food as offered by our farm shop and café. www.occombe.org.uk

One Voice specialises in food and drink, working with national, regional and local media, we can help any South West business looking to increase sales and awareness of their products and services. www.onevoicemedia.co.uk

Otter Brewery was, and is, a labour of love. David and Mary Ann McCaig's dream was always to produce a small and consistent range of distinctive beers full of integrity, flavour and provenance. Otter is now one of the South West's most successful independent breweries. www.otterbrewery.com

Pipers Farm was started by Peter and Henrietta Greig in 1989. Today, Pipers Farm helps to sustain 30 farming families who believe in offering their customers the best and healthiest meat that is a pleasure to cook, sensational to eat and excellent value. www.pipersfarm.com

Riverford grows and delivers award-winning affordable organic fruit and veg freshly picked on its Devon family farm straight to customers' doors. Ordering is easy and flexible – as well as fruit and veg, choose from a range of organic milk, eggs, meat and more. www.riverford.co.uk

The Tamar Valley bordering Cornwall and Devon, is one of the most beautiful and historically significant areas in the UK. In 1995, the Tamar Valley was designated an Area of Outstanding Natural Beauty (AONB) making it one of 40 in England and Wales. In its heyday, 15,000 people were employed in horticulture and market gardening. In 2006, the Tamar Valley was given World Heritage status. www.tamarvalley.org.uk

Plymouth Gin was founded in 1793 and has been providing the Royal Navy with gin ever since. The distillery is located in the medieval heart of Plymouth, called the Barbican, next to Sutton Pool www.plymouthgin.com

Devon County Council works in partnership with 'Food and Drink Devon' to provide support for Devon's food and drink businesses see: www.lovetheflavour.co.uk DCC also sponsors a number of key food events including the Exeter Festival of South West Food and Drink and delivers high profile campaigns to encourage visitors and locals to buy more local food. www.devon.gov.uk

Biographical details

Carol Trewin was both Farming Editor and then Food Editor at the *Western Morning News* based in Plymouth. Prior to that she had worked for Radio 4's Food programme, Woman's Hour, the BBC World Service, and was editor of Radio 4's Farming Today. She produced On Your Farm, Costing the Earth, Walston Goes Walkabout and Over the Counter. She was manager of Cornwall Taste of the West and for two years ran a £3 Million Food and Drink project. She was also a freelance journalist and wrote for many publications including *Food Illustrated, The Field, British Farmer and Grower, Inside Cornwall, Food and Devon Today*. In her spare time she wrote two award winning books: *Gourmet Cornwall* and *Cornish Fishing and Seafood*. Carol lived in Devon for over 20 years at Torquay, Rattery and Horrabridge. She died of leukaemia in October 2009 at the age of 56.

Adam Woolfitt has been a photographer for most of his life and his work illustrated both *Gourmet Cornwall* and *Cornish Fishing and Seafood*. He has travelled very widely and has contributed to *National Geographic* and many other magazines for over 30 years. He writes on digital photography for the *British Journal of Photography, Image Magazine* and *Photo District News* in New York. He was Chairman of the Association of Photographers and is an Honorary Fellow of the British Institute of Professional Photographers and co Founder of IDEA (The International Digital Exhibition and Awards). He lives in London. **www.adampix.com**

James Crowden was born in Plymouth and raised on the western edge of Dartmoor around Tavistock. His ancestor Zacharias Pascoe lived on the moor as a tin miner for over fifty years and led a tinners' riot in Chagford in 1793. James began work plucking turkeys in the Tamar Valley near a cherry orchard. He joined the army, travelled extensively in the Middle East and has spent a winter in Zangskar, deep in the Himalaya. He is a poet and has written more than a dozen books including *The Bad Winter, The Wheal of Hope* and *Ciderland*. **www.james-crowden.co.uk**

Ann Wilson lives in North Devon and came to the food and farming industry via nursing and publishing. Over the years she has worked with many of the South West's finest artisan food and drink producers, farm and speciality food shops and hospitality outlets. She is now a free-lance food and business adviser.